UNITARIANS AND INDIA

UNITARIANS AND INDIA:

A Study in Encounter and Response

By SPENCER LAVAN

Introduction by EUGENE PICKETT

Third Edition

EXPLORATION PRESS

Chicago, Illinois

Cover photo by Roger W. Holmes from "My Gandhi" by John Haynes Holmes, Copyright © 1953. Used with permission from Harper & Row, Publishers, Inc.

The Rev. John Haynes Holmes, minister of the Community Church of New York, visited Mohandas K. Gandhi in New Delhi Oct. 12, 1947, some three-and-one-half months before the latter's death. This photograph was taken by Holmes' son Roger, who accompanied him on the trip. The elder Holmes was one of the first Americans to appreciate the world-historical mission and significance of the Indian leader.

Exploration Press of the
Chicago Theological Seminary
5757 South University Avenue
Chicago, Illinois 60637

Printed in the United States of America

Third Edition, 1991

ISBN: 0-913552-46-1

Library of Congress Catalog Card Number: 90-86029

UNITARIANS AND INDIA:
A STUDY IN ENCOUNTER AND RESPONSE

Table of Contents

Preface

The adventure of historical researching was stimulated in me years ago at Harvard Divinity School when I studied American Unitarian History under Professor C. Conrad Wright. A term paper on the liberal religious Hindu movement, the Brahmo Samaj, written during my Ph.D. program at McGill University and published in two issues of *Faith and Freedom* in 1967-68 gave me a first insight into the significance of that movement for the modern history of India.

The work for this book began in January 1972, and was carried on primarily at the Unitarian Universalist Historical Archives at the Andover-Harvard Library at Harvard Divinity School. The first months of work brought me into contact with two new colleagues, both interested in and working on aspects of the same subject. Pamela Price, while writing a Master's thesis at the University of Wisconsin on the early ministry of Charles Dall in Calcutta, did painstaking research in the Dall papers and American Unitarian Association letterbooks which provided me with a better understanding of how to go about working with the Dall materials. David Kopf, professor of history at the University of Minnesota, had just completed two years of detailed research on the Brahmo Samaj while directing the American Institute of Indian Studies in Calcutta. His counsel and insights throughout my work have been of great significance. We three each presented papers at a panel session during the Bengal Studies Conference in Toronto in May 1972. There, through our interaction, the ideas for this book began to take shape.

Many other persons were of assistance to me in my work. The Reverend Alan Seaburg, curator of manuscripts at the Unitarian Universalist Historical Archives at Harvard Divinity School, and Professor C. Conrad Wright were both helpful in turning up valuable document and suggesting new places to look. Professor Neil Jordahl, then librarian at Meadville/Lombard Theological School, was most cordial in his assistance with the dusty Sunderland papers stored at that Chicago library. Mrs. Alice Sunderland Wethey, granddaughter of the Reverend Jabez T. Sunderland, and Mr. William McNitt (archivist for the Michigan Historical Society) were indispensable in their aid with Dr. Sunderland's personal papers. I am grateful to the family of John Haynes Holmes for allowing me to consult his papers now stored at the Library of Congress.

Research for a study such as this one may be likened in part to detective work, as I found when almost by accident I uncovered some previously unknown documents. For these I am appreciative of the cordial hospitality provided by Mr. Bayard Tuckerman of Westport, Massachusetts, a descendent of the Reverend Joseph Tuckerman, and to Mrs. Mary Harding, of Jamestown, Rhode Island, a descendent of the Reverend Charles Brooks. Both welcomed me into their homes to read over documents.

Materials from chapters four and six were previously published under the title "Rajah Rammohun Roy and the American Unitarians: New Worlds to Conquer, 1821-1824," in *West Bengal and Bangladesh* (edited by B. Thomas and S. Lavan), Michigan State University, East Lansing, 1973. The first chapter on Jabez Sunderland was published in the *Proceedings of the Unitarian Historical Society,* Boston, 1975. The second chapter on Jabez Sunderland was previously published in the Bengal Studies Papers for 1976, *Patterns of Change in Modern Bengal,* edited by Dr. Richard Park (Michigan State University, 1977). In addition, a brief article entitled "Rammohun Roy and the Reverend Jared Sparks" was published in *Bengal Past and Present,* Vol. XCIV, Part 1, No. 178, January-June 1975, by the Calcutta Historical Society.

Professor Dilip K. Biswas of Presidency College who assisted in making this latter publication possible represents my direct link with the Brahmo Samaj tradition. Our meetings in Calcutta and Montreal were most helpful in broadening my understanding of the Samaj and in seeking its landmarks and those of Calcutta Unitarianism. Mr. Sati Kumar Chatterjee, also of Calcutta, offered a different perspective on the Samaj and especially on the work of Keshub Chunder Sen. Portions of his personal library made accessible to Western scholars have provided a great asset in my work. Mr. Devison Marbaniang, current missionary among the Khasi Unitarians, provided me access to historical materials during a visit to Shillong in 1972. I must also mention the genuine excitement, interest, and generosity of the Khasi Unitarian community during my visit with them.

While much could be said of how English missionaries and the Hindu Brahmin elite of Calcutta came to affect each other, the specific task of this study is to examine how the theology and organization of Unitarianism, unknown as a concept or as a church in the year 1800, came to play a role in the encounter of a Bengali Hindu elite, a Madrasi low-caste community, and a newly developing religious reformation movement centered both in Boston and London. The motif of interaction and acculturation which I presented in my previous writing on the Islamic Ahmadiyah movement is crucial to understanding the purpose of this study, which is to point up how people and organizations affect and relate to one another. While the emphasis in this book will be on the role of American Unitarians in relation to India, the role of British Unitarians is by no means neglected. No one reading carefully through the material on the four American Unitarian spokemen can fail to be impressed with the role of the British throughout the story, but the significance of the Americans and their impact is the focal point of the history.

In any research project there are numerous details which must be omitted. The notes to this book provide assistance to those seeking greater detail or further clarification of points not fully developed in the text.

In conclusion, I offer special thanks to a former Tufts student, Jennifer Lee Pacheco, who typed the final manuscript, and to my family — wife, Susan, and children, Jonathan, Daniel, Timothy, and Joanna — for their love and care during the years of this work.

Tufts University
February 1977

A Preface To The Second Edition

Since the original publication of this book in 1977, a definitive work by Professor David Kopf, *The Brahmo Samaj and the Shaping of the Modern Indian Mind* has appeared. Published in 1979 by Princeton University Press, the book extends to more than 400 pages including a lengthy bibliography.

The reader who has begun a study of liberal religious movements in India and of Unitarian connections with India from America and Britain with the present book, or who has been stimulated by learning of the encounter of Unitarians with the Brahmo Samaj, will be even more stimulated by reading the Kopf volume. Where *Unitarians and India* has examined principally four Unitarian ministers and four major Brahmo leaders in the context of their encounter and acculturation, Kopf's study goes beyond many earlier summaries of Brahmo teachings or one-dimensional descriptions of its leading figures. Kopf does not present the movement in chronological sequence, a factor which makes it sometimes difficult to follow all the characters. However, after reading my general article on the Brahmo Samaj in Robert Baird, *Religion in Modern India*,

(South Asia Books, Columbia, Missouri, 1981) or the present volume, Kopf's study will be genuinely exciting, challenging and informative for the reader.

Of particular interest will be Kopf's chapter on famed poet Rabindranath Tagore, grandson of Dwarkanath (Rammohun's contemporary) and son of Debendranath, institutional developer of the Samaj. Here Kopf breaks new ground by describing in detail Tagore as a Brahmo, astutely demonstrating how Tagore used his literary works to raise central religious issues that Brahmos as liberals, reformers, and frequently as nationalists were deeply concerned about.

With the inauguration in 1984 of the Unitarian Universalist India Fund and the renewal of interest in liberal religious movements in India through the International Association for Religious Freedom to which both the Unitarian Universalist Association and Brahmo Samaj belong, the study of Unitarian historical connections with India and the study of the complex history of Brahmo personalities is again a matter of consequence within the association. The opportunity to offer *Unitarians and India* for republication is therefore especially exciting at this time.

Spencer Lavan
Brunswick, Maine
March, 1984

A Preface To The Third Edition

The opportunity to reprint *Unitarians and India* for a third time is an exciting prospect for its author. While the book remains of interest to a relatively small audience, it has been included on the reading list about Unitarian history required by the Ministerial Fellowship Committee of the Unitarian Universalist Association. More significantly, the book has served as a stimulus to two recent graduates writing dissertations for the Doctor of Ministry degree at Meadville/Lombard Theological School in Chicago.

In 1988, Calcutta native and Brahmo Samaj member Sunrit Mullick expanded on my discussion of Protap Mazumdar's 1893 and 1900 visits to the United States to write in detail and analyze the significance of Mazumdar's 1884 visit while offering a complete bibliography of his writings and a list of Brahmo and other Indian students who have attended Meadville since 1900. Mullick's dissertation, *Protap Chunder Mozoomdar in America: Missionary of a New Dispensation* is available from the Meadville/Lombard Library. While a student at Meadville, Mullick also served as a Brahmo "missionary" by stimulating the interest of his roommate, John Andrew Ritan, in the Brahmo movement and in the theology of Keshub Chunder Sen. Ritan studied Bengali, travelled to Bangladesh and lived in Calcutta after completing his manuscript, *Pilgrimmage to the Saints: Theology of Pluralism in Keshub Chunder Sen's New Dispensation.* Ritan is currently a parish minister in Atlanta while Mullick is working in Calcutta as Director of Project India, an effort to coordinate Brahmo and Unitarian activities in South Asia.

It is always inspiring for a teacher and scholar to know others have become interested enough in his subject to expand and even correct his work. In this case, there is another connection since the author became Dean and Chief Executive Officer of Meadville/Lombard in September, 1988 and before that, served on Mullick's thesis committee as a visiting scholar. With the development of the Holdeen Fund and India program of the Unitarian Universalist Association, there has been more interest in understanding why the UUA and International Association of Religious Freedom should have an India connection. The reprinting of this book offers that link with our past.

I wish to dedicate this printing of *Unitarians and India* to my mother, Fay Lavan and my late mother-in-law Pauline Kohlberg, both of whom have given of their love and support to me, my wife Susan, and our children over many years.

Spencer Lavan,
Chicago, Illinois
January, 1991

INTRODUCTION

The reprinting of this book by the Unitarian Universalist Association in 1984 is a mark of a new chapter in the story of Unitarians and India. This new chapter includes strengthening our ties with Unitarians and other liberal religious groups in India through the International Association for Religious Freedom and the establishment of the Unitarian Universalist India Fund.

The connections between the thought of India and of America are significant. Hindu and Buddhist teachings greatly influenced the Transcendentalism of Ralph Waldo Emerson. Ten years before Emerson's historic Harvard Divinity School Address in 1838, Rammohun Roy founded the liberal religious Hindu movement, the Brahmo Samaj. There was a continuous American Unitarian presence, in the person of the Reverend Charles Dall, in Calcutta from 1855 to 1886. While maintaining close ties with the Brahmo Samaj, Dall was also involved in establishing schools and educational reform programs. Dall introduced the works of Unitarian preachers such as William Ellery Channing and Theodore Parker to India. There is also the earlier connection with the Unitarian Christian Church in Madras. And perhaps our strongest and most continuous connection has been with the Unitarian Union of the Khasi Hills in Meghalaya.

American Unitarians were concerned not only with religious reforms but also with educational and social reforms and political activities. The Unitarian Minister, Jabez Sunderland, was a strong spokesperson against British injustice in India. And later John Haynes Holmes became a prominent supporter of Gandhi and his philosophy of non-violence.

For the first time American Unitarians are able to make an appropriate response to the concerns expressed by Rammohun Roy in his first correspondence with American Unitarian leaders in 1824. He suggested that American Unitarians could be most helpful in India not by sending ministers to convert the Indians but rather by making educational opportunities available and by promoting social reforms that would improve the lives of the people. It is in this spirit that the Unitarian Universalist India Fund is being developed. This Fund, established by a bequest of Jonathan Holdeen, to be administered by the Unitarian Universalist Association, is for the benefit of the people of India.

Beacon Press, the publishing house of the Unitarian Universalist Association, has fostered our India connection over the years by publishing such important works as *Gandhi: An Autobiography; A Tagore Reader,* from the works of Rabindranath Tagore; *The Kabir Book: Forty-four of the Ecstatic Poems of Kabir;* and most recently a work by the noted Indian psychoanalyst, Sudhir Kakar, *Shamans, Mystics and Doctors.*

Dr. Lavan's book tells the intriguing story of the interaction of Unitarians and India. The reprinting of this book will help us to understand each other better. It can help us move beyond our particular and parochial concerns to a greater understanding of the common concerns of liberal religion in North America, Great Britain and India.

Eugene Pickett
25 Beacon Street
Boston, Massachusetts
May, 1984

CHAPTER ONE

Unitarians and India:
Encounter, Response, and International Vision

Unitarians in India? Unitarians as missionaries? This monograph addresses itself to these two questions. Most readers will begin by asking themselves how a religious movement which has throughout the twentieth century prided itself on being non-missionary, individualistic, and accepting toward the religions of others could have a history in India and a missionary history at that. In the total perspective of India's religious life, the role that Unitarianism played was a minor one. In the total perspective of English and American Unitarianism, the India story in its entirety is virtually unknown.

Why should anyone bother to tell the story then? As a piece of Unitarian and Indian religious history which has stretched over a period from 1818 to the present, the story in its details provides fascinating insights into the characters, organizations, theology and faith of American and English Unitarians as well as their counterparts in Calcutta and Madras, India. The encounter begins with a series of letters between the early English religious liberal Thomas Belsham and a low-caste Madrasi Unitarian named William Roberts. It concludes with John Haynes Holmes' visit to Gandhi during the bloodshed of 1947 in New Delhi. Between 1818 and 1948 (the year of Gandhi's death), the study touches not only on events relevant to Unitarianism but on Unitarianism in relation to critical events of human history. In this sense *Unitarians and India* is a chronicle of the role of Unitarianism in the History of Religions. It is an examination of ways in which English and American religious liberals have reacted and responded to a situation in one corner of the world — South Asia.

Most history is written from one perspective. It describes events or personalities within the limitations of a city or even one culture or language area. If it is a history of colonialism or imperialism or of traditional missionary efforts, the perspective is often colored by the fact that one group or power has dominated or is dominating another.

The history of Unitarians and India moves beyond one-dimensional vision and attempts to speak relevantly to a newer anthropological concept, that of "acculturation." Acculturation has been defined as "culture change that is initiated by the conjunction of two or more autonomous culture systems."[1] It is that process by which two or more individuals or cultures have a significant impact on one another. Although acculturation has occurred often in human history, historians presenting one side or the other of an issue have generally used the term "influence" to emphasize the dominant position of one side over the other.

By applying the concept of "acculturation" to Unitarians and India, one immediately removes this history from the frequently one-sided approach of missionary history and at the same time, one immediately realizes that the history of Unitarians and India is not traditional missionary history. It is a story of developing inter-relationships among men and women on three different continents who unexpectedly discovered they had much in common and much worth sharing. Clearly their assumptions about religious truth differed as did their levels of tolerance and understanding for each other at various times. No one can look at this story in its details, however, without being impressed by the profound impact that Indian religious liberals such as Rammohun Roy, Keshub Chunder Sen, Protap C. Mazumdar, and Rabindranath Tagore had on English and American Unitarians. Nor can one escape being impressed by the significance that Channing, Henry Ware, and Theodore Parker had upon a mid-nineteenth century emancipated generation of Bengali Hindus, or the fact that a Unitarian minister, the Reverend Jabez T. Sunderland, was the first American to speak publicly at a meeting of the Indian National Congress, the early middle-class Hindu nationalist movement.

A study in encounter and response moves beyond the usual missionary assumptions to explore how each party in the encounter felt about the other and reacted to the other. Daniel Howe, historian of early and mid-nineteenth century Unitarians, has asserted that despite the smallness of the "church," one cannot fully understand the intellectual history of New England or even of the United States without taking Unitarianism into account. One is also unlikely to find any thorough history of modern India which does not discuss Rammohun Roy and the Brahmo Samaj as an "awakening" force for a new India. Even if one divests the history of Unitarianism or of the Bengal renaissance of its mythology, one cannot help but maintain the overriding significance of each movement for its own national culture and history.

That the religious liberals of India, England, and America happened to discover one another, just as each was beginning to organize and crystallize sentiment, was a remarkable coincidence. Even through the misunderstandings and excessive expectations each side had from the other, something dynamic occurred which demonstrated an openness between Unitarians and Brahmos not experienced by Indians in any earlier encounter with missionaries and seldom encountered in any later experience. Even as one observes the early controversy over whether the British Government in India should stress Oriental or Anglo education, a controversy in which the evangelical missionary faction and subsequently Thomas Babington Macaulay supported and won out for English education, one is struck by the fact that those supporting the movement for Fort William College and the resurgence of Indian languages and literature never intended to create open or equal relationships between themselves and Indians.

This is not to say that all relationships between Unitarians and Brahmos or Indian Unitarians were developed on equal or always agreeable terms. William Adam and Rammohun Roy, two major and closely associated figures in this study, disagreed sharply in matters of education and religion. American and British Unitarians were so involved in their own struggles to survive during the 1820s that they could not conceive of developing a mission response to the "Brahmo" religious liberalism of Rammohun in the proportions suggested by William Adam. In the 1850s New England Unitarians Charles Brooks and Charles Dall were similarly defensive about what conversion to Unitarianism demanded and neither could accept a totally open relationship with "young Bengalis" who were not prepared to become Christian. Jabez Sunderland, who demonstrated the most diplomatic skills in bringing together the three branches of the Brahmo Samaj during his 1895 visit, in setting the Khasi Hills Unitarian church fully into gear, and in 1913, in presiding over the all-India Theistic conference at Lahore, showed both leadership and sensitivity to the needs of Indians. Winning the hearts of an Indian intelligentsia from Bombay to Calcutta through his outspoken position on their behalf and against the British, he went so far that many Western critics dismissed his position as too extreme. John Haynes Holmes moved even farther afield, arguing his support for the Gandhi movement and Mohandas Gandhi before the American public primarily on grounds of ideological affinity with passive resistance rather than from a profound understanding of the problems India had emerged from or would face in the future.

The Missionary Problem

Most Unitarians do not realize that throughout the nineteenth century the American Unitarian Association believed that, within the scope of its financial limits, it should propagate its form of Christianity among those not ordinarily able to hear it. Mid-twentieth century Unitarians and Universalists have had little understanding or sympathy for Christian missions. In general, the expansion of religious liberalism in America and England has occurred when people have "discovered" a Unitarian church or fellowship to whose religious openness they can respond. If most present-day Unitarians and Universalists were to think about it, however, they would have to agree that most "converts" to religious liberalism carry an air of superiority and sense of enlightenment about their religious decision not unlike the attitude of excitement nineteenth-century Unitarians felt but were able to carry out in a more traditional missionary context.

The circumstances which brought Rammohun Roy and William Adam to the attention of American Unitarianism, to those who naively believed that the mission of American Unitarianism against Calvinism could easily be transposed to Rammohun's battle against Hindu Vaisnava polytheism, were circumstances of coincidence. But, it was Rammohun's Christian missionary opponents in India working for the greater glory of Christ who first brought Rammohun to Christian theological journals in England. It was from there that Unitarian periodicals began to review his works. And it was from these English Unitarian periodicals that American ones such as the *Christian Register* began to take up the cause. The attitude about a missionary effort as expressed in the minutes of the American Unitarian Society for the Propagation of the Gospel in India was a strongly conservative one. Although excited at the prospects in India, American Unitarians made only a token financial commitment after long delays due to slow communications and after they had established with certainty that the monies would not be wasted.

In the mid-nineteenth century, thirty years after the founding of the American Unitarian Association, a more traditional commitment to a mission program began. This was the start of the thirty-one-year Charles Dall missionary effort in India and the period when American Unitarian missions to the American Indians and later to the Japanese were widely supported. The Dall kind of mission failed to make any headway in areas other than education. Although reported in detail in the *American Unitarian Association Journal* in its early years, the work of both Dall and the mission received hardly any notice in either England or America after 1865. Yet, the years of Dall's ministry were years of increased Unitarian interest in non-Christian religions. The Transcendentalist movement, and especially Ralph Waldo Emerson, were deeply affected by the scriptures of Hindu and Buddhist faith. Unitarian Samuel Johnson, minister in Salem, Massachusetts, undertook a major two-volume work, *Oriental Religions*, published in 1879[2] but included only a brief chapter on Rammohun Roy and the Brahmo Samaj and no reference to Unitarianism in India. Less than a decade earlier, James Freeman Clarke, minister to Boston's Church of the Disciples, had published his *Ten Great Religions: An Essay in Comparative Theology* in which he argued for the superiority of Christianity as the most progressive religion.[3] Clarke mentioned neither Unitarianism nor any reform movement within Hinduism and in fact emphasized many of what he considered to be negative features of the Asian faiths he discussed from his Christian bias.

The work of Clarke, Johnson, and the transcendentalists must yet be studied in the context of the Free Religious Association and the movement for a more liberal understanding of Unitarianism developed in the Western Conference during the latter decades of the nineteenth century. Certainly the Free Religious Association, a sharply individualistic reaction against the post-Civil War conservative of establishment Unitarianism was a precurser of ecumenical Unitarianism, of the age of the 1893 World's Parliament of Religions, and subsequently of the International Association of Religious Freedom. While by 1900, the feeling of religious brotherhood was the idealism underlying much of this inter-religious activity, the financing and logistical support came almost entirely from the West and, with the exception of the All India Theistic Congress movement tied closely with the Indian National Congress and social reform assemblies, Hindus, Buddhists, or Muslims were seldom in a position to set the time or take the initiative in international religious relations.

The world parliament kind of activity discussed in detail in Chapter Ten coincided with the decision of the English Unitarians to send the Reverend Jabez Sunderland (an American, though born in England) to India in 1895, not to reestablish a Unitarian Christian mission but to explore conditions in the three Brahmo Samaj groups with an eye toward improving their affectiveness as a liberal religious force among Hindus. This kind of decision represented a major shift from the conversion emphasis of Charles Dall in the 1850s which, when it succeeded, usually managed to produce a convert whose perspective was so different from Dall that it might have been better in the long run had he not been converted.

International ecumenical activity such as a World Parliament or an International Association for Religious Freedom movement re-inforced stereotypes in another way, however. It removed the day-by-day activities and commitment even of one as eccentric as Charles Dall and replaced that regular activity and commentary at the home office with a biennial or triennial congress. Correspondence might pave the way for such a Congress, but daily or weekly intercourse of American Unitarians with Brahmos or Khasis was virtually neglected. The two trips of Sunderland to India, in spite of their substantial impact, were limited in time and scope. The American Unitarian Association sent a delegation of five to attend the Brahmo Samaj centeniary in 1928. John Haynes Holmes met Gandhi only twice — once in London, once in Delhi.

Can this kind of contact justify the claim of this study that the efforts of Unitarians for and in India and the reciprocal response by such persons as Rammohun Roy, Keshub Chunder Sen, Protap Chunder, and Rabindranath Tagore were significant social and cultural intercourse? The methodology of the monograph observes how and why Unitarians became involved with India. It also examines Unitarian activities from a variety of Indian, American and English sources and has employed both historical and anthropological method. It has been written to tell the American Unitarian as well as the English Unitarian side of a history concurrently being prepared on the religiously liberal Brahmo Samaj movement. Professor David Kopf, author of a social, cultural, and organizational history of the Brahmo Samaj, has examined the individual Brahmo leadership in far more detail than has this study.[4] The Kopf study and this one, placed back to back, mirror the same events through the eyes of friendly yet competing forces. To some extent the two studies span different eras and emphasize different periods more fully. But, both present a much neglected approach to the study of history — the study of how people interact with each other when they represent differing backgrounds and cultures and when they meet on each other's grounds. Despite their limitations, Unitarians were, from the beginning, open to this kind of interaction. Just as William Roberts, the Madras Unitarian, read and appreciated Joseph Priestley and Theophilus Lindsey, while Rammohun corresponded with Henry Ware and William Ellery Channing, Unitarians would react with amazement and respond equally anxious to become familiar with the Vedantic pure theism Rammohun Roy so strongly stressed in his reform movement.

In the mid-nineteenth century Charles Dall's introduction of Channing and Parker to the emancipated Hindu generation, "Young Bengal," or to Hajjom Kissor Singh, a lone Protestant seeker in the Khasi Hills, took interaction a further step. Channing and Parker alone were not an influence, however. Shakespeare, Milton, and Wordsworth, for example, were all part of the English education meant to bring "enlightenment" to the new generation of Calcutta Brahmins. That Charles Dall was willing to discuss the New Testament and a human Christ with hundreds of these young men while introducing them to the works of early Unitarians such as Channing, Dewey, and Ware meant that Dall was willing to provide them one step in their educational development — seen from a Western point of view, of course. The numbers actually affected by Unitarian Christianity were few although the impact on those, Keshub Chunder Sen, Protap C. Mazumdar, and other Western oriented leaders of the Navavidhan (New Dispensation) Brahmo Samaj was considerable.

In the case of the Khasi Unitarian movement, the line of communication or "influence" came first from a liberal Brahmo Hindu to Hajjom Kissor Singh and then through the works of Channing sent by Charles Dall. Finally, through correspondence between Singh and the Reverend Jabez Sunderland, strengthening over a thirty-five year period and including Sunderland's visit to the Khasi Hills in 1896, a two-way acculturation experience occurred. The impact of Sunderland and of other British Unitarians, notably the late Margaret Barr, who devoted more than thirty-five years of service to the Khasi people, has been enormous on that small community.[5] Sunderland's involvement with Brahmos, the Indian National Congress, outspoken editors such as Ramananda Chatterjee, and nationalists like Lajpat Rai affected his acculturation and encounter far more widely than that of Singh or of any of those that Sunderland personally encountered.

The legacy chronicled in *Unitarians in India: Encounter and Response* lives on in the international vision and work of the International Association for Religious Freedom. The Brahmo Samaj was the earliest and until the late 1960s the only non-Western, non-Christian member of the movement. With Congresses held in Europe and America, Brahmo participation in the International Association for Religious Freedom has been minimal in recent decades. However, the International Association for Religious Freedom has grown beyond the confines of Christianity to renewed relations with religious liberals of eastern Europe, Japanese Buddhism and Shinto, and Indian Islam. Its membership involves the Unitarians of the Khasi Hills and of Lagos, Nigeria. In the 1970s, the International Association for Religious Freedom is undertaking a major inter-religious dialogue, a dialogue of mutual search in which Asians must play an equal part with Americans and Europeans. Such is the nature of liberal religious encounter for the 1970s.

The history which this study will examine is that of an interaction of individuals, none of whom, with the exceptions of Rammohun Roy, the Tagore family, and Mahatma Gandhi, was vastly important for world history or even the history of the country from which he came. The significance of the interaction and encounter which each participant in this study had upon others and the effects of those encounters was indeed profound. As the unfolding history will show, the role of Brahmoism and Unitarianism had intellectual and organizational impact in each respective locus. The impact that each had on the other as well as on religious forces with differing perspectives means that the shockwave effect of each group went well beyond the confines of its own membership. In India, the Brahmo missionary program and approach was taken up by the militant Hindu Arya Samaj movement, the Ramakrishna mission, and the Islamic Ahmadiyah sect, each of which interacted both positively and negatively with other religious and secular organizations. In America, the Unitarians, after breaking with Congregational Calvinism in New England, evolved programs of theological change and social development within the denomination. Unitarian leadership provided a nucleus for social reform movements throughout the nineteenth and twentieth centuries. Like the Brahmos, American Unitarians also represented the *status quo* among its membership as well as the upper-class elite of Boston society. If the Brahmo Samaj and American Unitarianism failed to win society to their ideals, if the two movements became increasingly ineffective as the twentieth century wore on, the reasons are clear. Despite the call in both for a religious commitment and sense of support or discipline, an open, eclectic theology and the right of the individual to question his own beliefs through a process of reasoning could only splinter religious liberals. When the chips were down, militant nationalism in India and a more fundamentalist Christianity in America as well as the new secularism would win the day. This study does not focus on the reasons why Unitarianism and the Brahmo Samaj failed to serve the needs of their culture and context. Its purpose is solely to study the interaction of two religious groups with an eye toward understanding how and why those groups and their leaders affected each other's lives.

CHAPTER TWO

The Vision of Religious Liberalism and The Age of Enlightenment

Vasco da Gama's arrival on India's shores in 1498 to bring the lucrative spice trade under Portuguese domination and Francis Xavier's arrival as the first great Catholic Christian missionary to Portugal's settled territory in western India half a century later signalled the opening of interaction between India and the West. Columbus had sailed West from Spain seeking a new route to the Indies in order to move against Arab and Turkish Muslim domination of the trade. But, the Portuguese were successful both on the sea and at key points along the trade routes to the East. This made them far more significant masters of the South Asian area until Portugal was taken over by Spain in 1580. The Dutch then became the new dominating force in the East Indies in 1595. The British East India Company was established in the area in 1600. Although the Portuguese never attempted a major political encounter with the Mughal Muslim rulers at Agra in North India, they planted a solid colony of Christians with conservative Catholic values at Goa. There intermarriage with the local population left a legacy which survives to the present day.

India had experienced far more militant invasions many times before. Following the Aryan invasion of India from Central Asia sometime between 1500 and 1000 B.C., the four-caste system and "Hindu" civilization and religion had started its development. The Aryan invasion, which is documented only through references in the Vedic Hymns, most likely composed by families of Brahmin priests as the settlements occurred, pushed an earlier indigenous "Dravidian" population into the southern third of the subcontinent and made these dark-skinned peoples a *sudra* or servant class. The Aryans themselves divided into three classes: Brahmins or priests, Ksatriyas or warrior, and Vaisyas or merchant-farmers.

Sometime in the early centuries A.D., "caste" (from the Portuguese word for "pure") came to be defined in terms of *jati* or birth. One was automatically a member of a specific caste or sub-caste simply because of where and in which family he or she was born. But caste could not be defined very exactly, in Western terms at least, because it represented a complicated set of dietary, marital, and occupational regulations. Thus, in Hindu society, one's role was defined in relation to those with whom caste custom prescribed it possible for one to marry or socialize. Relations with persons of higher caste were always deferential and conceived of as on a fee-for-service basis. Travel far from one's home or outside of India which would mean eating with or relating to potentially polluting non-Hindus could signify loss of caste. Such humiliation was suffered by many Brahmins and other high-caste Indians such as Mohandas Gandhi in the late nineteenth century when they travelled to England to be educated. Even in the context of the early nineteenth-century Unitarian situation in India, caste became an issue for Calcutta Brahmin Rammohun Roy and low-caste Madrasi William Roberts (Moodelliar Vellazha) whose only relationship with each other was carried on through the Scottish missionary William Adam and through correspondence with British and American Unitarians.

The encounter of the Aryan Hindus with Islam was a difficult experience, and began around 1000 A.D. Invading Muslim armies and the ruling dynasties in North India were ideologically committed to strict monotheism, the Islamic sense of community (*umma*) and the law of God (*shari'a*) by which an Islamic state operated. The indigenous Hindu population was not organized either militarily or as a religiously-united community to respond vigorously against the second-class status assigned to them as *kafirs* or non-believers. The Hindus themselves were divided because of the long-developed caste system in which a huge majority of the population was low-caste servants, artisans, and peasants with no stake in or commitment to Brahmanic Hindu society. Although hundreds of thousands of these low-caste Hindus converted to Islam, and although Muslim dynasties ruled large portions of the subcontinent between 1000 and 1700 A.D., the Muslim population never exceeded 20 percent of the total population.

The high point of positive interaction between Hindus and Muslims, as well as with the early arriving Portuguese from Europe, occurred during the reign of the liberal Mughal emperor, Akbar, who succeeded in unifying much of the subcontinent between 1560 and 1605. While his three successors, Jahangir, Shah Jehan, and Awrangzeb continued the Mughal architectural and artistic splendor begun by Akbar, they each took increasingly rigid positions toward non-Muslims. As a result of their anti-Hindu policies, tensions between the two major religious communities of India grew substantially during the seventeenth century.

While the religious history of North India records the roles and teachings of such notable and saintly reformers as Chaitanya, Ramananda, Kabir and Guru Nanak during the fifteenth and sixteenth centuries, the eighteenth century, a period of enlightenment in the West, was very much a "dark ages" century in India. Though these earlier reformers had pressed for a new understanding of the *bhakti* or devotional Hinduism, and a rejection of class, caste, and sex discrimination, their devotees and successors seem to have been unable to carry their reforms forward even a few decades later. If there was any "reform" in Hinduism at all, it was caused by the presence of Islam itself, the Persian high court culture Islam brought to India, and the continuing challenge posed by the Mughal rule.

With the death of the last great Mughal, Awrangzeb in 1707, Muslim rule continued from Delhi while the Portuguese settlers, who began as traders, undertook a more systematic exploitation of India from bases on the west coast. Soon they were joined by the French, British, Dutch, and Danes who, during the eighteenth century, each attempted to partake of India's wealth through general economic exploitation. The British East India Company (founded in 1600) began its trading in India by a series of raids on the west coast through which they made only small inroads on Dutch and Portuguese trade. The Company's impact developed finally when they moved from the west coast to the northeast and settled in the small village of Calcutta, Bengal, in 1698. They also managed settlements in both Madras and Bombay, differing from the Dutch and Portuguese in policy by encouraging their settlers and traders to develop their own local government, while the Dutch and Portuguese maintained control of their colonies entirely and strictly from home. During the half-century from 1750 to 1800 when it was not clear which internal force — the weakening Mughals, the Sikhs of Northwest India, or the Maratthas (Hindus of West India) — would become the controlling indigenous power, the British East India Company became in effect a fourth indigenous power. The ability to make immediate decisions when needs and conflicts arose gave the Company, in all its locations, far more flexibility than that available to the other Europeans. Under the leadership of

Robert Clive, the Company organized local armies and succeeded in defeating both other European and indigenous opposition. By 1800, the East India Company was the major foreign power on Indian soil.[1]

Once established as rulers throughout large portions of the subcontinent, the Company appeared to have little interest in or concern for the individual members of the indigenous population except as a source of revenue or, in a few cases, as servants who could assist the small staff of British to help exploit the land. During the decade of the 1770s, however, under the governorship of Warren Hastings, a new elite of civil servants arrived in India, people such as Sir William Jones whose interest in Sanskrit, Persian, and Arabic learning influenced the Unitarian Joseph Priestley in far-off Pennsylvania. The new elite of English civil servant was fascinated by the origins of Hindu and Muslim civilization which had once set the cultural tone of India. Those who began to pursue the study of ancient languages and culture were soon described as the British "Orientalists."[2]

The earliest systematic and scholarly presentation of Hindu scripture and religion to the West was made by those Englishmen who came to India to teach and to be taught. Many of the interpretations these scholars made of what they saw in India bore the Christian prejudice and for some decades were not answered accurately or apologetically from within the Hindu or Muslim communities. The fact of an English scholarly presence, however, and the British fascination with record keeping brought several social issues to the surface in both the Indian and English consciousness. The glimmer of an age of enlightenment for India was about to begin.

The British East India Company, Religion and Education

While the British East India Company was the major foreign ruling force in India after 1800, the Company was by no means the only ruler. Wherever princely states existed scattered throughout the subcontinent much like the states of Germany prior to 1870, the Company welcomed local rule coupled with submission to its general policies. Gradually, Company power moved across North India until in the 1840s Punjab was wrested from the Sikhs, a religious minority community.

During all this period the Company officers were responsible to Parliament in London, reporting there in order to renew its charter from time to time. In many matters, however, it operated with virtual independence. Following the "Mutiny" of 1857 in which many Europeans were killed, power was transferred directly to the English Crown. The Mutiny was without doubt a militant uprising by both Hindus and Muslims against the way in which the Company was governing in India.

This is not to say that everything the British brought to the subcontinent before 1857 was of no positive use. In the context of education and religion some significant things happened, one of which was the rise of a small liberal religious movement. Because the eighteenth century had been one of turmoil within India's Hindu and Muslim communities as well as one of exploitation by the first forces of colonialism, there is little one can report of religious development during Europe's age of "enlightenment." It was when the British began to develop learning resource centers, most notably Fort William College, as places where Company civil servants could be educated, that a new generation of Indians began to respond to new forces at work in their environment.

In 1797, the Marquis Wellesley, a conservative English aristocrat, was sent to Calcutta as Governor General, a position he held until 1805. Fearing French expansion under Napoleon into India and believing many of the Company's civil servants to be unprepared for their duties, Wellesley proclaimed in 1800 the formation of Fort William College whose purpose it would be "to fix and establish sound and correct principles of religion and government in their minds at an early period of life . . . which could . . . provide for the stability of British power in India.[3] Wellesley envisaged a college modeled on Oxford or Cambridge with a staff of professors teaching Arabic, Persian, Urdu, and Sanskrit as well as courses on Muslim and Hindu law, English jurisprudence, and traditional European studies such as the Classics.

An interest in Oriental Studies had started several decades earlier with a loosely-established Asiatic Society of Bengal. Following the founding of Fort William College, the two institutions were brought more closely together and the work of Asiatic Society founder Sir William Jones had left uncompleted at his death in 1794 could now be completed by an organized group of scholars concerned with a broad variety of problems posed by the British presence in India. These problems emerged on two levels: those elicited by scholarly interest in antiquity and those which would help the Company servants govern more effectively.

The East India Company did not at first welcome Christian missionaries to Bengal. The Company was more concerned about financial profits and had no interest in being pressed about its ethical practices by either Christian clergy or local converts. Those most interested in Oriental studies and a renewal of ancient Hindu culture, however, happened to be religiously-educated missionary-oriented English civil servants. One group of missionaries headed by William Carey, formerly an indigo planter, arrived in 1800 in the small settlement of Serampore, an enclave near Calcutta. They were prepared to undertake missionary work and publications in many languages among the Indians while under the protection of the Danish rulers there. Serampore subsequently fell into British hands in 1801 when the Danish, believed to be siding with the French against England, were considered easy and legitimate prey for the Company.[4]

To understand the vision of religious liberalism in India and how it originated, one must look to the events and activities of the Asiatic Society, Fort William College, and the Serampore missionaries. The impact of these organizations combined with an increasing number of young Hindu intellectuals learning English, and undertaking academic studies while teaching indigenous languages at Fort William, to start a new pattern. The educational encounter at Fort William was not a sudden enlightenment leading to a repudiation of either Hindu or Christian orthodoxy. It represented rather a developing realization by a new generation of Hindus of the benefits of English education as well as a renewed awareness of potential value in long-forgotten Hindu roots. The intersection of these forces has been described as the "Bengal Renaissance." It was from this renaissance that Rammohun Roy, the short-lived Unitarian movement, and the Calcutta Brahmo Samaj all emerged.

Unitarian Origins: England

In 1818, Unitarianism was not yet organized in either London or Boston. Liberal sectarian dissent of various kinds had stirred religious controversy in England as early as Henry VIII's break with Rome in 1534. Henry himself, however, persecuted radical Anabaptists and came into conflict with Presbyterians during the remaining three years of his reign. One century later, the Puritans under Oliver Cromwell were in control of the country. A Calvinist conservative Christian movement, the Puritans, themselves dissenters both in England and in America, were notably intolerant of forms of religious dissent other than their own. It was during the Puritan reign in the 1640s that Unitarian ideas first took root in England.

The theological position which gave rise to a growing Unitarian awakening in eighteenth-century England was that known as "Socinianism," which had permeated England from the continent during the early years of the Reformation. The term "Socinian" was applied to those holding the views of Faustus Socinus, an Italian who had immigrated to Poland during the sixteenth century and had there developed a Unitarian following when advocating that Jesus was not God but the greatest man who had ever existed. Although Socinus maintained he was a fully believing Christian, his position on Jesus was far more radical than the "Arian" one generally attributed to early American Unitarians. The Arian view held that Christ was "of like substance" with the Father but not "of the same substance." Hence he was a divine-human clearly superior to other men but not to be understood as part of the godhead of a Trinity.

The earliest articulate English Socinian Unitarian was Francis Biddle who wrote in the 1640s that the doctrine of the Trinity could not be upheld in Scripture. Although imprisoned for his writings, Biddle was set free by Cromwell in 1651 at which time he organized a congregation of his followers. He soon discovered numerous allies. The publication of Unitarian works continued until a new period of suppression set in following the Restoration and the Act of Uniformity in 1662. For twenty-seven years all dissenters suffered severely until the Act of Toleration of 1689 and the ascension of William and Mary to the throne.

Three major figures independently supporting the liberal religious position were the poet John Milton whose *Paradise Lost* raised suspicions as to his orthodox views, the scientist Sir Isaac Newton, and the philosopher John Locke. The latter broke ground especially in the area of individual rights and personal freedom of expression setting the stage for the American Declaration of Independence a century later. While none can be claimed legitimately for organized Unitarianism, each made such a major impact on seventeenth and eighteenth century English thought that liberal Unitarian ideas could only benefit.

The true founder of English Unitarianism was Theophilus Lindsey, an Anglican chaplain who came across a Unitarian text in the mid-1760s. Although comfortably situated, Lindsey felt increasing pangs of conscience about remaining as an Anglican pastor while holding a basically Socinian position on the Trinity. A meeting with Joseph Priestley, minister of a dissenting church in Leeds (later the discoverer of oxygen and an emigré to the United States) led him to his final break with his Anglican congregation. After a period of great struggle, Lindsey succeeded in organizing a purely Unitarian congregation in London in 1774. The Essex Street chapel included Benjamin Franklin in its congregation and emphasized simplicity and pure teaching in religion. The new church attracted many educated and influential people, and received such generous financial support that when Lindsey fell ill in 1778, he was able to hire an associate minister, John Disney.[5]

Lindsey's friendship with Joseph Priestley continued, becoming especially close after Priestley was burned out of his home and church in Birmingham by a mob in 1791. Priestley first took refuge as minister of a congregation in Hackney, but in 1794 he moved to Philadelphia and later to Northumberland, Pennsylvania, where among many other things he wrote in 1799 a book entitled *Comparison of the Institutions of Moses with those of the Hindoos and other Ancient Nations*,[6] which introduced a new vision of liberal religious encounter with the the religious traditions of India. In some 300 pages, Priestley engaged in the comparative study of Hinduism and Judaism in a scholarly, open, and sensitive manner. Although one of his purposes was to refute a current theory that the five books of Moses had their origins in the five ancient Vedas, Priestley went systematically through all secondary sources on the sacred Hindu religious and philosophical texts presenting their views as explained by such eminent scholars as Sir William Jones. Jones had provided the first English translations and commentaries of the Hindu texts, and was responsible for stimulating a reawakening of interest in the Sanskrit and Persian medieval cultures of India, both in India and Europe.

Comparing the different attitudes toward Hindu customs and institutions reported by the French scholar Langles and by

Jones, Priestley stated his agreement with the first part of Jones's preface to the Hindu text, the *Laws of Manu*, but disagreement with later comments about the impact of the Vedas on Moses. It is significant that Priestley chose to engage in the scholarly study of comparative religion without missionary or polemical purpose. He compared the opinions of scholars and urged his readers

> to judge for themselves, from the copious extracts which I shall lay before them from the Hindoo books, and the testimony of travellers of greatest credit, such as are allowed to have been the best informed concerning the religion, the customs and the government, of Hindostan.[7]

Priestley's study of Hindu religiousness, as he understood it, preceded by two decades any direct involvement by English and American Unitarians in the religious life of India. While his writings had no direct impact on the missionary activity and religious encounter that was to follow during the century and a half from 1820 to 1970, it was indicative of an open attitude and vital interest that English and American religious liberals would always have toward the faiths of others and of Hindus in particular.

Unitarianism in New England[8]

Unitarian Christianity developed in a different context in America and apart from Joseph Priestley's isolated experience in Pennsylvania, the movement emerged slowly from Calvinist Puritanism in eighteenth-century New England. The Massachusetts Bay Colony had first been settled in 1630 by English Puritans who were extreme in their Calvinistic fervor, excluding Baptists and Quakers for holding views which gave people the opportunity to make religious decisions for themselves. In the Puritan view church and state were entirely interrelated. Because God predestined the fate of every person, overt conversion experience was seen as proof that one had been chosen by God for salvation. In Calvinist theology, Christ, the son of God, was the instrument by whose atonement individuals were to be saved from sin. In Puritan society of the Massachusetts Bay Colony, the conversion experience, church attendance, and strict belief were cardinal to one's standing in the community.

In the course of 150 years, however, the extreme position of Boston Calvinism shifted for many to an Arminian view which recognized each individual's responsibility to choose consciously between "good" and "evil" in living a Christian life. Such an Arminian view was not uncommon among certain of the Boston-area clergy in 1780. The "Arian" position, held during the early nineteenth century by most American Unitarians, asserted that Jesus, although far more than an ordinary man, was not "of like substance" with the Father and therefore was not the Son of God in any literal sense. Both Arminianism and Arianism helped shape the New England Unitarian position. These radical religious views caused the alienation of Unitarians, whether in Boston or London, from the "orthodox" Christians of many denominations. The "orthodox" still insisted on belief in the Athanasian creedal formulations (the formulations which William Roberts, isolated in Madras, India, also rejected) as requisite for being a true Christian.

Most early English Unitarians, however, were reacting more against an Anglican backdrop than a Puritan one. They were considered by their opponents as "Socinian." But even many American Unitarians of Arian persuasion did not consider themselves "Socinian." This term was applied, as noted previously to those holding the views of Faustus Socinus, a sixteenth-century Polish Unitarian, who believed that Jesus was the greatest man who had ever existed. This position was clearly distinguished from the "Arian" which described Christ as greater than men but less than God. This was the major point of theology differentiating English and American Unitarians at the turn of the nineteenth century.

In the Boston-Cambridge area, the issue between the more conservative Calvinist and the more "Arminian" and "Arian" Christians developed over the specific issue of whether a Calvinist or an Arminian should succeed to the chair of Hollis Professor of Divinity at Harvard. When the liberals won this skirmish in 1805, they discovered that they could not sit back to allow their position to develop slowly and quietly. The Calvinist party, led by the Reverend Jedidiah Morse of Charlestown, Massachusetts, continued attacking the liberals, among whom was the Reverend Henry Ware, Sr., who had become Hollis Professor. By 1818, as Calvinists continued to exclude Unitarians from their pulpits, although the open procedure of monthly pulpit exchanges had long been accepted, the cleavage moved beyond the clergy and theologians into the congregations. Throughout the Boston area, congregations split along conservative-liberal lines and in some instances, court cases determined whether the "Unitarians" or the "Congregationalists" would retain the church property.[9]

Liberal Religion: England, America and India

To pull together the threads of liberal religious development in all three countries to see how each movement interacted with the other, it is best to begin with Sir William Jones, who arrived in India in 1783 and provided the earliest translation of the sacred Sanskrit Hindu texts read in America by Joseph Priestley and by increasing numbers of British East India Company civil servants sent to India from England. Jones, founder of the Asiatic Society of Bengal, served as the father of a movement of revivified learning for both Indians who had lost their spiritual heritage and for Europeans seeking a knowledge of the land in which they were living. After 1800 the development of Fort William College as the base in which this study was carried out was a second step opening a Western style of academic education to Hindus capable of studying in English. The College in Calcutta as well as the arrival of a printing press from England for a Christian evangelism program in India added to the educational and social reform measures in the Charter Renewal Act of 1813. The act opened up a new opportunity for Serampore missionaries situated in the small Danish colony recently taken by the East India Company.

Three noted leaders were among the missionaries, the Reverend William Carey, publisher William Ward, and teacher Joshua Marshman. The latter had opened boarding schools with the aid of his wife and had established himself as Serampore's educational specialist. The three men were not prevented from their missionary-oriented pursuits, even after the British, who prior to 1813 regarded such activities as illegal, took over in Serampore. Even before the recognition of missionaries, however, Governor General Wellesley was already developing plans for an Orientalist College in Calcutta which was soon to make use of the talents of several missionaries including Carey, Marshman, and Ward.[10]

They had already been thinking and writing about a reformation for India in which the Sanskritic past might be intellectually recaptured. A reformation of this kind would also open the way for Christian understanding and conversion. The Serampore missionaries, Baptist in their orientation, were far more sympathetic toward a resurgence of traditional Indian learning than were other evangelicals such as Charles Grant. Grant, an important political figure in the Company, believed firmly that the heathen of India must be converted to Christianity. He further asserted that European classical education was the only route to enlightenment for the Indian people. This was a theme which would later be reechoed by the noted essayists Macaulay and Trevelyan.[11] Thus, initial attempts by the British at educational reform in Bengal were related to missionary efforts on behalf of Christianity. These efforts could not help but call to the attention of literate and sensitive Bengali Hindus the crying need for reformation at all levels of their culture.

Just as Joseph Priestley's writings opened the first awareness of an interest in Indian religiousness to American and English Unitarians (at that time referred to as "liberal Christians"), so Rammohun Roy, born in Bengal in 1772 of Brahmin origins, played the major opening role on the Indian side. Rammohun Roy has long been glorified as the "Father of Modern India" and has been considered by Westerners and Indians as totally original in all that he said and did. Although any study of the impact of Unitarianism in India must focus first on Rammohun, it must also begin with the realization that Rammohun's ideas and attitudes were first shaped by his encounter with Christian missionaries and the faculty at Fort William College in Calcutta.[12] David Kopf's assessment of Rammohun Roy suggests that

> His work as a Westerner has been lauded by generations of admirers, who have glorified him . . . Perhaps no other Bengali, with the exception of Rabindranath Tagore, has been so thoroughly identified with the cultural self-image of the people. The aura surrounding this man has exerted so profound an influence on later historians that he is frequently portrayed as a virtual god-man containing within him the seeds of a regenerated India.[13]

It would be well here to introduce more fully the cast of characters involved in this history. On the Indian side, Rammohun Roy plays the lead role as both a religious reformer of the Hindu tradition and as a "Unitarian" gadfly to the Christian missionaries. At Rammohun's side stood Dwarkanath Tagore, the country Brahmin who built a small family fortune into a great one. Together they would help finance first a small Unitarian movement and later the Hindu reform movement, the Brahmo Samaj. With the isolated low-caste William Roberts of Madras, these three would stand alone among millions on the subcontinent as outright supporters of a liberal religious faith. They were quick to gain supporters both because of their personalities and leadership and also because the advent of European education would open the minds of the generation of young Bengali Hindus emerging after 1830.

On the English American side, their counterpart and contemporary would be the Reverend William Adam, Baptist convert to Unitarianism, religious and social reformer, publisher and educator. Adam left an indelible mark for liberal Christianity in Calcutta, a mark to be picked up in 1854 by the Reverend Charles Brooks of Newport and in 1855 by the thirty-year missionary ministry of the Unitarian minister, Charles Dall.

The second generation on the Bengali Brahmo side includes many figures. Central was Debendranath Tagore, son of Dwarkanath and father of the noted poet and novelist Rabindranath. The second Tagore would carry on the Brahmo Samaj as a conservative liberal reform movement and stand in opposition to the encroaching Christian missionaries. Tagore's disciple Keshub Chunder Sen would change the direction of the Brahmo Samaj into a missionary faith with a strong social service dimension. According to M. M. Thomas, "it was he (Keshub) who shifted the emphasis (on Christ) from the teachings to the teacher." The impact of Western thought, Christianity, and particularly the writings of Channing and Parker were most evident as influences on Keshub. Keshub's cousin and successor, Protap Chundra Mazumdar, would take the Brahmo Samaj to England and America on four trips and between 1874 and 1900 open up a new dimension of interaction among the three liberal religious movements.

The later phase of liberal religious interaction involves first and foremost the Reverend Jabez T. Sunderland, sent as a reconciler by the British Unitarian Association to the thrice-splintered Brahmo Samaj. His first visit to India in 1895 also was the first stage of a developing relationship with the Khasi Hills Unitarian movement under the leadership of Hajjom Kissor Singh. With the entry of Jabez Sunderland begins the period of concern with political issues in India particularly by American Unitarians. This effort would culminate in John Haynes Holmes's activity on behalf of Mohandas Gandhi and through his correspondence with the Indian leader.

While many more figures and encounters enter the story of Unitarians and India than are introduced here, these are the principal characters whose lives, ministries, and writings focused on developing a new liberal religious vision in India, England, and America. It is with the senior of these figures, Rammohun Roy and William Roberts, that this history begins.

CHAPTER THREE

The Madras Experience: William Roberts

The first Indian identifying himself as a Unitarian Christian was a low-caste Tamil Hindu, Moodelliar Vellazha, who called himself by the Christian name William Roberts. On Christmas day, 1816, he initiated an extensive correspondence with the Reverend Thomas Belsham, minister of the Unitarian Society in London who served there as successor to and biographer of the noted Reverend Theophilus Lindsey. Through this letter, the story of Roberts's "conversion" to Unitarianism and the founding of the first Unitarian congregation in India started to unfold.[1]

Roberts, born somewhere in the Carnatic of South India, lost both parents during the Hydar rebellions of 1780. Before he was even ten, he moved to Madras where he was taken in by a Muslim trader who later sold him as a slave to a European ship officer. Freed because of the sudden death of his officer-owner, Roberts continued working for the ship's captain and received back pay for his period of enslavement. During subsequent years of travel, Roberts first converted to Islam, but in the summer of 1789, while he was living with the Captain's family in England and learning English, he was baptized a Christian at St. James church in London. During that time Roberts first became acquainted with both the Bible and the *Book of Common Prayer.* When he returned to Madras in 1790 as the servant of another Englishman, Roberts pursued the study of English to better understand the Bible.

> Whenever I had leisure the Bible was in my hands. The first thing that struck me and I stumbled at, was the Creed of St. Athanasius in the Common Prayer Book. The persons of the same power and attributes, yet separately God and Lord, yet altogether no more than One God, was a thing too hard for me to make anything of. . . The more I considered the harder it seemed to my reasoning power; for I had not the wisdom to consider the contents of the Bible without the Common Prayer Book, and no notion of the corruptions of Christianity in the reformed churches.[2]

Roberts's religiously isolated life was evident from his statement to Belsham that it was not until after he was acquainted with the Bible in English that he discovered Danish missionaries in Ceylon had already translated it into his native language, Tamil. On a return visit to England in 1793 Roberts discovered the writings of Priestley and Lindsey after a young woman servant in the house in which he too was working read to him from a Unitarian tract.

The next year, Roberts carried a library of Unitarian theological works with him back to Madras. In discussions with both Protestants and Roman Catholics, Roberts's Unitarianism was dubbed "a refined heathenism." Although alone in his beliefs, he was all the more a confirmed Unitarian whenever he read and studied the Scriptures both in Tamil and English. In 1797, Roberts ordered from London Priestley's *History of the Corruptions of Christianity* and *Early Opinions Concerning Christ*, Lindsey's *Apology and Sequel*, Clarke's *Scripture Doctrine of the Trinity*, and Sale's well-known early English translation of the *Qur'an*. These works not only stimulated his religious curiosity further but showed him to be something of an innocent comparativist, knowledgeable in two languages and exposed to the teachings and practices of Hinduism, Islam, and Christianity.

During a final journey to England in 1806, Roberts gained copies of Priestley's *Church History*, *Institutes of Natural and Revealed Religion*, and *Comparison of the Institutions of Moses with those of the Hindoos.*[3] While purchasing these and other more recent books by Lindsey, Roberts received an invitation to meet the Reverend J. Joyce of Camden Town although Roberts unfortunately had to return to India before the meeting could take place. While one would wonder why Roberts did not take the initiative in meeting either Lindsey or Belsham, his failure to do so can be understood when one appreciates his own sense of inferiority coupled with a serious determination to serve those with whom he was socially equal and linguistically compatible. He wrote Belsham:

> Though my poverty and mean situation in life and also my disqualification and incapability to teach, be two great impediments, yet as far as lay in my power, I always made a point of answering, and instructing, and giving all the information I was master of to all those of my countrymen who would.[4]

So it was that Roberts began conversion and the organization of a Unitarian religious community. His first congregant, Meguel

Annathy, a "sickly" seventy-five-year-old man, "originally a convert to Roman Catholicism from Heathenism" operated a Tamil school for the children of Unitarians. After preparing a Tamil prayerbook modeled after that of Theophilus Lindsey, and purchasing a burying ground, a "small place of worship" was opened on December 19, 1813.

Usually Roberts would conduct worship. In his absence, Annathy would lead prayers and read scripture. "Here we baptize, administer the Lord's supper, give marriage, and bury our dead," Roberts reported. "We shall be very glad to have a regular Unitarian minister to do all these for us; but we do not know from what quarter we can look for such a blessing, for we are poor and helpless." Indicating that both inquiries and opposition had come from Europeans and Indians, Roberts concluded his first letter to Belsham with a series of requests for support while praying encouragement to the Unitarians that their religion might "become the means of enlightening the whole world with rational Christianity."[5]

While neither British nor American Unitarians organized themselves into an association of individuals who could mutually support each other through their associated churches until 1825, both groups had several publications, the *Monthly Repository* and *The Christian Reformer* published in England and *The Christian Register* and *The Christian Disciple* (called *Christian Examiner* after 1824) in Boston, plus *The Unitarian Miscellany and Monitor* of Baltimore, in which the first American Unitarian reaction to Rammohun Roy appeared. The response to Rammohun as well as that to William Roberts began slowly in the pages of *The Christian Reformer* in London in 1818 and in the pages of the newly published *Christian Register* in Boston in 1821.

With so much effort in the domestic struggle against a hostile orthodoxy and in the support of publications espousing the Unitarian cause, news of William Roberts's request for help in far-off Madras, exciting as it may have appeared, came as something of a shock. When he sent a letter of support and a parcel of books for Roberts to translate into Tamil, Belsham explained the nature of the British Unitarian problem in 1818 in this way:

> I stated that it was not within the purview of our society to send out missionaries. And that for my own part, I could not see how they could be of any use. That Roberts appeared to me to be fully

competent to teach the youth in the Christian doctrine; and that if he could get two or three young men of good talents and character, with proper instruction from him, they would be much better qualified to teach the Gospel to their countrymen than any missionary we could send from England.[6]

In his request that a missionary be sent out from England, Roberts expressed the feeling, which was to remain throughout the uncertain history of the Madras Unitarian movement, that the small, poor community whose members came from low-caste origins could barely survive without paternalistic assistance from England and America. Belsham's response, in return, set the tone for most future British Unitarian interest in India. Financial and publication support seemed feasible, but sending English missionaries seemed remote and undesirable. The American attitude, however, would eventually be far more positive and aggressive.

Subsequent correspondence demonstrates the profound effect English Unitarianism was to have on Roberts and the Madras movement. Writing later in 1818 but before having heard from Belsham concerning limited support, Roberts wrote,

> The Reverend Theophilus Lindsey has lighted our lamp; the Reverend Dr. Joseph Priestley has supplied this lamp with pure oil in abundance; the Reverend Thomas Belsham has taken a lively interest to stir up the wick of this lamp: may the Reverend Thomas Madge, and the most respectable and benevolent English Unitarian Society at large give hand, encourage, assist and hold up this most glorious and pure lamp till Indian superstition be no more.[7]

The spirit moving Roberts and his little Madrasi community was indeed marvelous to behold. With the death of his friend Annathy, the school was turned over to a Trinitarian whose salary Roberts had to pay partially from his own pocket. After projecting publishing expenses for Unitarian tracts in Tamil and exploring ideas on how to expand his community he commented on subtle opposition saying, "The Trinitarians (both black and white), teachers and disciples, persuade themselves that when William Roberts dies, the name of Unitarians will cease here. . ."[8]

The lead articles in the *Christian Reformer* for January 1818 and 1819 describing William Roberts and his church and Thomas Belsham's limited response did not go unnoticed by the readership. One articulate observer took Belsham to task for his statement that the possibility of inducing anyone to "submit to the difficulties and perils of a missionary life in order to propagate pure and uncorrupt Christianity . . . is an event *more to be desired than expected.*" "And why not *expected*?" the reader retorted. The Moravians, Baptists, and Methodists had carried on missionary work without even being asked to. While recognizing that Unitarians did not consider all Heathen subject to damnation if they did not become Christian, he went on to argue that "if Unitarianism be worth believing, it must be worth propagating." Urging that Unitarians not appear lukewarm or indifferent, for to do so would be to repudiate the cause of Christ and his apostles, he called upon the Unitarian leadership to respond to Roberts who had so eloquently written his praises to Lindsey and Priestley.[9]

By June 1821, Roberts wrote that he had two new large families and two other converts from Catholicism now in his congregation. His notes on the Gospels and Acts were ready for use by the congregation. Additionally, Roberts had prepared two boards, one containing "the list of false readings and mistranslations in our Tamil New Testament . . . and another list containing questions to the Trinitarians taken from the *Christian Reformer.* Both lists were made available in his school at Pursewaukum for all to read or copy. On the matter of incorrect readings of the Scripture, Roberts reported that he now had access to three different Tamil translations, the most recent prepared by the Calcutta Auxiliary Bible Society in 1771. Citing critical words left out of certain passages Roberts also quoted such passages as Ephesians iv:32 where "instead of 'God for Christ's sake hath forgiven you,' it is 'God in Christ hath forgiven you,' " or in I Timothy i:12 the Tamil read "I adore Jesus Christ our Lord" rather than the accurate "I thank Jesus Christ our Lord."[10]

Roberts must have amazed the English Unitarians as a budding scholar of the New Testament. His letter of June 1818 with its report of two newly published tracts had also showed him to be something of a comparativist. The first of the two for which Roberts was seeking support for publication was entitled "Thrunagalachothy" or, in English, "A Seasonable Light." The work was an attempt to present a critical position against both theological Christianity and traditional Hinduism. In the first chapter, for example, Roberts argued against the idea that man could exist "in a separate state before his birth on earth (an attempt to repudiate the Athenasian creedal position on Christ). In the second he strongly opposed image worship in a statement directed against both Hinduism and Catholicism. Another chapter argued that the "soul" was nothing more than the life principle and against the Christian and Hindu idea that the soul could exist independently of the body. Three chapters explored the relation to the Christian Trinity of the Hindu *Trimurti* or Trinity and its belief in Brahma as creator, Vishnu as sustainer, and Shiva as destroyer. Each of these Gods of Hindu mythology, Roberts demonstrated, was really an Old Testament figure. In the case of Shiva, he surmised, "that he is no other than the first created man, Adam (Gen. 2:7). Shiva's destroying power consists of inflicting death on his offspring. This originates from his having eaten the forbidden fruit." The penultimate chapter repudiated Hindu vegetarianism as superior to the eating of fish or animal foods while the final chapter was an outline of Christianity including the Ten Commandments and Lord's Prayer.[11]

The second of Roberts's tracts was a series of more than eighty questions and answers leading the reader not only from Hinduism to the excellence of Christianity but onward to the truths of the Unitarian Christianity of Priestley and Lindsey. As for news of the Madras mission, the English Unitarian *Monthly Repository* carried regular reports from Roberts for the next decade including the important fact in 1823 that William Adam, the Unitarian minister and supporter of Rammohun Roy in Calcutta, was now corresponding with Roberts on a monthly basis. By mid-July 1823, Roberts reported that he had published and distributed new tracts including accounts of Rammohun Roy's Unitarianism and his *Precepts of Jesus.* Another letter that year reported Roberts's first contact with an "English-American Unitarian gentleman," Edward Poole, who had visited the church at Christmas.[12]

That Roberts was taking every opportunity to gain support was evident from his statement that sent Poole home to Philadelphia with Tamil tracts, greetings and requests for more materials from America. Aware also that William Adam might possibly receive British Unitarian support for his work with Rammohun in Calcutta, Roberts requested that Adam be allowed to extend his mission to Madras. He realized again, however, that the poverty and low-caste standing of his community with its lack of European constituency would probably mean that neither Adam nor any other missionary would be sent. Another letter from Roberts to British Unitarians written late in 1824 detailed the structure and problems of the congregation now grown to twenty families primarily of "parish" or servant caste.

> Most of the men are gentlemen's servants, such as butlers, cooks, butler's mates, cook's mates: three of them are drummers in the company of the Nabob, one is a Lascar in the company's service, three are teachers. . . The women in general manage their home affairs, and take care of their children. Most of the men, and some women, can read; several of them have purchased Bibles for themselves. . .

Roberts stressed the significance of education for the children of the members' families and the prejudicial difficulties some had faced when placing their children either in regular mission schools or in schools open to Muslims or upper-caste Hindus. He then concluded this detailed letter with another plea for support.

> Above all, in behalf of us and our much debased countrymen, we earnestly entreat . . . all Unitarian and Christian ministers and people to unite their God-like zeal, love, and charity together, to bless Madras also with Unitarian missionaries, and specially with one, if possible before I am no more. . .[13]

William Roberts, the first Indian Unitarian Christian, was a man of drive and determination, limited in resources but working constantly for the religious cause in which he deeply believed. Compared to the more famous Rammohun Roy of Calcutta, William Roberts received little attention from his British and American counterparts. Ironically, however, while Unitarianism in Calcutta and its Hindu counterpart the Brahmo Samaj rose, divided, and declined over the decades, the small Unitarian movement in Madras has persisted as one continuous church to the present day.

From the perspective of this study, Roberts was a minor character. He and his little community set the stage, however, for the religious liberals such as Rammohun Roy and William Adam who would indeed make a significant impact on early nineteenth century Indian life.

RAMMOHUN ROY

CHAPTER FOUR

Rammohun Roy

Rammohun Roy, born a Brahmin in 1772 and later dubbed the "Father of Modern India," was an impressive and outstanding person whether in his own time or in any other.[1] He was original in much of his thinking even if obviously a product of the culture in which he was raised. Rammohun was capable of expressing himself well in both English and Bengali; he was learned in Arabic, Persian, and Sanskrit; and he was at least somewhat familiar with Hebrew and Greek as a result of his work with the missionaries. His contemporary Ramram Basu had already explored ideas of religious reform within Hinduism before Rammohun became active in his own campaigns. However, Rammohun's sense that religious Hindus needed to return to a purified "Unitarian" monistic Vedantic system, as opposed to the prevalent polytheism, came alive in him not only because of his contacts with Orientalist scholars such as H. H. Wilson, but also because of the Sanskrit pundits with whom he studied in his youth. Rammohun's exposure to Islam, Tibetan Buddhism, and certain schools of Western as well as Indian philosophy opened him to some eclectic interests. Rammohun was enough of a "Renaissance man" to work in his religious writings and activities at reforming Hinduism as well as attempting to clarify the meaning of Christianity.

By raising religious and ultimately social and political questions about such issues as *sati* (widow burning) and caste practice, Rammohun did not ingratiate himself to orthodox elements of Hindu society, even though pressures for these social reforms were made as much to the British rulers as to Brahmin Hindu society. Further, as Professor David Kopf has asserted,[2] Rammohun's expressions for reform were limited to his writings. He did not engage much, if at all, in educational reform institutions or societies. Of thirty-two works Rammohun wrote in Bengali, only three dealt with social questions and each of these pertained to *sati*, though two other works raised questions of caste responsibility. Moreover, Rammohun's first ten works in English were concerned solely with Vedantic religious questions or were translations of *Upanishads*. After 1820, Rammohun began to publish far more in English on issues such as women's rights, freedom of the press, inheritance, and rights to ancestral properties, but even so, twenty-five of Rammohun's forty English publications dealt with primarily religious issues.

Rammohun was considered significant on three levels not only by the English Unitarians who discovered his writings in 1818 but also by the American Unitarians who discovered him in 1821. Rammohun's interest in translating basic Hindu religious texts and commenting upon them while reinterpreting them to meet the needs of the times first attracted Western liberal religious attention. Then Rammohun's campaigns on such social questions as *sati* had a natural appeal on ethical and humanitarian grounds. Finally, Rammohun's writings on the New Testament and his controversy with Joshua Marshman and other Baptist missionaries at Serampore brought out major Unitarian support, spiritually and financially, for Rammohun's efforts.

When Rammohun Roy began his study of Jesus, he was already a liberal reformer within his own tradition. Writing in English as early as 1816 in the preface to his "Abridgement of the Vedant," Rammohun spoke of

> the injurious rites, introduced by the peculiar practice of Hindoo idolatry, which, more than any other Pagan worship, destroys the texture of society, and together with compassion for my countrymen, have compelled me to use every possible effort to awaken them from their dream of error.[3]

Rammohun's use of the term "pagan" is fascinating in this context, as he was not yet even exploring the texts of Christianity. Yet, in the same introductory passage cited here, he indicates that although a Brahmin, he had been sensitive to the study of various sects and castes of Hinduism, "observing the superstitious puerilities into which they have been thrown by their self-interested guides."

It was thus that Rammohun took up his study of Christianity and, after considerable research, found, as he himself said, "the doctrines of Christ more conducive to moral principles, and better adapted for the use of rational beings than any other."[4] It was in this spirit and out of a personal background that Rammohun undertook writing *The Precepts of Jesus*, in which he set out the crucial human and ethical passages of the Synoptic Gospels as the best way to introduce the New Testament to his countrymen.[5] For his efforts as a non-believer, Rammohun was roundly attacked by the Reverend Joshua Marshman, editor of the evangelical publication, *The Friend of India.* This attack led Rammohun to compose three rebuttals or "Appeals" in addition to a series of other publications through which he attempted to clarify his views of Jesus.

M. M. Thomas, the Indian Christian scholar, has provided a useful reference in setting out what he called the "three fundamental ideas of Rammohun's religion."[6] The first is Rammohun's monotheistic faith and his emphasis on the unity of God, which Thomas assumes Rammohun first learned as much from Islam as from Vedanta. Second is that morality is the essence of true religion and that moral degradation results from the practice of polytheism and idolatry. The third point is that rationalism was a basic tool in the development of Rammohun's religious outlook. While the former two principles showed through his work on the Vedanta and Upanishads, it was Rammohun's use of biblical critical principles, rather in advance of his time and unusual for the context in which he was living, which brought a keen use of rational technique to his work.

By the time he was working on the *Precepts*, however, Rammohun articulated the idea that no human being could truly understand the nature of ultimate reality through philosophical reasoning. It was thus that he decided

> to leave speculative doctrines of religion aside and adhere to the notion rationally arrived at, 'of the existence of a supreme superintending power, the Author and Preserver of this harmonious system' and to concentrate on the discovery of a morality which will 'reconcile us to human nature and . . . render our existence agreeable to ourselves and profitable to mankind.'[7]

Because of his emphasis on the moral teachings of Jesus as a base for religiousness, and because of his repudiation by Marshman for taking portions of the scripture out of context, Rammohun came to the attention of American and British Unitarians. "These precepts," Rammohun wrote in the preface of his book,

> separated from the mysterious dogmas and historical records, appear . . . to contain not only the essence of all that is necessary to instruct mankind in their civil duties, but also the best and only

means of obtaining the forgiveness of sins, the favour of God and the strength to overcome our passions and to keep his commandments.[8]

Thomas finds all Hindu religious writers who did not convert to Christianity less than adequate theologically and justifies Marshman's criticism of Rammohun on the grounds that Rammohun would allow law to be sufficient and to justify and sanctify mankind. By contrast, the purpose of Paul's teachings and the doctrine of the church was to press faith over law. It is on this point of theology that one must take exception to Thomas' approach to Hindu religious liberals influenced by the life and teachings of Jesus. While he gives them credit for opening the way to Christ for many Indians, Thomas also belittles the liberal application of the teachings and spirit of Jesus when it deviates from acceptable Christian theological molds or is worked eclectically into some form of Hindu faith. Thomas is perceptive in making distinctions among the liberals, all of whom were members of Rammohun's Brahmo Samaj founded in 1828. He realizes that when one moves from Rammohun to Keshub Chunder Sen to Protap Mazumdar that the emphasis moves from "the teachings to the teacher."[9] Similarly, Thomas points to two implicit criticisms of Rammohun's theological position found in Keshub's later utilization of Jesus. The first is that Rammohun's approach to the Gospels was basically secular or academic in nature. Second, he attacks Rammohun's deistic or unitarian faith which could give no credence to the idea of divine incarnation nor compromise a strict monotheism. But Thomas has neglected Rammohun on subjects of concern to this study: the organization of a Unitarian church in Calcutta, the struggle of and between Rammohun Roy and William Adam (an encounter in acculturation itself), and the final decision by Rammohun to establish a Hindu-based Brahmo Samaj rather than to join a Christian Unitarian movement.

The Unitarian Discovery of Rammohun

Rammohun Roy's reputation reached America by way of England and the Reverend Thomas Belsham, the English Unitarian who had already corresponded with William Roberts of Madras. Writing in the same 1818 article as that from which he quoted William Roberts's letter of introduction, Thomas

Belsham commented on his awareness, through Christian missionary sources, that "the great doctrine of the Unity and unrivalled supremacy of God" was also "making a triumphant progress among the higher castes of Hindoos in the great and populous city of Calcutta."[10] Describing Rammohun Roy as a "learned, eloquent and opulent Brahmun," Belsham expressed genuine excitement that Rammohun had

> by the proper exercise of his own understanding, discovered the folly and absurdity of the Hindoo mythology and of idol-worship, was led by a conscientious sense of duty to proclaim this important discovery to his countrymen, and has publicly taught the doctrine of the divine Unity and perfection to the native Hindoos, and has entered his protest against their impious, barbarous and idolatrous rites . . . and it is said that many hundreds of the native Hindoos, and especially of the young people, have embraced his doctrine. He does not profess to be a Christian.[11]

Belsham's statement indicates his own belief, typical of English Christians of that time, that there was little if any good in orthodox Hindu Vaisnavism, that religious tradition which he dubbed a "folly and absurdity." Belsham was also enthusiastic at finding that Rammohun, though not a Christian, was a religious rationalist urging belief in the Vedantic doctrine of Divine Unity. Thus Belsham was led to the belief that Rammohun was already developing a religious reform movement in Bengal even though there was no factual evidence to support this view.

Strongly organized religious reform would hardly be the case even a decade later. But of even greater interest to the English Unitarian was the news that Rammohun was about to undertake the study of the gospel "with twenty other learned Brahmuns . . . with the greatest possible attention and impartiality; in order to discover their real meaning."[12]

In 1819, readers of the *Monthly Respository*, already introduced to Rammohun Roy by a letter published in 1818 by one of Rammohun's English admirers, were presented a major review of five of his works on Hinduism published during 1816 and 1817. One of these books had already been published in London. The books reviewed included Rammohun's *Abridgement of the Vedant*, translations of the *Kena* and *Isa Upanishads*, *The Defense of Hindu Theism in Reply to the Attack of an Advocate for Idolatry*, and *An Apology for the*

Present System of Hindoo Worship. Citing biographical data on Rammohun provided him by the English editor of the *Kena Upanishad,* the reviewer enticed his Unitarian readers further by quoting from a recent letter of Rammohun's to John Digby, a former civil servant and friend in India:

> The consequence of my long and uninterrupted researches into religious truth has been, that I have found the doctrines of Christ more conducive to moral principles, and better adapted for the use of rational beings, than any others which have come to my knowledge.[13]

Continuing his letter, Rammohun stressed to Digby how much he wished to convince Brahmins of how superstitious and miserable their religious rites and domestic ceremonies were. However, in his attempts to point out to them that the doctrine of Divine Unity was at the very basis of the Vedanta, Rammohun was opposed and rebuffed. Indicating that he had now received support from a few friends, although not the large numbers which Thomas Belsham had previously indicated, Rammohun appeared in his letter to Digby to be seeking outside support. Although the reviewer of Rammohun's works was not sufficiently versed in Hindu religious doctrine to know whether Rammohun had proven his point, the reviewer found the numerous obvious passages in the Upanishads, such as "God is indeed one and has no second," adequate. Clearly the Unitarian reviewer knew nothing of the totality of the Vedas or the Vedantic tradition. He accepted as an accurate judgment Rammohun's conclusion that while most Brahmins knew better, they also knew their means of livelihood would be destroyed should "the rites, ceremonies and festivals of idolatry" be suspended. Commenting on the doctrine of Vedanta itself, the reviewer wrote of Rammohun's position:

> The doctrine of the Vedant that 'God is everywhere and every thing is in God' which is, it seems pleaded in behalf of Hindoo idolatry, amounts to no more, according to Rammohun Roy, than 'nothing is absent from God, and nothing bears real existence except by the volition of the conceived existence of the universe, which is acted upon by him in the same manner as a human body is by soul.'[14]

The point here, as well as of a subsequent article in the *Monthly Repository* of January 1820, by the French Bishop

Abbé Gregoire, was that it presented Rammohun and his work from a sympathetic yet biased, even polemical, point of view. Writing in support of Rammohun, the Abbé Gregoire commented that

> Whatever be the abstract merit of Rammohun Roy, there is probably throughout India no Brahmin who is less a Brahmin and less a Hindoo than he; and thousands of dupes who have suffered the loss of their caste have been less offenders against the peculiarities of their religion than he.[15]

Praising Rammohun for his opposition to caste, the Abbé made the important point that "Far, however, from wishing to lose his Brahmanical dignity, it is upon *that* he founds his enterprise; asserting that it is his duty as a Brahmin, to instruct his countrymen in the sense and in the real commands of their sacred books."[16]

Thus it was that as a reformer of Hinduism who clearly wished to remain part of his tradition, yet for whom Christ and Christianity had increasing meaning, that English and American Unitarians, via the pages of the *Christian Register* of Boston in 1821, came to know of Rammohun Roy and his work. The letter to John Digby published in the *Repository* review set the stage for Rammohun's further research into Christian teaching and doctrine. What Rammohun did not expect from his study of Christianity was the emergence of a major controversy.

Acquainted with Christians in Calcutta for four years before beginning his *The Precepts of Jesus* in 1820, Rammohun had learned some Hebrew and Greek.[17] Deeply concerned about ethics and morality, Rammohun studied the Gospels in order to determine the ethical teachings of Jesus and to separate the "essentials" from accretions, which he believed the Baptist missionaries stressed in their presentation of Christianity. The study was clearly related to his earlier presentations of the Vedanta, for Rammohun wrote in the preface to *The Precepts of Jesus* that in separating the ethical teachings from the bulk of doctrinal material he could reach out to the universal religious concerns of mankind. "This simple code of religion, and morality," he wrote,

> is so admirably calculated to elevate men's ideas to high and liberal notions of one God, who has equally subjected all living creatures, without distinction of caste, rank or wealth, to change, disappoint-

ment, pain and death, and has equally admitted all to be partakers of the bountiful mercies which he has lavished over nature, and is also so well fitted to regulate the conduct of the human race in the discharge of their various duties to God, to themselves, and to society, that I cannot but hope the best effects from its promulgation in the present form.[18]

Rammohun's interest in the study of Christianity was polemical to the extent that he wished to point up what he saw as the essential teachings of Christ, just as he had written about the Vedanta to point up what he believed were the essentials of Hinduism. In his universal interests, which he never fully pursued in the study of Islam or Buddhism, he far surpassed the Unitarian Christians of London or Boston, many of whom accepted Rammohun as a Unitarian Christian on the basis of his writings in the *Precepts* and his subsequent controversy with Joshua Marshman.

From an orthodox Christian point of view, as expressed by M. M. Thomas, Rammohun was to be faulted for separating the teaching of Jesus from the historical events of his life, death, and resurrection; for ignoring much of the Gospel of John in favor of the Synoptic; and for failing to understand that the message of the New Testament in its entirety was a message of salvation from sin. Rammohun believed that the teachings of Jesus alone were sufficient to "reconcile us to human nature and render our existence agreeable to ourselves and profitable to the rest of mankind."[19]

Such an expression of his faith in Jesus Christ was directly in the rationalist and Arian tradition being developed by English and particularly American Unitarians. Arguing that it was the words of Christ which led to his works and his works which led to his authority among his disciples, Manilal Parekh, writing of Rammohun, has stated:

He sealed his Precepts with his blood and through the love that he thus showed invested them with not only that authority but even divine power, without which they could have been but a dead letter or what is worse an infinitude of burden which no human being could bear for a moment.[20]

Parekh, an Indian Christian writing long after the controversy, has agreed with Marshman who saw the teachings of Jesus as proofs of his power and grace to save. For Marshman, the two leading doctrines of the New Testament could be summed up:

That God views all sin as so abominable that the death of Jesus Christ alone can expiate its guilt; and that the human heart is so corrupt that it must be renewed by the Divine Spirit before a man can enter heaven. . . Without these two dogmas, what is the Gospel?[21]

Rammohun, who had tried sincerely to explore the truth of religious morality in his *Precepts*, was deeply hurt by the attack of Marshman in the *Friend of India* journal. That any seeker after truth should be faulted in such a narrow way was difficult for Rammohun to understand. He felt compelled to respond as did Marshman in return. In all, Rammohun wrote three increasingly long responses, *An Appeal to the Christian Public in Defence of the Precepts of Jesus*, *The Second Appeal*, and *The Final Appeal.* In *The Second Appeal*, Rammohun pointed to Marshman's "seven positions" on the authority of Scripture to prove the deity of Jesus, positions that stressed the omniscience and omnipotence of Christ. The argument between the two seemed at this point to be about the two natures of Christ, Marshman stressing the divine nature at the expense of the human, Rammohun emphasizing the human as that which was essential for all humankind.

Most of the controversy with Marshman took place during 1820 and 1821 during which time Rammohun wrote and published all but the *Final Appeal.* In addition, the first two issues of the *Brahmanical Magazine* published anonymously by Rammohun were used as a broadside to defend Hinduism against the attacks coming from Christian missionaries. For Hindus, even if Rammohun represented the most liberal segment of that community, a new day was dawning. One of their own was willing to stand firm against the outsiders. Joining William Adam, soon Rammohun would make one of those Christians an ally with him and with Unitarianism.

CHAPTER FIVE

The Unusual Career of William Adam

During the controversy with Joshua Marshman, the scholarly and dynamic Rammohun Roy was not estranged from all Christian missionaries in Calcutta. His interest in Christianity kept him in close touch with several others, two of whom, the Reverend William Adam and the Reverend William Yates, both "well reputed for their Oriental and classical acquirements" according to Rammohun, sought out the controversial Brahmin to assist them in a new translation of the New Testament into Bengali. They had accepted Rammohun's suggestion that a new translation was needed. As Adam himself reported in a letter to the supporting Committee of the Baptist Missionary Society, June 11, 1821, Rammohun had asserted that the two earlier translations by a Mr. Ellerton and the well-known missionary Dr. Carey "abounded in the most flagrant violations of native idiom."[1]

The work of translation went well until the three men reached the third verse of the first chapter of the *Gospel of John.* At first the group agreed that the Greek preposition *dia* could be translated "through" and all were willing to render the phrase, "All things were made through Him." However, Yates soon feared that if *dia* was not translated "by," the heresy of Arianism might be implied. He quickly withdrew from the project leaving Adam and Rammohun Roy to finish it. During the process, the two became close friends and Adam decided that there was indeed no proof of the Trinity in the New Testament.

Given the context and the times, this was a major and courageous decision for Adam to make. In accepting Arianism, and therefore Unitarianism, he was cutting himself off from the Baptists who had educated him and brought him to India as a missionary. By allying himself with Rammohun Roy, he was choosing to befriend and support a man whose reform attempts in Hinduism and whose writings on Christianity had made him an enemy of both Brahmins and Englishmen. Conversion by a "heathen" was more than enough to bring sharp derision on the former Baptist now dubbed by his evangelical friends as "the second fallen Adam." The pleas of William Roberts in Madras and the initial writings of Rammohun on Hinduism and Christianity had brought interest but relatively little active response from American and English Unitarians. The "conversion" of William Adam, however, with the ensuing controversy in Calcutta and the ream of correspondence that was to follow the organization of a Unitarian Society in Bengal brought on a multitude of activities including published correspondence and perceptive articles about possible missionary efforts in the publications of Boston and London Unitarians.

By the autumn of 1822, *The Monthly Repository* published not only a series of letters by a London Baptist minister strongly opposed to Adam's activities in Calcutta, but also responses by London Unitarians and, later, responses by Adam, too. The key document was Adam's letter to the Baptist Committee in Calcutta dated September 21, 1821, and published in London during 1823. He explained that while he was discharging his duties as a missionary he began to wonder how he could convince Hindus to give up their belief in "idolatry" while still teaching them the "Trinity." Adam explained further that these doubts had led him to a close scrutiny of the Scriptures, the result of which study had convinced him that he could no longer teach Trinitarian doctrine to Hindus. "In order to prevent all misunderstanding," he continued,

> I beg to assure you that the supreme, underived, independent deity of Jesus Christ, and the distinct personality of the Holy Spirit, are the only doctrines belonging to my former system of belief which I feel compelled to reject; and that although my first doubts respecting them were suggested by conversing with intelligent Hindoos on the principles of *natural reason* . . . yet it is not on that ground alone that I have finally rejected them.[2]

Though reason had brought him to his decision, Adam still placed revelation above reason. Now an Arian in the truest sense, Adam, without using that heretical epithet, stressed that he still believed Jesus Christ to be the only-begotten Son of God, that he believed in the immaculate conception, and that he also believed in Christ's twofold nature as Son of God and Son of Man. Adam also emphasized his belief in the resurrection, Christ's ascension into heaven, his role as intercessor with the Father, and his being the atoning sacrifice for all people. The stumbling point was that Adam had sincerely concluded, in the tradition that Rammohun had himself developed, that "there is only one God and Father of all, who is above all, and through all, and in us all, so there is only one Mediator between God and men."[3] The tone of Adam's letter was, he asserted, "guarded and conciliatory," and by it he intended to ameliorate the Baptists' hostility. He admitted to the editor of *The Monthly Repository*, however, that he did not expect any positive change in the Baptists' attitude toward him.

The letter to the Baptist Committee published by London Unitarians in 1823 was accompanied by a longer letter from Adam in which he expressed the fact that his views had since become more liberal. "The simple humanity of Christ's person and the unpurchased mercy of God, are doctrines which, since writing it, have fully recommended themselves to my understanding and my heart."[4] Adam also stood firm against the numerous charges which had been published against him by the London Baptist minister Joseph Ivemey.

Adam: Man and Missionary

William Adam, an exciting but neglected figure in Unitarian history, has perhaps been neglected because his career spanned so many dimensions for such short periods and because it seems to have ended unfulfilled. Though he lived during the heart of the nineteenth century, his career was something of a prototype of the mid-twentieth century Unitarian minister. His interests and talents were diverse. A convert from orthodox Protestantism, his outspoken attitude on social questions and governmental actions was far more typical of the present day than of his own time. In many respects William Adam can be compared closely with William Ellery Channing and Theodore Parker in American Unitarianism.

Born in the last decade of the eighteenth century, a native of Dumfermline, Scotland, Adam attended St. Andrews School until he was accepted as a ministerial candidate by the Baptist Missionary Society. In 1815, he became a student at Bristol and a year later he attended Glasgow until his departure for Serampore in 1818. Two months prior to leaving for India, he was married to Phoebe Grant, older daughter of famed missionary Charles Grant and older sister of the wife of the Reverend William Yates.[5] While residing in Calcutta, Adam began the study of Sanskrit and Bengali, but after about a year, he began an arrangement of living six months each year with William Carey at Dignapore. Late in 1818, he joined with

William Yates and some other missionaries to establish the Circular Road Church where he remained a member and relatively obscure junior missionary until the translation issue and his heresy trial in 1821.[6]

The translation project with Rammohun and Yates took place during the winter of 1821, terminating on March 21 in the debate over the translation into Bengali of John 1:3. Adam has claimed in all his letters as well as in an 1861 interview with Charles Dall that even Yates had great doubts about the Trinity at the time of the translation but, possibly afraid of the consequences to himself and his career at being allied with Rammohun Roy, Yates became an even stauncher defender of his Trinitarian Baptist views and led the council at the Circular Road Church which denounced Adam's heresy in September 1821. The church's attitude toward Adam was clear from its pronouncement about him:

> That Mr. Adam, having expressed sentiments which are entirely opposite to the fundamental doctrines of the Gospel on which it is established do, in justice to the glory and character of Christ, and to express its own entire disapprobation of such sentiments, exclude brother Adam from its communion and privileges, but with the most sincere desire that he may, through Grace, at length perceive his error and return to the Truth, when the Church will be truly glad to receive him again, as sorry now to exclude him.[7]

Adam appears to have been somewhat foolhardy to make such a commitment to ideology, cutting himself off from friends and family in a distant land. Yet, he seems to have had the courage of his convictions, sticking to and refining his new beliefs even at the cost of continuous battle and uncertain financial future. While working with Rammohun during the next five years and corresponding with English and American Unitarians to gain support for his mission dream, he served as a clerk with the Crittenden, McKillop Company in Calcutta. He seems surely to have believed, as the most zealous convert to any new idea would, that Unitarian Christianity and Rammohun Roy were the religious future for Bengal, for Adam stood by both for years to come.

Reflecting on the translation project, Adam has insisted that Rammohun knew no Greek or Latin, where many Bengali writers have suggested he did, and that he had studied Hebrew for perhaps only six months. At the time of the project, Adam asserted, Rammohun held "high Arian views," calling Jesus "the first born of every creature" and "high as the angels of God and even higher than they" in his already published *Precepts.*[8] A year later in his published sermon, "The Claims of Jesus," Adam expressed similar views:

> He is as far below the unoriginal Jehovah as the derivation of nature can place him — and he is as far above every other existence as the immediateness of that derivation can raise him. Such then is Jesus — the first and only being begotten in the womb of a virgin by the immediate power of God and the first and only being raised from death to life by the immediate power of God.[9]

The reaction against Adam's conversion and Roy's writings as well as against the commencing of a Unitarian Committee was considerable. From the perspective of an historian, the threat posed by Unitarians was really not much more than that which Baptists and Anglicans posed to each other. Yet, beyond the articles which Joshua Marshman published against Rammohun, William Yates also published, in the name of the Baptist mission, a series of essays attacking both Adam and Rammohun. Answering the charges that the *Precepts* distorted Christian teaching because they took Jesus out of his Biblical context, Adam replied that missionaries frequently distributed the New Testament without the Old, the Gospels without the Epistles and even particular Biblical stories in tract form. How were Hindus given these texts to know whether they were the whole or part of Christian Scripture?[10] In response to the charge of Marshman, supported by Yates, that Rammohun had overlooked the "grand design of revelation" and the doctrines issuing from revelation, in stressing the practical part of the Gospel, Adam answered that the only doctrines Rammohun sought to exclude were those which Jesus Christ did not really teach.[11]

The conclusion of Adam's lengthy letter stressed how ineffective most missionary work in India had been since the arrival of the first two Baptist missionaries some thirty years before. One would think that from the negative experiences missionaries had undergone, they "would have anxiously sought to cherish the slightest tendancy to Christianity in such a person as Rammohun Roy." Finding errors in his presentation of Christianity, Adam suggested that they might have attempted constructive criticism instead of using "opprobrious epithets, injurious imputations and the most barefaced calumnies employed to bear him down." Concluding his letter in anger, Adam wrote,

> I am compelled to say that they know neither their own spirit, nor the spirit of the master whom they profess to serve, and that judging not by their professions, but by their conduct in this particular case, they might, without any breach of charity, be supposed to have come to this country not to spread Christianity but to retard its progress.[12]

Adam as Journalist

William Adam found allies in the English political press which supported Rammohun and the right of Unitarians to organize in Calcutta quite apart from the truth or falsehood of their theology. *The India Gazette* in 1824, reviewing the Adam letter to Yates, asserted boldly that Rammohun had bested Marshman in the battle while the *Bengal Chronicle*, editorializing twice during October, 1827, stated that

> Whatever may be the merits or demerits of Unitarianism as compared with the more orthodox faith, surely even the most bigotted Trinitarianism would not be infatuated enough to deny that it would be a wonderful step in the religious advancement of the worshippers of wood and stone, to make them worshippers of one great universal cause even in the Unitarian form![13]

The support of the press may well have been due to the fact that Adam became involved with it as early as 1825 when James Sutherland, then editor of the *Bengal Chronicle*, avoided suppression of the paper by admitting to the authorship of certain anti-government articles published there. Adam succeeded as editor, serving for more than a year until he had a major disagreement with the owner. In January, 1827, Adam started *The Calcutta Chronicle*, assisted by Sutherland as co-proprietor and co-editor. Adam spoke out strongly against the Calcutta Stamp Act in an editorial and soon received word from the Government that the *Chronicle*'s license to publish had been revoked. In March 1829 Adam became editor of *The India Gazette*, a task to which he devoted himself full time for several years after the collapse of the Unitarian mission project. According to the founder of the competing *Englishman*, *The Gazette* changed from being "an indifferent spectator of local events" to a "calm yet scrupulous and honest investigator of every question of interest . . . that could possibly be offered to the consideration of a community growing in extent and intelligence."[14] By November 1829 its circulation had increased from 350 to 569 and by 1830 it went from bi-weekly to daily with a tri-weekly supplement.

The editor of the *Englishman*, in placing judgment upon Adam and the *Gazette*, was accurate in stating that its politics were "ultra-radical," a term he believed also applicable to the Anglo-Bengali community to which the *Gazette* meant to appeal. He admired Adam's courage in constantly discussing questions of Government policy "undeterred by any fear of the displeasure of authority, or any anxiety for the applause of the multitudes."[15] Toward the end of 1833, however, the English owners of the paper were forced to sell it during a financial crisis. It was subsequently bought up by Dwarkanath Tagore, Rammohun's close friend whose son, Debendranath, would next lead the Brahmo Samaj. Dwarkanath merged the *Chronicle* with the *Bengal Harkaru*, though Adam continued to edit the tri-weekly edition which continued under the name *Calcutta Chronicle* through 1834. During these years, Adam received as much as 1400 rupees a month as a clerk for McIntosh Company and as editor. It is little wonder that he did not appreciate the token support offered by the American Unitarian Association and the British Unitarians who never felt themselves quite in a position to respond to his far-sighted plans.

Adam as Government Servant

With the closing of the *Gazette* and the failure of the mission, William Adam turned to what was to be the most illustrious part of his career. In 1835, he was hired by Lord William Bentinck, Governor General of Bengal, to conduct a major investigation into the state of vernacular education in Bengal and Bihar. Adam had grown tired of the widespread English assumption that the native population was illiterate and uncivilized. He had written articles in the *Gazette* maintaining that such an assumption was wholly false and would ultimately lead the English into great difficulties. Adam insisted that the native population was largely self-taught and "civilized."[16]

Lord William Bentinck, an enlightened and sensitive governor, requested Adam to submit a proposal for his study which

Adam, in his typical methodical manner, did in ten major points. The purpose of his effort he stated in strongly moral terms:

> It is assumed that the Government is desirous of encouraging education amongst all classes of its subjects, whether Christians, Mahomedans or Hindoos, as a means of improving their condition by a better knowledge of the arts of life that minister to human wants; of purifying and elevating their character by moral and intellectual instruction, and of qualifying them at once to appreciate the benevolent intentions and salutary measures of Government, and to give these measures the moral force derived from the support of an intelligent and instructed population.[17]

There was no assumption of education for independence here. Adam's concern was direct and humanitarian within the framework of British rule in India. A discussion of practical details followed. Adam suggested that education in the vernacular where possible would be desirable as a means of keeping religious and communal groups together. The place to begin was with a study of existing community institutions, developing plans to work with them and helping them to improve their approaches and facilities without actually taking them over. The study in each community would be conducted with the aid of leading *mullahs* and *pandits* who would assist with actual tasks of enumeration and would assist Adam in evaluating what was happening in each institution. The radical openness which Adam proposed for the study was unique for a European in his time. He described how he would situate himself at a district headquarters for a period, go to each village for a few days, and enter

> freely into communication with parents, teachers, and pundits on that subject, examining schools both common and learned.[18]

Proposing a salary of 700 rupees a month for himself and expenses for a staff of six amounting to 218 more rupees a month, Adam concluded his proposal with further details of travel expenses and related estimates to which the Governor promptly and positively responded. Bentinck described Adam as a man of "great industry" with "high character for integrity," whom Bentinck felt would need three years to complete the massive study.

Adam's work was subsequently published as three separate but related reports dated 1835, 1836, and 1838. Following the British practice adopted by census takers, Adam provided copious detail on such matters as schools, students, teachers, books, language medium, female education. The summary of his basic conclusions appeared in the second chapter of the 1838 Report in which he called for strong government financial support for extensive educational development throughout Bengal and Bihar. Standing strongly in support of vernacular education as the base from which to build, Adam set forth a program in which the Government would take the lead in the adoption and direction of measures aiding "development of the native character, native society and native institutions."[19]

Such a plan would usually develop through consultation with indigenous communities, urging new vigor and commitment to established institutions without interfering or dictating as such. Adam foresaw problems in such a liberal program, however. In their present situation, he believed the indigenous population of India could only understand commands and operate from a stance of obedience. Illustrating this by example from his own visits to villages where he had attempted openness and equal intercourse with local residents, Adam concluded that centuries of suppression had led rural populations to view any government as an "instrument of power" rather than an "organ of law." Religion was the only area in which Adam felt that local communities would vigorously assert themselves against governmental interference.

What first step then might be best for the government to undertake? A requirement for an elementary school in every village would go beyond mere recommendation. Schools would push villagers too poor and illiterate to realize that their own children should have an education even if they had not. Adam, however, understanding the complexity of the caste system and of village life, knew well that such a proposal might be rejected by upper as well as lower caste Indians. Any Government plan would have to operate, therefore, by "slow and almost imperceptible steps."[20] A second concern raised by Adam pertained to the question of what would happen to community involvement once the Government began to build schools, to pay teachers, and to order books? A staunch believer in community involvement, Adam contended that total government involvement would not ultimately produce a healthy educational system.

Perhaps most significant of his recommendations was Adam's call for a massive infusion of funds for public education. "If all other resources fail," he wrote,

> there is still one left, the general revenue of the country on which the poor and the ignorant have primary claim, a claim which is second to no other whatsoever, for whence is that revenue derived but from the bones and the sinews, the toil and sweat whose cause I am pleading? Shall *L*10,000 continue to be the sole permanent appropriation from a revenue of more than twenty millions sterling for the education of nearly a hundred millions of people?[21]

The sensitivity and awareness shown by Adam both in conducting the study and in setting forth his results and philosophy follow quite logically from his earlier courageous stances as a missionary and as a newspaper editor. Adam had devoted twenty years in India to gaining a perceptive understanding of the land and its people.

Throughout his three reports, Adam had always attempted to support his arguments with judicious quotes from important government figures. At the conclusion of this third report, he quoted Lord Moira who, during his term in Calcutta in 1815, had already said that it was time for the government to move beyond the law and order to a more "enlarged and liberal policy" of administration. "The moral duties require encouragement," he wrote.

> The arts which adorn and embellish life will follow in ordinary course. It is for the credit of the British name that this beneficial revolution should arise under British sway. To be a source of blessings to the immense population of India, is an ambition worthy of our country. In proportion as we have found intellect neglected and sterile here, the obligation is the stronger on us to cultivate it.[22]

As Adam completed his momentous reports, he continued to hold down several government jobs during 1838. The most significant of these was as Secretary to the Committee on Road Convicts. It was apparently the practice of the Government to set native prisoners to work on the road in fetters. Adam was in charge of improving their working conditions by provision of food, clothing, and medical aid, which, according to Adam, improved vastly during his tenure with the committee. In the same year, Adam was appointed to the Stationers Department to ferret out abuses. At this time Adam appears to have been earning as much as 1600 rupees a month.[23] Having sent his family to America in 1834, Adam now felt that he had sufficient funds to leave India, and thus, he proceeded to America where he arrived sometime during November 1838. Since his official resignation as Unitarian missionary in a letter to the Boston-based Society for the Promotion of Christianity in India in 1829, Adam had continued corresponding with some of its members as well as with the Reverend Jared Sparks, by then a professor at Harvard. The Society had met infrequently during the past nine years, voting in 1830 to send some money via London to the mission in Madras, but voting in 1837 during a debate on what to do with the Calcutta funds, not to send missionaries to the Sandwich Islands or even to Calcutta.

Adam in America

Shortly after his 1838 arrival in Boston, Adam addressed the Society for the Promotion of Christianity in India, delivering his famous lecture "On the Life and Labours of Rammohun Roy."[24] In response to questions on the prospects for Christianity in Bengal, Adam stressed that prospects were not good for although "intelligent Hindoos were throwing off superstitions of the country," they were not embracing Christianity. Adam's suggestion, nowhere as grandiose as those he had proposed fifteen years earlier, was that the American Unitarian Association send an "agent" who could build up a circle of European supporters which in turn might extend an influence to the local population. That there was free religious discussion in Calcutta, Adam was assured. How far one could go beyond that, his unwary successor the Reverend Charles Dall would also wonder some twenty years later.

Whatever Adam may have said of the "life and labours of Rammohun Roy" and of his own work in India, it only had the effect of convincing the Bostonians that they even should no longer support the Madras mission after the death of William Roberts in 1839. On June 5 of that year, the organization voted itself out of existence, turning over all its funds to the Benevolent Fraternity of Unitarian Churches, the Boston mission to the poor and the social work agency created by Joseph Tuckerman in 1826.[25] Domestic missions had clearly begun to take precedence for American Unitarians. Perhaps the only positive reflection to be made about the decision was that it took the society even longer to dissolve itself after its purpose had failed than it did to establish itself at the time Rammohun and Adam needed support.

Adam's courageous character and his profound understanding of Rammohun's life and reforms as well as of Indian social problems emerge from two other writings published in 1839 and 1840. The first of these appeared in *The Christian Examiner* as a lengthy review of Malcom's *Travels.* This was the same Unitarian publication which had written so much of Adam and Roy fifteen years earlier. Malcom had devoted a long section of his book to Rammohun and the Brahmo Samaj, although his visit to Calcutta was brief and had occurred some years after Rammohun's death. Adam found it both incorrect and "inconsistent with itself on the whole presenting a distorted, prejudiced and imperfect view" of Rammohun and his impact as reformer and leader of liberal Hindus in Calcutta.[26]

Quoting four pages from Malcom, Adam began a direct attack on much of what Malcom had had to say of Rammohun Roy. "He did not abhor to abomination of the Veda and the monstrosities of its thirty-three millions of gods in as much as such monstrosities and abominations are not found in the Veds," Adam wrote

> As a Unitarian, it was his express object and endeavor to revive among his countrymen in Bengal, the pure forms of faith and worship taught in the Veda, which, in his opinion, were as distinct from the absurdities of the modern Hindu mythology, as is the New Testament from the legends of the Romish church.[27]

Malcom had dubbed Rammohun a "Unitarian Hindu" as against "Unitarian Christian" to which Adam responded that one might as well add "musalman" (Muslim).

> In the strict sense of these terms, he was none of the three, for he held only what is common to all, without admitting or denying what is peculiar to each. He believed that the Unity of God, taught equally in its purity by Unitarian Christians, by Unitarian Hindus and by Musalmans, was the great and fundamental doctrine of all religions.[28]

As such, Rammohun was a Unitarian in the truest sense, or better, though Adam did not use the designation, a "Universalist." Adam came down hard on Unitarian Christians, however, asserting that they tend to "exaggerate the importance of the doctrine from which they are named and characterized, take in general a very narrow and inadequate view of its comprehensive bearings, especially in idolatrous, polytheistic and atheistic communities."

Adam was especially opposed to Malcom's characterization of the Brahmo Samaj as of no use, compared to what might have been accomplished had Rammohun founded a good school. Citing Malcom's obvious ignorance of Rammohun's contributions to education and social welfare, Adam traced out, step by step, how Rammohun had been a major influence on British decision-making in these areas, and especially how Roy had opposed the purely Oriental education first suggested by Lord Amherst for Sanskrit College.

Malcom's biased characterization of the Brahmo Samaj service probably disturbed Adam most of all:

> After all this miserable carping, Mr. Malcom winds up with exclaiming, 'Such is the boasted reformation of Rammohun Roy'! He attends a single service of two hours' duration, conducted in a language which he does not understand, and is dependent for every idea he receives on the interpretation of a gentleman whose vocation brings him almost daily into hostile conflict with those whose religion he is called on to explain, and against whom his feelings are embittered.[29]

It appears from Adam's strong stance in this article that his views had liberalized considerably since his "conversion" to Arian Unitarianism in 1821. His encounter with humankind at the most basic levels of Indian society, his relationships with such Indians as Rammohun and Dwarkanath Tagore and his realization of the ineptness of many missionary and East India Company enterprises, had affected him considerably. But Adam's strongest response to social injustice certainly appeared with the publication of his *The Law and Custom of Slavery in British India.*

In this work, written as a series of letters to Thomas Foxcroft, a New England acquaintance, Adam again demonstrated his ability to use sources convincingly, using his profound knowledge of the Indian situation in impressive analysis. Indicating near the start that slavery was only one of many evils under which India suffered and that its effects were far less in their reach than some other evils, slavery in India still created a bad influence leading to injustice, degradation and suffering.[30]

> Although not a citizen of the United States yet, as a citizen of the world — a far higher and nobler title — I look upon every slave in every country as an injured and oppressed fellow man; and from the bottom of my soul, I wish God-speed to every attempt based on Christian principles . . . to strike off the fetters of the slave.[31]

Although the British were proud that no slavery existed in the West Indies and were quick to criticize Americans for continued slavery in the South, Adam asserted, they did not admit that there were some 800,000 slaves working for the British East India Company. Then, proceeding to detail seven categories of slavery, Adam criticized British legislation of the 1770s condemning criminals to slavery and sending them abroad.

In his conclusion, Adam came to the defense of the British, however, citing numerous examples of how they had reformed certain institutions and practices of the Indians which by Western Christian standards were clearly inhumane — female infanticide, *sati*, sacrificing babies to the Ganges, etc. At the same time, Adam strongly stressed that the British had always made the administration of justice in India subservient to the collection of revenue. Respect for the indigenous population was notoriously lacking among civil servants. It was easy to see in fact why, despite British pretensions to justice and fair play, that slavery could still flourish in Bengal.[32]

Adam argued that slavery should be abolished because it was the Government's duty "as the common protector to shield the weak from the strong, the poor from the rich, and to give the slave the lawful possession, hitherto unjustly withheld, of his own body and the fruits of his own labor." If one were to count numbers of slave owners who would lose their rights, Adam continued, justice would surely be with the slaves who were far more numerous. And, if one were to object about government interference in the private property of slave owners, one could also argue that in a "civilized" country individual human rights surely took precedence. "Let it be further observed," Adam concluded,

> that slavery in India has not been legalized by a formal enactment of the British Parliament, nor even of the British Indian Government, but by a mere interpretation, and as I firmly believe and maintain,

> by a gross and palpable misinterpretation of a rule of law which, it is admitted by the expounders, makes not the slightest mention of, or allusion to slavery.[33]

William Adam thus was an early advocate of an abolitionist position, writing on American soil, as an Englishman, about slavery in India. The effect of his antislavery arguments reached no farther than did his pleas for vernacular education supported by Government in India or his pleas for a vital Unitarian mission. Nor were his views on slavery so popular among Boston Unitarians in 1840. Certainly from this moment forward, the remainder of Adam's career was destined for even greater disappointments. In 1846, he was called to serve as first minister of the new Unitarian Church in Toronto, but one year later he moved on to the far more prestigious First Church in Chicago where he served until 1849. At some point, Adam became sharply disillusioned with American Unitarianism and returned to England. Nothing is known of this last phase of his career other than the interview Adam had in 1861 with the Reverend Charles Dall, at which time Adam made it clear that he had repudiated Unitarianism and no longer considered himself a minister.

Such was the career of William Adam and the effect it had on the history of English and American Unitarianism. A thorough and rational explorer of ideas and systems, he remained throughout his life controversial, relatively little known apart from his role in India, raising serious questions about existing and established beliefs and practices, but more often refuted and ignored by those he sought to convince. What William Adam did not know was that he was to set an example for other Unitarians who were also ambitious to bring religious reform to India.

CHAPTER SIX

Unitarianism in Calcutta 1820 — 1833: Encounter and Acculturation

It may appear from preceding chapters that Rammohun Roy was argumentative, and that he involved himself in matters above and beyond those in which Calcutta Brahmins would engage in 1820. This was not the case even in the eyes of Christian opponents such as Marshman. From the start, the missionaries asserted that they were not opposing Rammohun on personal grounds but only because he was distorting true Christianity. The Reverend William Adam, one of Rammohun's staunchest supporters, "was never more thoroughly, deeply, and constantly impressed than when in the presence of Rammohun Roy."

In 1838, five years after the death of Rammohun, Adam wrote:

> in friendly and confidential converse with him . . . [I knew then] that I was in the presence of a man of natural and inherent genius, of powerful understanding, and of determined will, a will determined with singular energy and uncontrollable self-direction to lofty and generous purposes. He seemed to think, to feel, to speak, to act as if he could not do all this and that he must and could do it only in and from and through himself. . . He would be free or not be at all. . . Love of freedom was perhaps the strongest passion of his soul, freedom not of the body merely, but of the mind.[1]

In his first address to an American audience, Adam told them of Rammohun at first hand. This was the earliest such account that American Unitarians would receive some seventeen years after their first acquaintance with Rammohun through the pages of *The Christian Register* and through letters from both Rammohun and Adam. Adam was pivotal in bringing Rammohun even more directly to the attention of English and American Unitarians. The controversy between Rammohun and Joshua Marshman, already at its peak in 1821, was just the beginning of an unexpected Unitarian offensive against the Baptist missionaries of Serampore. It was an opening also for a renewed and reformed Hindu self-consciousness, the seeds of which Rammohun sowed in his *Precepts of Jesus* and especially in the *Brahmanical Magazine.* It was in England and America, however, that Rammohun had found, with William Adam, Unitarians of like mind who had offered strong spiritual if not financial support.

The Formation of the Calcutta Unitarian Society

A close allegiance between Rammohun and Adam developed following an incident that occurred in Calcutta late in 1821. Adam described the meeting

> One day in the hot season, about mid-day, I was engaged in my usual studies, when I was informed that a native gentleman was at the gate of my compound and desired to see me. This was an unusual hour for a call. I went to the gate and found that it was Rammohun Roy, whom I instantly requested to alight from his carriage and enter the house. The unusualness of the hour was fully justified by the explanation he gave me. On invitation, he had been to see Dr. Middleton the Bishop of Calcutta. Rammohun Roy's house was probably about two miles from the Bishop's palace and my dwelling was intermediate between the two. He called on me both for refreshment to his body and sympathy in his mental trouble. His first request was that he should be permitted to remove his turban, which was of course granted, and the second that he should have some refreshment, but that before it was brought and he partook of it, my servants should be sent away, since if they had seen him eat under my roof they would have bruited abroad that he had lost caste. This was promptly and quietly attended to, and when he felt cool and refreshed, he proceeded to state what had disturbed his mind.[2]

The cause of Rammohun's distraught state was his interview with the Anglican bishop of Calcutta, who had attempted to persuade him to accept Christianity after a lengthy argument which appealed to the possibilities for fame and materialistic success. As Adam further commented, "he was asked to profess the Christian religion, not on the force of evidence, or for the love of truth or for the satisfaction of his conscience, or for the benefit of his fellow men, but for the sake of the honour, glory and fame it might bring him. This was utterly abhorrent to Rammohun's mind. It alienated, repelled and disgusted him."

The insensitivity of the bishop, the attacks of the editor of *Friend of India*, the Baptists' utter rejection of Adam for his theological heresy, and the warmth of Adam to Rammohun in a moment of need all served to bring Adam and Rammohun closer together in search of a solution to resolve their mutual religious needs. Where Rammohun tended to present his ideas personally through publications such as his additional *Appeals* and *Brahmanical Magazine*, Adam was an institutional man. In September 1821, in conjunction with Bengali Brahmins Dwarkanath Tagore, Prusunnu C. Tagore, and Radhaprusad Roy, as well as a number of English and Scottish merchants and civil servants, Adam and Rammohun founded the Calcutta Unitarian Committee. The initial purpose of the committee was not to proselytize but to be a source of education and information "respecting the evidences, the duties, and the doctrines of the religion of Christ." Besides a program for teaching which included the establishment of Roy's Anglo-Hindu school, Rammohun financially supported the creation of a Unitarian press which would undertake publications in both English and Bengali. Although Adam played a major part in the organization of these projects, they could never have started without the strong financial backing Rammohun was able to offer.[3] By January 1822 Adam had rented a house where weekly services were to be held. His organizational talents also emerged as he began regular correspondence with Unitarians in London, Boston, and Baltimore, seeking financial and missionary support for the new Calcutta project.

Adam reported on the controversy in Calcutta in letters to a young Unitarian minister in Baltimore who had gained fame when William Ellery Channing of Boston had preached the sermon at his ordination in 1819. Adam could have chosen a no more sympathetic ear than that of the Reverend Jared Sparks from whose pulpit the controversial broadside, "Unitarian Christianity," had been preached. In 1821, sitting at almost the southern extremity of an essentially New England-based Unitarian movement, Sparks had begun his own journal, *The Unitarian Miscellany and Christian Monitor*, which in its issues of February 1822 and June 1823 reported on both the Rammohun Roy "Jesus" controversy and on the conversion of William Adam to Unitarianism.[4] Articles on Adam's conversion and his "Arian" sermon, "The Claims of Jesus," preached before the Unitarian society in Calcutta, as well as editorial support for Adam's work, also filled the pages of the more widely circulated *Christian Register* throughout 1822. In addition, Adam, attempting to make as wide a circle of contacts as possible, wrote to William Ellery Channing, noted minister of the Federal Street Church in Boston, whose controversial

Baltimore sermon, "Unitarian Christianity," Adam and Rammohun Roy had recently published in Calcutta along with Adam's "The Claims of Jesus." Since Channing was on sabbatical in Europe when Adam's letter arrived in 1823, it was forwarded to Professor Henry S. Ware, Sr., at Harvard Divinity School, who was interested both in the question of missions and the particular situation of Rammohun and Adam about which he had been reading in *The Christian Register*.

To gain a more factual perspective on what was really occurring in Calcutta, both in the view of Rammohun and of Adam, Henry Ware addressed twenty questions to each in a letter dated April 24, 1823. In the meantime, the second Boston-based Unitarian publication, *The Christian Disciple*, offered its readers two major assessments of the Calcutta situation during 1823.[5] During the summer a critical assessment of Christian missions appeared in an article reviewing the publication of Channing's "Baltimore Sermon" and the recent sermon of Adam, both published at Rammohun's Unitarian Press. And the November issue carried a more significant thirty page analysis of Rammohun's writings including the 1816 translation of the *Kena Upanishad* and the more recent *Second Appeal* and *Final Appeal*, both written in response to Baptist opposition to Rammohun's views on Jesus.

It was not difficult for the reviewer in *The Christian Disciple* to sympathize completely with Rammohun against Dr. Marshman. After discussing the arguments pro and con, he commented,

> How are we to wonder that the Baptists are spending their thousands for nought when there is not a Brahmin boy in his elements, but has the logic enough to see through the immense chasm between Dr. Marshman's premises and conclusions? We blush for the discredit into which our glorious faith is brought, when we picture to ourselves a well-informed Hindoo turning over the pages of Dr. Marshman's work, under the idea that they present a just exhibition of the Christian system and of the manner in which its advocates maintain it; and we reflect with deep concern upon the probability that the introduction of Christianity into India will prove to be greatly obstructed and delayed, by the prevalence of that contempt for it, which cannot fail to have been thus produced.[6]

Despite the difficulties Rammohun had experienced, the reviewer was led to assert that Rammohun's works on Christianity were far more than the mere passing project of one man. "We think," he concluded, that any important revolution in the belief of the Hindoos will begin with the Brahmins; that whoever among them will embrace Christianity will do it because he sees good reasons; and that those reasons will, for the most part, be exhibited to them in the writings of sensible and learned men in the original or in translations.[7]

It is clear from the attitude taken in this review that Boston Unitarians were primarily concerned with supporting Rammohun as a Christian rather than as a Hindu reformer. Indeed, William Adam, it was finally suggested, might be just the man to start the project of disseminating the "true Christianity, Unitarian Christianity, in India."

But the Boston Unitarians wanted much detail before they would begin to commit themselves to such a missionary effort. They were not yet organized as an association and, besides, Unitarians had mixed feelings about the purpose and effectiveness of mission work. This attitude had certainly been demonstrated in *The Christian Disciple*'s comments about Joshua Marshman and Serampore Baptists.

Two letters from Rammohun and one from Adam published in 1824 helped to resolve some questions. The first of these appeared prior to the answers to Henry Ware and was published in the pages of *The Christian Register*, May 7, 1824.[8] A year earlier, David Reed, its editor, had written Rammohun asking the following questions:

(1) How far the doctrines of the *Trinity*, *native depravity*, and other kindred doctrines of Calvinism, as held and taught by the present missionaries, are obstacles to the introduction of Christianity among the Hindoos?
(2) Whether there appears to be an insuperable obstacle, in the manners, habits, or present beliefs of the native Hindoos, to the rational and simple doctrines of Christianity, as inculcated by Unitarians?
(3) Whether gentlemen who should inculcate the doctrine of the Divine Unity, and the most plain and simple doctrines of Christianity, would probably meet with such success, either with Hindoos or Mussalmans, as would justify any measures that might be taken for the support of such teachers in any part of Hindoostan?

In an answer dated January 13, 1824, and thus the earliest published response of Rammohun Roy to an American,[9] Rammohun expressed deep gratitude that the editor should have taken note of his work and should have expressed agreement with the free discussion of religious and political ideas Rammohun had undertaken. In response to the first question, Rammohun reaffirmed that the doctrine of the Trinity as taught by the missionaries had "not only rendered their labour unsuccessful, but has exposed the name of Christianity to ridicule among enlightened Hindoos and Moosulmans."[10]

To Reed's second question, Rammohun offered the recent tract of P. K. Thakoor (Tagore), "Humble Suggestions to his countrymen who believe in the *One True God.*" This tract, now believed to be the work of Rammohun himself but published under the name of his friend and co-supporter in the Unitarian movement, Rammohun quoted from, saying,

> We should feel no reluctance to co-operate with them [Unitarian Christians] merely because they consider Jesus Christ as the messenger of God and their Spiritual Teacher; for oneness in the object of worship and sameness of religious practice should produce attachment among the worshippers.

Referring Reed to the "enlightened" Hindus who had joined with Europeans to form the Calcutta Unitarian Society, Roy expressed sharp criticism of the 'ignorant' who should find neither the Trinitarian nor the Unitarian structure religiously meaningful. What Unitarians ought to consider, Rammohun continued, was sending teachers of a high moral quality who could teach English literature and the sciences to help

> improve the understandings of the present ignorant generation, and thereby improve their hearts in the progress of time, that the cause of truth must triumph over false religion, and the desired comfort and happiness may be enjoyed by men of all classes.[11]

In response to Reed's third question Rammohun replied that while his own studies of Christian Scripture had demonstrated the validity of Divine Unity, these views were further substantiated when studied by "many unbiassed [*sic*] sensible, and independent Hindoos." Nowhere in Rammohun's response was there talk of undertaking missionary work. His concern was for the enlightenment of Western education, social reform, and religious values which would demonstrate qualities of universalism.

This was substantiated further by the somewhat limited twelve pages of response from Rammohun to Henry Ware published in Cambridge also during 1824. Where Adam wrote some 125 pages of response, answering in detail questions about current missionary efforts in Bengal, and describing the low-caste types of Hindus and Muslims who had been converted, Rammohun, claiming ignorance of any details, seemed reluctant to deal in any controversy. In the letter to Ware, Rammohun reemphasized that education was far more desirable than the emphasis on a ministry or preaching to convert. Perhaps overly optimistic in his assessment of how far an educational program could go, Roy asserted that even in the lowest classes "two-thirds of the native population of Bengal would be glad to see their children educated in English learning."[12] In response to a question as to whether his new translation of the Bible into Bengali was free from sectarian influence and was accurate, Rammohun described the difficulties of his work with Yates and Adam stating, "I beg to assure you, that I, (though a native of this country) do not recollect having engaged myself once, during my life, in so difficult a task, as the translation of the New Testament into Bengalee."[13]

In a letter written to the Secretary of the Unitarian Fund in London as early as January 1822, less than five months after he and Rammohun had organized the Unitarians of Calcutta, Adam had urged a much grander program. Tracing the opposition of Christians to his renunciation of the Trinity and his own excommunication from the Circular Church in Calcutta, Adam justified his letter to the English Unitarians, even knowing nothing of their organization or possibilities, out of the zeal of his conversion. Clearly committed to the notion of a Unitarian mission in India, Adam pointed up the advantages that English Unitarians would have in promoting such a program. Stressing first that the East India Company Act of 1811 - 1812 now allowed missionaries and missions to operate, he emphasized that English Unitarians would be allowed the same rights in India as they were at home, orthodox opposition notwithstanding. "This country has particular claims upon you as Christians," he continued.

> Here is an immense population subject to the British Government, but ignorant of the Gospel, and unblessed with those elevated and purifying hopes which it conveys. You are possessed of the light of Christianity of which they are destitute; and you have free access to them for the purpose of communicating it if you will avail yourselves of that privilege."[14]

Detailing the varied Indian populations and the various advantages Unitarians would have in promoting their views with each, Adam continued explaining the qualifications and kind of support a Unitarian missionary should have. In a grandiose plan, he suggested for a start that missionaries go at least to Calcutta, Madras, Bombay, and Colombo, and that each place have a staff of four men. In addition, Adam recommended sending a printer, a paper maker, a letter founder, and a school teacher to assist in the propagation.

The annual report of the English Unitarian committee, written in part in response to Adam's letter, and the news of what had occurred thus far in Calcutta, suggested that a mission of far more limited scale than that proposed by Adam would soon produce great results. "The committee contended that it would shew the reasonableness of religion to possess a mightier force than all that the authority of governments, or the zeal of multitudes can give to machinery which they employ for the diffusion of a corrupt system."[15] The committee, however, put off for two years any concrete decision of support and when support was voted it was in the amount of only $600 a year to Adam rather than for the missionary program Adam had sought.

The American Response

Henry Ware's twenty questions on the "Prospects of Christianity in India" gave William Adam an opportunity to expand on his suggestions to the English Unitarians. He took 120 printed pages to make his points. Impressed, as were their English counterparts, leaders of the American Association, newly founded in 1825, began serious review of the Calcutta Unitarian situation based on the articles about Rammohun Roy, his writings on Hinduism and Christianity, and his published letters as well as those which had come from William Adam. Activity now developed in Boston on two levels. Theory about the validity of a missionary enterprise was articulated, on the one hand, by the Reverend Joseph Tuckerman and Professor Henry Ware. On the other hand, deliberate planning was initiated, slowly and conservatively, through the founding of the Society for the Promotion of Christianity in India by such noted Boston area Unitarians as Channing, Tuckerman, Henry Ware and his son, and Andrews Norton. The first meeting of this new society was held on April 11, 1825, at the home of

Lewis Tappan, a Boston merchant who was to serve as its treasurer. The first public meeting of the new association, however, gathering delegates from many Boston area churches to support the India program was not held until May 1826. Moving conservatively in its support of a missionary program for India, the Boston group finally voted in November 1826 a ten-year annual commitment of $600 toward the salary and expenses of William Adam. They did this, however, only after receiving new word on the growth of the Calcutta mission by both Indian and European Unitarians and learning from London that the British Unitarian Committee had voted during 1825 to make a similar token commitment.[16] Such slight support from the two groups from whom he had expected much more all but dashed the hopes of William Adam who was convinced that much could be done to make the Unitarian ideals he so deeply held work in the Indian environment. This was one of the causes for the faltering of the movement in Calcutta.[17]

Given the domestic struggles in which New England Unitarians were still engaged, justification for even token foreign missionary work required considerable explanation. Such a defense was developed through a series of articles, the first of which appeared in *The Christian Examiner* (successor bimonthly journal to *The Christian Disciple*) which published a Joseph Tuckerman essay in the spring of 1824 discussing why Unitarians had previously refrained from engaging in foreign missions. Commencing with the thesis that Unitarians did have a responsibility "to extend their sympathy to the heathen of the world," Tuckerman suggested that Unitarian inaction in missions had heretofore been because (1) Unitarians believed that anyone could be saved, regardless of whether he was a Christian or not; and (2) Unitarians had been critical of the way in which Christian missions had been conducted — the waste of excitement, money, and life, as Tuckerman expressed it. Let Unitarians learn from these errors, he insisted. Instead of sending twenty or thirty men, let Unitarians spend their money training two or three Christians "without narrowness of bigotry." A few like this would "raze the whole foundations of Brahmanical faith." Although these two latter phrases would appear to be in contradiction to one another, in Tuckerman's perspective, the limitations of Hindu Vaisnavism were as much to be overcome as the limitations of evangelical missionaries in India. Admitting that Unitarians had been primarily concerned with domestic missions and that there was much to do to defend their cause at home, Tuckerman suggested that his colleagues might meet the criticisms of the orthodox that Unitarians were indifferent to missionary work by meeting the new challenge presented by Rammohun and Adam from India.[18]

William Ellery Channing, always dubious of religious associations and missionary outreach, offered the same criticisms of missions in a short essay, "Remarks on Associations" as well as in a later essay, "The Universal Father"[19] which stressed the universal nature of God's laws and love which are available to all people. Joseph Tuckerman's tract, "Letter on the Principles of the Missionary Enterprise," written at Chelsea in June 1826, proposed a new era for missionary work in which Christians could unite in extending the work of "our religion." He called again on the American Unitarian Association to cooperate with Unitarian Christians throughout the world and pleaded in particular for support in Calcutta.[20]

Tuckerman's most significant article appeared in the September-October 1826 issue of *The Christian Examiner.* "Is Rammohun Roy a Christian?"[21] asked Tuckerman, feeling the answer had an important bearing on whether American Unitarians should support a mission and the extent of patronage for that mission. There was strong evidence, Tuckerman argued, that Rammohun Roy was a Christian even though Trinitarians would never be satisfied that he was. Using Rammohun's writings only — The *Precepts of Jesus* and the *Three Appeals* — Tuckerman pressed his case. Referring to the introduction to *The Precepts* he wrote, "It was not made certain by this publication that Rammohun Roy was a believer in the divine authority of our Lord. But it was made most certain that he esteemed the Christian precepts to be above all other precepts and that he was most solicitous to persuade his countrymen that in obeying the precepts they would find their happiness."[22]

The attacks on Rammohun by the Reverends Marshman and Carey of Calcutta in which they referred to him as a "deist," an "infidel," and a "heathen," when his rejection of idolatry was publicly known, was an outrage. "It might have been doubted whether he was a Christian," wrote Tuckerman, "but not that he was a heathen." Tuckerman went on to assert that Marshman's *Friend of India* had no grounds for attacking Rammohun who had expressed no doubts about the truth of the gospels. In fact, Rammohun had not understood the differences between

Unitarians and Trinitarians until "the divine teacher had made them clear." Finally, Tuckerman pointed out that Rammohun had refused to compare Christian and Hindu miracles, believing Hindus would minimize the importance of Christ's few miraculous feats. Instead, Rammohun had stressed that the central issue was the teachings of Jesus which to him stood above all other religious teachings. Quoting numerous passages from Rammohun's *Final Appeal*, Tuckerman reiterated his insistence that there was no justification for attacking the Bengali reformer's understanding of Christianity.

At the close of his essay, Tuckerman showed a sympathetic understanding of Rammohun Roy's desire to retain his Hindu caste status in order to retain his property and influence in India. Actual conversion would have identified Rammohun with low-caste converts to Catholicism. This would have given Muslims, true Unitarians in their own right, the impression he was a Trinitarian thereby to misunderstand his purpose. Tuckerman reasoned further that since Unitarian Christians were such a small group in Calcutta, it would seem senseless for Rammohun to cut himself off from Hindus, Muslims, and orthodox Christian contacts by taking so controversial a step. Let Rammohun Roy remain a Brahmin, Tuckerman concluded, for "yet he lives in the spirit of Christianity and believes the truth as Jesus has expressed it. . . Let him who has done or is doing more for the cause of the gospel of Christ, cast the first stone."[23]

While Tuckerman seemed to understand the issues preventing Rammohun from an all-out conversion to Christianity, he failed truly to understand all that was involved in Rammohun's reformation for his own community. Tuckerman and Adam were both too facile in pinning the Christian label on Rammohun. They could not help but be impressed that Rammohun and two Englishmen, G. J. Gordon and W. Tate, had each subscribed 5000 rupees to the permanent fund for the Calcutta Unitarian society while Dwarkanath Tagore, Prusunna Tagore, and two others had each subscribed 2500 rupees. Writing Boston about his own views of the new religious community, Rammohun may well have stirred further excitement about his being Christian when he stated:

> The interest which the friends to religious truth in America and England have taken in the promotion of our common cause, has successfully put in operation the feeling and spirit of those in Calcutta, who have that interest at heart. They have raised, in a

period of less than a month, about 30,000 rupees in support of a perpetual mission in Bengal; and have directed their attention to the direction of a long-comtemplated chapel, in the centre of this town. As far as my knowledge of them extends, I feel authorized to assure you, that the intelligent part of the Hindoo community has every inclination to join, or at least support us; though many of them may perhaps have objections to the honor of being called Christians, from aversion to a change in name, and especially looking to the outcaste converts at Serampoor, who, among the natives for several years, have passed by that appellation.[24]

That Rammohun had found and had been warmly received by allies in America and England was certainly evident. Up to 1826, Rammohun was certainly struggling with questions of Christian identity although at no point, in line with his statement to *The Christian Examiner*, would he, or most of his friends, have wished to have been identified with low-caste converts. A social reformer, certainly appalled by the bad effects of caste in India, Rammohun could never make a clear decision to act against caste restriction. This was evident, for example, in William Adam's description of their meeting at his home. Even when Rammohun decided to go to England and thereby be the first Brahmin to cross the ocean, he went as the appointed representative of the puppet Mughal emperor, Akbar II, and with the title "Rajah."

A letter from William Adam to Ezra Stiles Gannett, President of the American Unitarian Association, written in early August 1826, continued to press for more support from America. After thanking Gannett for his letter and a package of books sent to Rammohun via a nephew of Gannett's visiting Calcutta, Adam asked Gannett in return to deliver a parcel of books and articles on Indian missions to Joseph Tuckerman, noting that he (Adam) no longer had firsthand contact with Christian missionaries. After offering congratulations on the formation of the American Unitarian Association and the new zeal he expected would follow, he wrote, "I trust the day is not far distant,"

when we shall have a British Indian Unitarian Association — not only an association so named — . . . one having direct relations with avowed and zealous supporters of Unitarianism in the three Presidencies of British India. O, what a wide door is open for Unitarians here if they would only enter and take possession! I trouble lest they bring on themselves the guilt of neglecting to communicate according to their ability the knowledge of the pure and unadulterated gospel of Christ to the numerous inhabitants of this vast continent.

With the strictest adherance to truth, I can say that the minds of many, both Europeans and natives, are prepared to receive the doctrine of Unitarian Christianity . . . and if a permanent Unitarian mission could be established in Calcutta, from it, the word of God might be made to sound forth to them all.[25]

In an earlier letter to Tuckerman attempting to explain why Rammohun was unable to decide between Christianity and Hinduism, Adam stated clearly what Tuckerman had already expressed in his essay on Rammohun. However, Adam added the further judgment, "I do *not* feel these reasons to be quite so convincing as they appear to him . . . I have no doubt that in his opinion they possess all the force necessary fully to justify him in the sight of God and his own conscience in the course which he has pursued."[26] For Adam and for Tuckerman, it was difficult to understand how Rammohun could be both a Hindu and, at least in spirit, a Christian. He had made public the fact that in his will everything not left to his two sons was left to Adam and the mission. Earlier, Rammohun had written a defense of his attending Unitarian worship services[27] but by 1826, in spite of his financial support, he did not attend any Christian service during a period when Unitarian services were not being held.

It must have been difficult for Adam to remain patient during this period. It was more than five years since Unitarians had organized in Calcutta and token English support was just arriving, while American support, newly decided upon, would not yet come for some months. Although Rammohun had already been generous in his support of Adam, the $1,200 which would eventually come annually from abroad was not nearly enough for Adam to support his family. Thus, early in 1827, Adam began a brief career as editor and publisher of the *Calcutta Chronicle*, a daily newspaper. The venture did not last long, however, for due to Adam's outspoken criticism of English East India Company policies, the paper was censored and suppressed.

The arrival of a large financial gift from England toward the building of the chapel had made it possible to renew Unitarian services in rented rooms attached to the *Bengal Hurkaru* newspaper and had also led to the establishment of a small theological library there. During the autumn as many as sixty to eighty attended English services, but Adam found strong opposition to conducting services in Bengali among the Brahmin leadership of the committee who asserted that only English, Persian, or Sanskrit would command respect while the use of the vernacular would be degrading.[28]

Adam and Rammohun had earlier run into conflict over the operation of Rammohun's Anglo-Hindu School. Adam wished it to be a mission school. He often disagreed with Rammohun about the style and manner of its management. In an attempt to reach the Bengali-speaking population, Adam began an unsuccessful series of lectures at the school after the Committee turned down the idea of Bengali Unitarian services.[29] During 1827, however, as attendance at English services was declining, the members of the Unitarian Committee renewed their support of the mission by forming themselves into a British Indian Unitarian Association whose purpose would meet the suggested requirements Adam had stated two years earlier.

Minutes of the dramatic reorganization meeting contained a grand program for religious worship, education, contact with Madras, and a library, as well as excerpts of letters of support from Unitarians in Boston and London and extensive excerpts from Henry Ware's Berry Street Lecture of 1826, which called upon the Unitarian clergy to support the Indian mission. All this would make it seem as if the mission would be well off the ground during 1828, but in fact the opposite was true. Within a few months, Rammohun, at the behest of a few of his close friends, had decided on a new approach, that of organizing Hindu Unitarians into the Brahmo Samaj or Society of God. Adam, in letters written during February and April 1828 takes credit for urging the Brahmin leadership of the Unitarian movement to go in that new direction. Whatever role Adam may have played in the creation of the new society, it was Rammohun, the Tagores, and other reform-minded Brahmins who commenced the worship on August 20, 1828. The service, as described by Adam in a letter to Tuckerman in 1829, demonstrates how the Brahmo Samaj helped intellectual upper-caste Hindus to reform their tradition without closing off religious, cultural, or caste identity.

> The service begins with two or three of the Pandits singing, or rather chanting in the cathedral style, some of the spiritual portions of the Ved, which are next explained in the vernacular dialect to the people by another Pandit. This is followed by a discourse in Bengali . . . and the whole is concluded by hymns both in Sanskrit and Bengali, sung with the voice and accompanied by instrumental music, which is also

occasionally interposed between other parts of the service. The audience consists generally of from fifty to sixty individuals, several Pandits, a good many Brahmins and all decent and attentive in their demeanour.[30]

There is little doubt, however, that both Adam and the European religious liberals were disappointed at this turn of events. On the one hand, they were willing to intermingle with a Hindu Brahmin elite in a Western and Christian frame of reference in which English was the medium of communication. The Brahmin leadership, it is interesting to note, which refused the use of Bengali in a Unitarian Christian context, found it quite acceptable as a medium at the Brahmo Samaj. Adam began to understand Rammohun's deeper purposes when he wrote Tuckerman,

> Rammohun Roy, I am persuaded, supports this institution, not because he believes in the divine authority of the Ved, but solely as an instrument for overthrowing idolatry. To be candid, however, I must add that . . . in my mind . . . he employs Unitarian Christianity in the same way, as an instrument for spreading pure and just notions of God, without believing in the divine authority of the Gospel.[31]

In founding the Brahmo Samaj, however, Rammohun Roy did not reject Jesus or the teachings of Christianity. But when Rammohun left for England in 1830, Adam had resigned his position as Unitarian missionary and the Unitarian movement had folded. During his three years in England, Rammohun was frequently feted by Unitarians, and when he died in Bristol, it was the Unitarian minister Lant Carpenter who delivered the eulogy.[32]

A hitherto unknown letter written by Joseph Tuckerman to William Ellery Channing while the former was in England in 1833 may perhaps touch the continuing aspect of misunderstanding which Tuckerman and his colleagues, with the best of intentions, had toward Rammohun Roy. Writing Channing that he had met with Rammohun on August 20, 1833, and that he had left him "in perfect health," Tuckerman described Rammohun as "the most advanced Christian I have met in this country" (England). "Most deeply impressive," Tuckerman continued,

> and affecting, was it to hear him, emerging as he did from the deep darkness and deeper pollutions of Hindooism, expounding our

religion by reference of it in all its precepts and objects to the spirit of the life of Christ; and bringing the laws and institutions, and the images, manners, sentiments and lives of Christians, to the standard of the gospel. I have met no one here, who has seemed to feel, as he felt, the greatness of the evil of skepticism, on the one hand, and the indifference to religion, on the other, which characterises great numbers of the upper classes of society here; and the narrowness, the bigotry and the party spirit with all its . . . evils which equally characterise the mass of all the sects of religionists . . . I never met with one in whom the indications were stronger than in him, of simplicity and truth. He retained his Brahmanical costume, abstained from partaking of the food which would expose him to a loss of caste . . . but his object in all this was that he might retain influence with his countrymen. He meant to return to Calcutta, there to show that Brahmins might travel in Christendom, and not lose caste; thus to induce intelligent men in his own country to travel into other lands and to bring the useful knowledge which they might acquire in other countries into their own.[33]

Closing these remarks, Tuckerman indicated that Rammohun had expressed a desire to come to America to meet Channing. "He felt that you had been a great benefactor to his mind and he had a true Christian love for you," Tuckerman concluded. Thus did Joseph Tuckerman reinforce what he had written of Rammohun seven years earlier. Perhaps it was the very Unitarian symbolically or literally that led Tuckerman and his colleagues to apply the term so readily to Rammohun Roy. Tuckerman almost seems to have been speaking contradictions by recognizing Rammohun's need to remain a Brahmin while yet insisting that he was the "most advanced Christian" he had met in England.

For William Ellery Channing, the life and meaning of Rammohun Roy went far beyond institutional or purely Christian concerns. Channing had been informed of Rammohun's death not only by Tuckerman but also by Miss Lucy Aiken, an English Unitarian correspondent. Perhaps more than any other American Unitarian, Channing most often expressed Rammohun's significance when he wrote Miss Aiken in December 1833,

I feel his loss deeply, I cannot name a stranger whom I so wished to see. Do treasure up your recollections of him, and give them to me and the public. I lived in hope that he was to visit this country, and now I can only know him by following him into the common country of all pure and noble spirits.[34]

Rammohun Roy, both as founder of the Brahmo Samaj and as initiator of a short-lived first Unitarian mission in India, remained a symbol of religious freedom and social reform for American Unitarians, as well as the subject of numerous lectures by American Unitarians visiting India. His American Unitarian contemporaries, Adam and Tuckerman, though stung by his move away from Unitarian Christianity, finally accepted it. Neither ever fully understood why someone as aware of the effects of Hindu Vaisnavism as was Rammohun would not seek to become an avowed Unitarian Christian. Indeed, it was not until Charles Dall joined the Brahmo Samaj while serving in Calcutta as a Unitarian missionary in 1872 that the first stages of rapprochement between the two institutions were truly possible.

CHAPTER SEVEN

Return to Calcutta: Charles Timothy Brooks and The Brahmo Samaj

The reformation Rammohun had undertaken in Bengal slowed but it did not die after his departure for England. Coincident with the rise of Company power and the 1813 Charter Act allowing more missionaries to enter Bengal, there had been a rising Hindu merchant class whose new wealth and social mobility had increased its own interest in English education. Some of the new merchant class, the Tagores for example, had responded to Rammohun's program for reform and had supported him. But Rammohun had been opposed by other Hindus, the most notable of whom were Raja Radhakanta Deb (1784-1867), Diwan Ramkamal Sen (1783-1844), and Bhavanicharan Banerji (1787-1848). These and other leaders resisted Rammohun's reforms, opposing legislation against *sati* through journals, articles, and their own organization, the Dharma Sabha. Incursions against orthodox Hinduism were to be resisted, they asserted. The old order was to be reestablished and followers of Rammohun were dubbed "half-liberals" and unscrupulous opportunists.[1]

The complete termination of restrictions on Christian missionaries by the Charter of 1833 caused three kinds of reactions to develop among Hindu populations in Calcutta. The first of these was a new push by reform movements such as the Brahmo Samaj to respond to the rational and more open approach of Hindu youth, many of whom were soon to be identified as "Young Bengal."[2] A second response was observed in the considerable anti-missionary propaganda of the vernacular press, while a third dimension showed itself in opposition not only to government schools in which Christianity was taught but also to missionary schools. The anti-missionary trend showed up in three particular ways: attempts to reconvert Christians to Hinduism, socio-economic discrimination against converts, and anti-missionary feelings which developed most sharply when missionaries attempted to engage in social reforms.[3]

Debendranath Tagore, the next major successor to Rammohun Roy in the Brahmo Samaj, established the Tattvabodhini Sabha in October 1839, for the explicit purpose of stemming the rapid growth of Christianity while familiarizing the Hindu population with its own scriptures through extensive publication. While Debendranath Tagore and his biographers have both stressed his contemplative side, it is clear that in his early days, Tagore was very much an activist as well. Rammohun's immediate successor, Ramchandra Vidyavagisha, had continued to perform divine services at the Brahmo Samaj during the 1830s even though the effectiveness of the organization on social questions had all but vanished. Much of the membership of the Tattvabodhini Sabha overlapped with that of the Brahmo Samaj, however. About 1842, Debendranath developed an alliance between the two organizations in which the Brahmo Samaj was clearly the more religious and devotional organization.[4]

The following year, Debendranath framed a covenant for the Samaj to which some twenty members subscribed in 1843, thus self-consciously making the Brahmo Samaj a new sect of Hinduism.[5] This statement of faith expressed the Brahmo theological position.

1. God is a personal being with sublime attributes.
2. God has never become incarnate.
3. God hears and answers prayers.
4. God is to be worshipped only in spiritual ways. Hindu asceticism, temples and fixed forms of worship are unnecessary . . . all castes and races may worship God acceptably.
5. Repentance and cessation from sin are the only way to forgiveness and salvation.
6. Nature and intuition are sources for the knowledge of God. No book is.[6]

During the 1840s the Brahmo Samaj progressed slowly. Because Brahmos maintained many traditional aspects in their devotions, Christian missionaries accused the Brahmos of behaving in a way that was inconsistent with their preaching. Brahmins, for example, did not give up the sacred thread, the traditional Hindu symbol of investiture when coming of age at this time even — though their new faith was anathema to traditional Brahminism.[7] From 1850 to 1854, the Brahmos began a modest mission of their own. In 1851, the Maharaja of Burdwan, later to become interested in Unitarianism after a meeting with Charles Dall, formed a Samaj within the palace complex. Instrumental in founding two Samajes during 1852 and 1853 was Rakhal Das Haldar[8] who was also a close associate of Dall's and later his travelling companion in England.

Charles Brooks' Exploration

In 1854, some twenty-five years after the demise of the first Unitarian mission in India, the Reverend Charles Timothy Brooks, a Unitarian pastor, reached Calcutta to represent the interests of the American Unitarian Association. In the intervening years the Brahmo Samaj had been formed, Rammohun Roy had left for England where he had subsequently died, and the English had consolidated their hold on Bengal as well as most of the rest of the subcontinent.

This renewal of a connection between the American Unitarians and the Brahmo Samaj in the mid-1850s occurred rather by chance. Charles Brooks, a little-known nineteenth-century Unitarian minister who was to serve his entire thirty-seven-year pastorate at Newport, Rhode Island, suffered, as did so many young clergy of the time, from various bronchial and pneumatic ailments brought on by overwork and the damp, cold climate. Born in Salem, Massachusetts, in 1813, Brooks was a graduate of Harvard College and Divinity School where he completed his studies in 1835.[9] Brooks was as much a scholar as a minister. Particularly fluent in German, he translated such works as Goethe's *Faust.* After sixteen years of ministry in Newport, Brooks succumbed to a serious throat and chest illness which forced him to give up all preaching and pastoral work just as the new church year was beginning in the fall of 1853. A close friend and ship-owner offered Brooks a round-trip passage to India which, while meaning exile from family and friends for almost a year, would give him a rare opportunity to visit Asia. Hence, on October 27, 1853, Brooks set sail for Madras and Calcutta on a new ship, the "Piscataqua," whose principal cargo was ice, regularly shipped from New England to India. The only other passengers on board were three missionaries and their families returning to India.[10]

The journey to Madras was anything but pleasant. Shortly after departing from Boston harbor, the ship was caught in a gust of wind. When the ship tilted sharply one way, the ice improperly stored in the hold, all tilted with the ship which left the ship lopsided for the remaining 143 days of the journey. During the entire trip, neither Brooks nor his fellow passengers could walk straight up. However, the considerable stretches of time were used for reading and for Hindustani and Tamil lessons from the missionaries, which Brooks exchanged for

Hebrew, German, and Italian lessons.[11] Brooks's diary details his brief two months in India.

The importance of Brooks's short visit cannot be overestimated, however, for it was the enthusiasm with which he returned to Boston that reopened American Unitarian connections with Calcutta and Madras. Brooks arrived in Madras in South India on March 20, 1854, and remained there until April 20. On the second day in Madras after visiting a Christian missionary who had been in Newport in 1846, Brooks began his quest for William Roberts, minister of the small Unitarian community and son of the founder who had first written Thomas Belsham in 1817. The search, through a city which had a population of 700,000 even in 1854, was not easy. "I was told he lived in Vepery," Brooks wrote.

> We drove out through the Elephant Gate through street after street, road after road, suburb after suburb, narrow ways such as I imagine those of Cairo or Canton, crowded with little bazaars in long rows and lazy natives sprawled on the piazzas which are screened by thatched and sometime tatties or tatters — pile after pile of native products . . . heaped and hanging round; tailors, shoemakers, carvers, shopkeepers all sitting in front of their doors.[12]

After commenting on how moved he was by scenes of poverty throughout the city, Brooks told of finding the Unitarian school but no sign of William Roberts. Leaving his card at the school, Brooks returned to his house where Roberts appeared the next morning.

The Madrasi impressed Brooks with his "good heart, spirit and great good sense." The young man, but thirty-three years old, thinking that Brooks had been sent as a permanent missionary, was deeply disappointed to find that the visit was to be only a brief one. Roberts was anxious for a "white man" to work with him because of the competition with other Christian groups. The Unitarian membership was poor, and easily tempted to become "rice Christians" by offers of free schooling from other churches. Roberts admitted the temptation to apostasize in order to earn a real living. His elder brother, Joseph, educated in England by English Unitarians to succeed William Roberts, Sr., had become a tutor to an orthodox Hindu family in order to make a reasonable living. The younger William had become a minister without any formal training as a tribute to his father's memory.[13]

Despite the difficulties that Roberts reported, however, another Unitarian chapel was under construction at Secunderabad under the leadership of seventy-year-old Abraham Chiniah and a small congregation had also been formed at nearby Salem. British Unitarians were presently nominally supporting both Madras and Secunderabad, Roberts and his schoolmaster receiving the equivalent of 300 rupees a year from the English as a gift. Compared to the 1,000 rupees William Adam received each month twenty years earlier when serving the Government of Bengal, Roberts's support was mere tokenism.

The following Sunday, Brooks attended Tamil services at the small Madras church during which the text of the sermon was taken from Acts 28:22, "Concerning this sect, we know that everywhere it is spoken against." After the service, Brooks joined in a discussion with the congregation, meeting, among others, three of the four living founders of the church. Later, in his report to the American Unitarian Association, Brooks was to plead for a contribution of $500 and an annual appropriation afterwards, which "would plant roses in the wilderness and kindle the star of hope in a dreary sky." He had been deeply moved by the little congregation which had already survived forty years in spite of desperate odds.[14]

At a visit to Roberts's home later in the week, Brooks had an encounter with Roberts and a Muslim friend Janay Jahan Khan about the New Testament and the Qur'an on the subject of "the Divine Unity." In what Brooks has described as a lively debate on Christianity and Islam, his Unitarian Christian paternalism became evident in his admission that he wanted to prove the superiority of Christianity.

> I also told him that Mohamet got his doctrine from Moses and his morality from Jesus. He smiled and shook his head as if that were a desperate assertion. And thus we talked in a most friendly manner fighting peacefully . . . I insisted that he must not confound Christians with the creeds of churches which he said he did not do.[15]

In Calcutta Brooks's stay was limited to three weeks. He arrived at the end of April in the worst heat of the season. Already long delayed by the difficulties of the ship and needing to return home by the summer's end, his visit was necessarily brief. Meeting first with Hodgson Pratt, "a young and zealous Unitarian, under-secretary of the Bengal Government," the two agreed to discuss further the possibilities of a new mission in Calcutta. Pratt feared possible disruptions of Christian missions should a new Unitarian controversy emerge but Brooks disagreed with this position. Brooks knew little of the Brahmo Samaj; Pratt, however, made it clear to Brooks that he held little sympathy with the Brahmos. "He also insisted," Brooks wrote,

> that we must give the Vedantists the local Hindoo philosophical Unitarians to understand at onset that we stood upon the Christian foundation and not merely on that of natural religion and reason.[16]

Pratt, lay leader of the mission begun officially under Charles Dall in 1855, represented a restatement of the Unitarian dilemma William Adam had experienced three decades earlier. The Brahmo attitude had crystalized during the intervening decades and the personal and Hindu self-consciousness which had been a factor in the founding of the Samaj and the anti-missionary program of the Tattvabodhini Sabha now colored the message Brooks was hearing from several of the young Bengal Hindu intelligentsia.

At Pratt's Brooks met a Reverend Bellew, whose sermon he had heard the previous Sunday and who was well read in Channing. There Brooks also met Gannendro Mohan Tagore, one of the two most significant Hindus that he would encounter. The other, Rajendra Dutt, told Brooks that he had not converted to Christianity because he was an only son whose mother wished to have orthodox funeral rites performed by him when she died. Brooks, however, was most impressed by Tagore,

> a young man who has become a Christian by his own reading and study. . . His appearance was very singular. He was clad in a long black (robe) like that of a Romish priest and a ruffle shirt . . . his small slender stature and prominent glowing eyes and black thick hair . . . made up a somewhat odd looking person. He soon got me to talking about Emerson, Parker and Channing of whom he had some crude and false notions among many just ones. He seemed to think that Emerson could appreciate St. John better than Channing could. . . (He) also had a notion of Parker's strongly maintaining a peculiar Divine inspiration as incarnated Christ. . . He was evidently fond of mysticism (for) he said he read St. John day and night.[17]

The Tagore whom Brooks met at Pratt's was another son of Dwarkanath cut off from his inheritance, he said, for converting to Christianity. His brother Debendranath's resistance to Christian incursions into the Brahmo Samaj during this same decade gives further evidence of the strong move away from even a liberal form of Christianity, or a mystical non-dogmatic form such as espoused by the Christian Tagore.

This same Tagore documented further the attitude held toward Rammohun Roy, a view which disappointed Brooks. Reporting on Rammohun as an intimate friend of his father, this Christian Tagore maintained that Rammohun had not been a Christian in faith, though he had been a Unitarian and had supported Unitarians philanthropically. "Finding the Precepts of Jesus consonant to his reason and benevolence," and holding the English Unitarians in high regard, Rammohun had let himself pass for a Christian Unitarian. This, Tagore insisted, was nothing more than the attitude a liberal Chinese would take toward Confucius.

Brooks was pained to learn that Rammohun was not so well regarded in Calcutta in 1854 as he was in Cambridge. Not easily disillusioned, however, Brooks noted that Pratt, Tagore, and Reverend Bellew understood Rammohun no better than he did. "I said, then, that their account impeached his honesty; oh, they said, that was simply Oriental accomodation, that he was one of those Vedantists, those Hindoo deists who pass for Christian just as some Unitarians have done in some other countries."[18]

At least two other aspects of Brooks's stay in Calcutta were far less controversial and more vital to his developing an understanding of the religio-cultural situation. Attending a meeting of the Bethune Society with Pratt, Brooks heard a lecture on Vernacular Education delivered by Lal Behari Day, a convert and noted preacher to the Calcutta Christians. Brooks had already been struck by the potential of "Young Bengal" after reading the essay by Shoshee Chunder Dutt[19] which was both critical and supportive of the new generation, many of whom formed the basic membership of the Brahmo Samaj. Brooks surmised that Lal Behari Day had chosen the subject of vernacular education in order to answer the criticism of Young Bengal for Bengali and its strong preference for English. "Young Bengal likes to condemn the Bengali language as incapable of being the medium of national regeneration having so long been wedded to a low and licentious literature," Brooks noted in his diary.[20] Lal Behari Day, while praising English as a medium, suggested strongly that much that was available in English could be translated into Bengali in order to reach larger masses of the population.

As for Dutt's essay on "Young Bengal," one passage struck Brooks sufficiently that he copied it into his diary:

> Our next charge against Young Bengal shall be that he has no religion; and we say this even of the best. Some are deists after Hume and Gibbon; a few we believe are Unitarian Christians on principle, but unbaptized; many are Vedantists: but of the bulk, it may be safely affirmed, that they have forsworn an old faith but have "not had time" to get a new one.[21]

Receipt by the American Unitarian Association of letters from two liberal Muslims, one of whom Brooks had met in Madras, further urged the sending of a Unitarian missionary who could be supportive of liberal Muslims. Another letter from eleven laymen of the Madras Unitarian Church in response to the Brooks visits elicited a gift of $50 "for the distribution of Christian books."[22]

While Brooks felt that his poor health and lack of time had prevented him from conducting the kind of thorough study he would have wished in Calcutta, his presentation to the American Unitarian Association Executive Committee revived their memory of the earlier attempts to missionize in India. One year later they would take the big step and initiate a new mission to Calcutta in the person of the Reverend Charles Dall. It is his story to which this study now turns.

CHAPTER EIGHT

A New Missionary Effort
The Controversial Mission of Charles Dall

What Charles Brooks communicated in his letters to the American Unitarian Association Executive Committee, published subsequently in the *Quarterly Journal*, brought significant response from clergy and laity alike, sufficient to make the subject of a mission to India the major topic of the February 1855 Executive Committee session. The Secretary of the American Unitarian Association, Henry Miles, had already corresponded with several candidates, the most impressive of whom appeared to be the thirty-nine-year-old Charles H. A. Dall, then a resident of Newton, Massachusetts.

Dall was born in Baltimore in 1816 but was educated in Boston where he lived with an uncle. A graduate (valedictorian) of Boston Latin School in 1833, Dall entered Harvard College where he appeared to be a sensitive, studious young man who, according to his biographer, suffered "peculiarities of manner and temperament" which seemed to alienate many of his classmates. From the college, Dall moved on in 1837 to Harvard Divinity School. While there, he served as Sunday School director at Hollis Street Church. When he graduated in 1840, Dall joined the increasing number of Harvard Unitarian graduates leaving New England. Dall was ordained in 1840 in St. Louis where he held his first pastorate under the Reverend W. G. Eliot.[1] While there is no record to substantiate who and what may have influenced Dall during his days at the Divinity School, it appears from his ministry in St. Louis, later ministries in Baltimore and Portsmouth, New Hampshire, and from an early unpublished lecture,[2] that Dall modeled much of his ministerial style after the Reverend Joseph Tuckerman, who was in the last days of his urban pastorate to the poor when Dall entered the ministry. Dall's primary concern seemed to be that of providing educational opportunities to the disadvantaged. While illness seemed to stifle his early career at every turn, his three inner-city ministries carried Dall through 1846 with some winters spent in the south and most of 1842 spent in Europe. While in Baltimore, Dall married Caroline Healey, a woman who would become well-known in her own right while Dall was off in India. Their first child, William Healey Dall, born in 1845, became a distinguished American scientist during the late nineteenth century.[3]

From 1847 to 1849, Dall served as minister in Needham, Massachusetts, until he was again struck by illness. Following the resignation of William Adam, Dall accepted a call and served as the second minister to the Toronto church from 1850 to 1854. When serious illness set in again in the fall of 1854, Dall resigned and moved to Newton, Massachusetts, where he responded to the news that Charles Brooks had brought back from India. Some of the language of Dall's letter of application and of the charge to him by the American Unitarian Association Executive Committee clarify the tone and manner in which the new mission project was undertaken. Reflecting on the earlier attempt at a mission in India, Dall wrote,

> I believe that a missionary spirit longing to embrace the world, struggles for expression in the enlarging heart of the Unitarian Church, not less, but much more than it did twenty-five or thirty years ago. . . And now *shall I be sent*, in a way to engage many hearts around me here to bless and be blessed by many there, — going with no wisdom but Christ's love to perishing men, and an utter faith in him as the single and only God-commissioned Saviour of the world?[4]

The clearly Christian and Unitarian tone of Dall's letter was very much on the conservative to mainstream side of the movement and very much outside the Transcendentalist thrust of the same period. While the American Unitarian Association chose to send Dall first to Calcutta where, among other tasks, he was to investigate the Brahmo Samaj ("Society of Vedantists"), he was also instructed to go to Madras, Secunderabad, and Salem in South India to make a judgment about the needs of the Unitarians there. "You go out as a *Unitarian* missionary," they wrote,

> because we have reason to believe that many will receive the Gospel as we hold it who reject the errors which we believe others have added to the faith once delivered to the saints. But you are not expected to carry more doctrinal discussions and secretarian strife to those distant lands . . . we need not remind you that, as a Unitarian believer in the Lord Jesus Christ, you will enjoy a great advantage in the simplicity of your doctrine, the intelligibleness of your faith, and its accordance with the correct and obvious teachings of Scripture.[5]

The missionary commitment of the American Unitarian Association in its 1855 charge to Charles Dall was clearly in the Pauline tradition and not in the spirit of dialogue or of free interchange. Avoid controversy and polemics, Dall was urged. Find out about the Brahmo Samaj movement and how it may be relevant to Unitarian concerns. But do not forget that you are carrying the true message of the Gospel. The spirit was therefore a mixed one. Educate, sell, and give away books on Unitarianism, interact freely with other missionaries, and report back to us regularly on the impact of your work. It was thus that Charles H. A. Dall began a thirty-one-year ministry in Calcutta.

The journey to Calcutta was not without its trials. During forty of the 110 days Dall was extremely ill. At Calcutta he had to be carried ashore in a litter. Nevertheless, he had the strength to write the American Unitarian Association just before landing on June 18, 1855, and again on July 3. But once settled, Dall found, as had so many others such as Brooks, Channing, and Buckminster that whatever may have caused Dall to suffer physically in New England all but disappeared in the tropical humidity of Calcutta. Dall seemed to thrive almost immediately, carrying on an extensive local ministry and later traveling throughout the subcontinent, returning to America only in 1862, 1869, 1872, 1875, and 1882.[6]

The record of Dall's work for the early years is far more extensive than for the later ones. His letters to the American Unitarian Association were published quarterly in considerable detail until the termination of the *Journal* in 1866. His own copious notes and records, letters copied and received, and his own unpublished letters to the American Unitarian Association, have survived far more fully for the early years, and to some extent for the final years. Dall's initial support from high-status English and American residents of Calcutta was certainly a significant early boost to his work. Writing the American Unitarian Association on July 3, two weeks after his arrival, Dall was able to report that he had already held two Sunday services with English, American, and "native fellowworshippers" in attendance. Dall's leading supporter was Hodgson Pratt, Superintendent of Government Schools, who had befriended Charles Brooks one year earlier. The American consul, Richard Lewis, with whom Brooks had also had an interview, was active and anxious, Dall wrote, to see the works of Channing spread throughout India. By August 8, Dall had written that after seven Sundays he had an active congregation of fifty, had rented a hall, and had one month earlier officially formed a "Society for the Propagation of the Gospel in India." Interaction with the educated Hindu community had also started, for Dall wrote, "Some Hindoos of education, and a few of the Society of Rammohun Roy, attend, and also meet me during the week for conversation. Of these native gentlemen, some contribute towards our expenses, many purchase our Unitarian books, and a few look earnestly towards Christianity."[7]

Dall's letter was accompanied by one from Hodgson Pratt, newly chosen president of the Society, containing a record of the meeting at which the Society had been organized. The entirely non-Indian Executive Committee was clearly determined to organize a successful Unitarian church in the city. As a result, both Pratt and Dall requested the American Unitarian Association to release the minister from travelling to Madras and south until the church in Calcutta was well-organized. Pratt, explaining the social and religious reasons why so few Hindus had converted to Christianity, extolled the virtues of Unitarian Christianity as a way out for English-educated Hindus, pledging support for Dall in his work but chiding the American Unitarian Association for paying Dall only one-third of the lowest salary received by any other missionary in Bengal.[8]

Pratt's postscript on the relationship possible with Muslims in Bengal as contrasted to Hindus was highly illustrative of the limited attitude of even a liberal, enlightened civil servant of the Government. Alluding to the fact that he had only referred to Hindus in his letter, he commented,

> You will perhaps be surprised to hear that the Mohammedans do not in any degree share in the progressive reforming spirit which has been so striking a fact in the case of the Hindoos during the last twenty or thirty years. The Mohammedans, though possessed of greater physical strength are now infinitely less active than the Hindoos; are sunk in sensual apathy and indifference, neglecting, with a few exceptions, their own literature and learned languages, while they regard with contempt the languages and sciences of the West.[9]

Thus, asserting that while Government Schools were opened to all Indians, only Hindus attended, Pratt explained why only

Hindus were to be found in Government positions open to Indians, and therefore, why only Hindus might be attracted to the Unitarian community. What Pratt left unsaid, and what it took Dall some time to realize, was that the "enlightened" and available numbers of Hindus in a condition any better than that attributed to Muslims was also miniscule. Further, he seemed unaware that even the Brahmo Samaj under Debendranath Tagore in its Bengali publications had been out of sympathy if not in direct conflict with any mission program for more than a decade. While it is true that Bengali Muslims might well have been described as Pratt described them in 1855, he seemed ignorant of the reasons for their condition and, in particular, of the fact that centuries in a Bengali environment had divorced much of the Muslim population from the Persian-Arabic roots so much a part of North and West Indian Urdu Islamic culture.

By August 22, 1855, Dall could write that despite his fifty active supporters, what impressed him most was the interest and "welcome given to our mission by the *native* mind." While he did not reject the support of Unitarian Christians, Dall believed his mission to be "for the long-degraded victims of the worship of false gods."

> No wonder that this people of one hundred and fifty millions of souls are deeply sunk in ignorance, intemperance, and licentiousness. They have not one temple erected to any of those virtues, not one to the only true God. Those who daily frequent my rooms in search of truth declare that self-denial, and the command laid upon the strong to bear the infirmities of the weak, are altogether peculair to Christianity. We American Unitarian Christians are sought and found of the Gentiles, and we shall gain our brothers by kindness erelong, if we are fruitful.[10]

In his own copy of this same letter, Dall listed the names of about twenty leaders, as he saw them, of the Calcutta Hindu community which he asked the American Unitarian Association not to publish. Overly optimistic about what their relationship might be, Dall saw them as "pioneers" in the Unitarian cause.

Among the most significant of these "pioneers" was Rajendra Dutt, the supporter of Debendranath in the Tattvabodhini Sabha and one of the two significant Hindus with whom Brooks had met in 1854.[11] Another was twenty-nine-year-old Raj Narain Bose (Basu), the son of one of Rammohun's disciples. He too had worked for the Tattvabodhini, translated the Upanishads into English, actively engaged with the Brahmo

Samaj, and held nationalist views.[12] Others included Perry Chand Mittra, Librarian and Secretary of the Calcutta Public Library, and a leading member of the Bengal British India Society and the British Indian Association, a champion of social justice, particularly in the continuing conflict with the indigo planters;[13] Rajendralal Mittra, at this time librarian of the Asiatic Society and also a strong supporter of peasant rights and promoter of vernacular literature, as well as joint founder with Hodgson Pratt in 1854 of an art school;[14] and Kissory Chand Mittra, another early social reformer.[15] In the long run, Dall's interaction with men of this calibre was to be in such religiously neutral but progressive institutions as the Bethune Society or the British Indian Association.

A further perusal of Dall's initial activities and contacts in Calcutta indicates his role as a "listener" at the General Conference of Bengal Protestant Missionaries and his continuing distribution of the works of Channing, Ware, Greenwood, Clark, and Eliot among the increasing number of Hindus who came to visit him. Dall expressly regretted that more than twenty-five years had been wasted with little evidence remaining of the work of William Adam. Dall also wrote of his first contacts with Muslims when attending the "General Meeting of the Mahometan Association" early in November.[16]

Dall's Unitarian Theology

Dall and his supporters believed publication to be an effective way of reaching the public. Thus, above and beyond the distribution of American Unitarian materials, Dall began publishing tracts and books, most notable of which were his "Discourse Occasioned by the Death of the Hon'ble Abbot Lawrence" and his ten lectures, *Some Gospel Principles*, designed to acquaint Calcutta with the nature of Unitarianism.[17] The former discourse must have been especially pleasing to Dall's predominantly mercantile and governmental servant congregation, extolling Lawrence as he did as the virtuous merchant and capitalist, a Unitarian Christian who had set such a fine example in New England.

> Yet he did it often in a way that shewed him to be moved, if by hopes of personal profit, still by a generous, aye, a religious patriotism; and by a belief that Providence, God's will, had designed those

> United States to become one people, industrious, intelligent and innocently happy by their own labor; by an industry which employs not only for good . . . but creates . . . and delivers the small farmer and his children from the danger of oppression.[18]

The *Ten Lectures*, besides being a statement of Unitarian theology, showed Dall's sensitivity to political and social issues. Already deeply concerned about abolition and temperance as a result of his inner-city ministries in America and his visits to the south, Dall also played on points of freedom of thought and expression as well as on individualism. A "people if allowed to read and taught to think, can constitutionally govern themselves," he wrote in the lecture on American Unitarianism. In the United States and Britain, rule by law and not by arbitrary will (perhaps an allusion to British rule in India) has worked for freedom, he commented.[19] His lecture on "Christian Liberty" stressed again the significance of dissent in religious history, pressing Dall's model heros for American Unitarian reform Henry Ware, Tuckerman, Channing, and Noah Worcester, the early nineteenth-century pacifist.[20]

Dall's Christology was very much in the middle-to-late Channing tradition and not at all of the Parker-Emerson transcendentalist vision. Basing his statements on the text John 18:37, "To this end was I born, and for this cause I came into the world, that I should bear witness unto the Truth," Dall began by asserting that Christ saves men only by the Truth, not by any favoritism or expediency. The "Truth," he insisted, is forever and everywhere the same, impartial and immutable. Thus Dall made clear his universalism over against the particularism of the missionaries. In the spirit of Channing's "Likeness to God," Dall argued that Christ's relation to God is like that of a reflector of his mental and moral likeness, analogous to the likeness of a child to its father. Christ's relation to people, however, is that of light and love to eye and heart. He shows the way to Truth. Therefore, God is love as Christ is love.

Dall took the occasion of this lecture, as he did so often in his contacts with the Hindu intelligentsia, to point to Rammohun Roy's call to men to receive the precepts and parables of Jesus as their guide to peace and happiness. This seemed to be Dall's key to developing a relationship on Christian terms with Brahmos and other Hindu liberals. For them, he argued that Rammohun was on the right track in his exposition of the message of Jesus. Dall stood firm against the orthodox clergy, concluding,

> Christianity is therefore no expedient: no mere *scheme* of Redemption. It is God's truth and God's love embodied in human life, for all time. Christianity is not *a* religion — but Religion; the Absolute Religion. Christ is Christianity; and Christianity is Christ.[21]

Pursuing his Unitarianism in other lectures Dall openly rejected the doctrine of the atonement as "heathen" in favor of a view that Christ was God's perfect image in man whose every word and deed is intended to show us the way to the Father. It is the morals Christ taught that are essential to salvation, Dall concluded, the simplicity and catholicity of the creed of Christ, a sense of human brotherhood which is the true church of Christ. "Protestantism absolves man from all allegiance short of God in religious things, just as democracy absolves men from all allegiance short of humanity in secular things."[22] Protestantism was the proclamation of individual freedom and had meaning for India because, Dall believed, it was the only force by which Indians could drive out their rulers. Christianity would never have come to India had it not been for the British, whose rule in India Dall saw to be unjust in many instances as compared with their rule in England.

Dall's sense of the breadth of Christ's message and life forshadowed what Keshub Chunder Sen, educated in Unitarian theology, would preach to the Brahmo Samaj a decade later. Dall's Unitarianism emphasized that God's truth had come to other men in other times and places than in Palestine. The era in India when the Vedas and Upanishads were revealed was an example of God at work; however, darkness had fallen on India in recent centuries until at last Christ's truth had now come.

Charles Dall's theology and religious message were liberal by the standards of his Christian missionary contemporaries. It was fascinating to the young Bengalis who came to discuss scripture and Channing with him, to attend his services at times and to participate in various associational meetings with him. But no matter how liberal Dall's views were, they were still Christian; there was no hedging that. His efforts to convert Hindus to Unitarianism, therefore, were necessarily limited by social and cultural forces around him.

Dall and the Brahmos

The ministry of Charles Dall was multifaceted. While there is little doubt that Dall's precise and at times petulant personality led him into many petty controversies during his thirty-one-year ministry, it is also true that Dall became engaged in many original enterprises and interacted with some of the most significant Hindu and missionary figures active in Bengal during the second half of the nineteenth century. Dall's perception of Bengali life and culture is a good point at which to start an examination of the significance of his work. His interaction with persons who were either converts or potential converts and his eventual controversies with all of them affords a second dimension for study. His lectures, his continuing defense of Rammohun Roy in controversies with Brahmos and others, his slowly blooming friendship with the youthful Keshub Chunder Sen, and his decision in 1871 to become a member of the Brahmo Samaj while remaining the Unitarian Christian minister in Calcutta, highlight the final phase of a study of his involvement with Hindu intelligentsia.

It is important also to observe a reverse impact. When Dall went to England in 1861, he took with him a Brahmo supporter, Rakhal Das Haldar. Previously, his first Hindu "convert," Philip Joganath Ganguli, had visited both England and America. Haldar, while a student in England, succeeded in introducing the early lectures of the young Keshub Chunder Sen to English Unitarians. Consequently, when the thirty-two-year-old Keshub arrived in England on a lecture tour in 1870, some two years after English Unitarian Mary Carpenter's return from India, social work with the Brahmos, among others, his impact and the resulting interchange between Brahmos and Unitarians went far beyond what Dall could develop in Calcutta alone. The impact of this interchange was to continue through the 1874 visit to England of Keshub's cousin Protap Chunder Mazumdar and the latter's three subsequent visits to America in 1884, 1893, and 1900, as well as through the social work and writings of Mary Carpenter and the publications of Sophie Dobson Collet about Rammohun Roy and current events at the Brahmo Samaj.

From Calcutta Dall expanded his work in different directions. While visiting Hodgson Pratt who had moved to Burdwan, sixty-six miles away, Dall was introduced to the rajah who, while living in the surroundings of an Oriental potentate, had grown up among Europeans and was almost European in his personal attitudes. Several impressive activities occurred during the first year of Dall's ministry. A chapter of the Brahmo Samaj had already been founded in the Burdwan palace precincts a few years earlier. While the rajah made it clear that he could never become a Christian he was so impressed with Dall's exposition of Unitarian Christianity that he invited Dall to send tracts and return for a preaching engagement. Because it was common practice for Europeans to visit schools and conduct examinations of Indian students, Dall was often called upon to perform this task. This he did at the rajah's boys' school in Burdwan.[23]

Early in January of 1856, Dall lectured to the Bethune Society and spoke to the prize day at Metropolitan College, a college attended by 700 Hindu students and the only one then started in India without government aid.[24] His address on self-reliance in education was subsequently published in Bengali and Urdu. In the tradition of his earlier inner-city ministries, Dall went daily to the School of Industrial Arts where he also discussed religious matters. By 1860, he had founded his own School of Useful Arts to meet what he believed to be a crying need for practical education. As early as 1855, Dall had impressed members of the Kidderpore Brahmo Samaj and while becoming a close friend of their leader Rakhal Das Haldar, he preached at Kidderpore every week for three months before the conservative wing of the group refused to allow him to participate any longer. Rakhal Das withdrew from the Brahmo Samaj as a show of support for Dall though he never actually "converted" to Christianity as Dall had wished. In addition, a Muslim convert, John Muatter, carried Unitarian materials to Peshawer in the northwest, while at Jessore in eastern Bengal, another Christian convert, impressed with Unitarianism, was preaching to Hindus. At Bali, some six miles up the Hooghly River, Chundy Churn Singha, director of a boys' school, was preaching and disseminating Unitarianism. He was frequently visited by Dall and was soon to produce one of Dall's closest followers and subsequently greatest problems, Joganath Ganguli.[25]

Dall's continued emphasis on the teachings of Rammohun Roy about Jesus and true Christianity caused conflict with Debendranath Tagore on the one side and Dr. Alexander Duff, leader of the Scotch Church in Calcutta, on the other. Debendranath had early informed Dall that "he would not hear the name of Jesus spoken in the Samaj." This was a direct result of Debendranath's beliefs that the basis for Brahmoism was Vedantic reformation and also because of a decade of opposition to Trinitarian Christianity through the Tattvabodhini Sabha. That Debendranath was on the conservative side of Brahmo opinion even as early as 1855 was evident from Dall's controversial role at Kidderpore and the presence on Dall's list of church visitors and financial supporters of such men as Rakhal Das Haldar, Rajender Dutt, and Kissory Chand Mittra. When Tagore no longer allowed Dall to speak to the Calcutta Brahmo Samaj and in 1857 informed Dall that he was no longer even welcome, Dall responded by organizing the Rammohun Roy Society[26] which eventually emerged as the Hitoishini Association. Its membership was primarily that of Brahmos interested in studying the teachings of Rammohun and Christianity.

The Hitoishini group pressed for different kinds of reforms than did the Brahmos. They felt the need for using Bengali in preference to Sanskrit alone. They invited Dall to participate with them, and his influence was obvious in two ways. First he encouraged them in the study of Channing and, later, Parker. As a result they began Bengali translations and included Channing's "Moral Argument Against Calvinism" in their journal. Second, Dall pushed their incipient proto-nationalist interests with his lecture "True Patriotism in Bengal" which the association paid to have published.[27] There was not much more that a foreign missionary could have said at this time which would have pleased progressive young Bengalis more. Stressing an identity theme by telling his listeners that Bengalis had a country worth living for, Dall criticized the wealthy zamindars (landowners) and rajahs who were doing so little for the 30 million inhabitants of a land so rich in resources. Bengalis, he continued, had motives for lofty patriotism. Praising the Hindu character for its potential, Dall laid blame on the Muslims for the atrocities of the "mutiny." If the Hindus had an obstacle to overcome, he continued, it was that of caste. The purpose of caste, he conjectured, "was to bring savage life to order. I love order and so I love caste as God ordained it but I hate much that man has made of it." A strong stand against the corruptions of Brahminism and a free press, he concluded, would do much, with help and sympathy, to make Bengal a great nation.

Dall, excited by his many contacts, vastly overestimated their significance in predicting how successful the Unitarian mission would become. In November, 1856, he began the first of many journeys staying several weeks in Madras, preaching twice to the Unitarian congregation of William Roberts, and writing to the American Unitarian Association that they were indeed as Charles Brooks had described them, "a little band of martyrs, not easily convinced 'how far into the night' of our self-love, as a body of Christians, their little taper throws its beams."[28] Returning to Calcutta a month later, Dall found the church and its attendance still intact, four discourses of Channing's, including the one "On the Death of Charles Follen," having served as the basis for Sunday worship in his absence. Upon his return, Dall had to answer newspaper attacks on the mission published in his absence by both Brahmos and orthodox Christians. He also produced a new tract, "The Christian Testimony of Rammohun Roy," in answer to a "Vedantist" attack published by the Bhoawaneepore Brahmos against Dall.[29]

By January of 1857, Dall wrote that he had been approached by members of five societies populated with "Young Bengal" types asking him to meet with them weekly "to take religious charge of them as a sheep having no shepherd." This included meetings every Monday, Tuesday, and Wednesday evenings plus the Bethune Society, Dall went on to write, "of three or four hundred young half-Christianized men, which meets on the second Thursday of each month; and my second annual course of public lectures on 'Gospel Principles' is to fill the next seven or eight Friday evenings." Dall had now moved out of his hotel into living quarters adjacent to the mission rooms, which were now also serving as reading rooms. All were located at No. 4 Tank Square in the center of Calcutta. During his remaining three decades, Dall would move again several times but he always remained in the center of the city. He spent the longest period at 24 Motts Lane with briefer periods in buildings at 79, 85, and 97 Dhurumtollah Street in the neighborhood where Rammohun Roy's Unitarian press and William Adam's newspaper office had been located.[30]

From the commencement of his stay, Dall had undertaken the study of Bengali, "Hindustani" (Hindi-Urdu), and Sanskrit. He believed Sanskrit most important to his work as it contained the roots and origins of all other North Indian languages. Bengali was also essential for intercourse with the kind of non-English-speaking people Dall wished to influence through industrial arts training schools and in the mufassil, or rural areas. In 1857, Dall began a period of study of the Bhagavad Gita with Rajah Radhakant Deb,[31] a conservative Vaisnava Hindu opponent of the Brahmo Samaj and a most unlikely contact for Dall. Born in 1783 and roughly a contemporary of Rammohun Roy, Radhakant Deb had been among the founders and staunch supporters of Hindu College. Moreover, he was strongly opposed to the irreligious and generally amoral life of many young Hindus and also to the effects of missionaries on education. In his opposition to missionaries, he had joined Debendranath Tagore in the Tattvabodhini Sabha, yet he was also a precurser of Rammohun in advocating education for women. His reaction to Hindu religious decline took him in the opposite direction from Rammohun, however. As a scholar of Sanskrit and the recipient of many awards, Dall could deeply appreciate Radhakant's help in translating the *Gita.* But his report of their theological discussions in a letter to the American Unitarian Association indicates his failure to accept Radhakant on his own terms.

> He is usually reputed one of the finest living specimens of a sincere highly educated idolater; and I went expecting to find him an eloquent pleader for the worship of sticks and stones. In this I was disappointed. He began the conversation with a hearty asservation of the existence of only one God. I asked him what name he would apply to the only God, and was not a little pleased to hear him say that his name was not 'Bruhm', the abyss of being, out of whom come Brahma, Vishnu and Shiva. . . The Hindoo Trinity. 'No,' he said, 'his name is Porom-Eeshwar,' (the Most High) which I recognized at once as the Bengali name for God, which the missionaries of all sects of Christians unite in according to Jehovah. . . . . . So far I had reason to be well pleased with the Rajah's faith, and almost began to hope that the reading of Christian books had taken effect upon him as he approached the close of a long life. It was near sunrise, and as we rested on the balustrade of his palace verandah and surveyed the beauty on every hand, I asked the old man what temple that was on the other side of the pond. Had he erected that to Porom-Eeshwar? 'No, no, that was to Krishna.' 'And who is Krishna?' said I. 'One of the sixteen chief incarnations,' he replied. 'What attribute of Porom-Eeshwar does Krishna embody?' I asked. He replied, 'O that is the Vedantist system, that looks for special truths in special deities. There is no need of that since everything is God, one thing as much as another.' The Rajah soon fell into the grossest pantheism, saying, 'I am God, you are God, this pillar is God. Let a man worship what he will, he cannot help worshipping God all the same.'[32]

Although Dall seemed to show a gross lack of understanding of a man like Rajah Radhakant Deb, yet it appears that within a few years Dall was almost totally rejected by the European-English-speaking community, his few close friends and supporters being primarily reformist Indian. The "Mutiny" of 1857 made him clearly aware of the abuses and injustices perpetrated by British rule and his response to these could not have endeared him much to the British establishment. Yet, with all his apparent awareness of the plight of the ryot peasant and the suffering of the Indian people in masses, Dall never acted radically as did his missionary cohort, the Reverend James Long, convicted in 1861 for his support of the indigo workers' rebellion and translation into English of the controversial book *Nil Darpan.*

Dall As Social Critic

Reflecting on the departure of Hodgson Pratt for England, Dall wrote the American Unitarian Association in 1858 that no one knew better than Pratt that the latter's $10,000 a year salary was paid in large part from the proceeds of opium raised in India to be smuggled into China. "None have known better than he, that the land tax was raised by much harsh treatment of the tillers of the soil, the 'peeled' and often tortured ryots."[33] Though no one would dispute, Dall continued, that British rule was on the whole a blessing to India, everyone knew also of the excessive abuses of civil servants and especially tax collectors. Describing some of the horrors of the "revolt," the murder of Europeans in Delhi, as well as the fact that "Hindoos are being blown from the mouth of British cannon by the 'bully boys' of England," Dall was appalled by the total support given to such British horrors even by a Christian publication like the *Friend of India.*[34]

In mid-September, Dall learned at first hand of the conditions under which ryot peasants worked when he travelled with Mahendra Nath Mukerji to the latter's schools at Gooberdinga, some forty miles northeast of Calcutta. Mukerji had met Dall early in 1856 and had slowly become an unconverted Unitarian, teaching much of what Dall had imparted to him in the Gooberdinga schools. Continuing to Dacca and other places in Eastern Bengal, Dall reported of his stays with indigo planters, likening life on the plantations and the hospitality to that he had received in the American South. Dall's sympathies and understanding were increasingly with the ryot peasant and poor Bengali, yet he always seemed to see some good coming from both sides of a situation. He reported in a letter early in 1858 that Bengal missionaries had a petition before Parliament to "exert its strong hand to stay the oppressions of the European planter, which they affirm are grinding the ryot to the dust." In his own experience, Dall had seen no such suppressions but claimed instead to have witnessed alleviation. For example, he approved of the daily courts held by planters to adjudicate disputes among ryots and to support the helpless. The peasant ryots, he asserted, preferred this system to the British courts and abided by their decisions. Of course, while Dall continued to observe that there was no one more wretched than the ryot, he seemed to overlook the fact that very few if any uneducated Indians found any justice according to the English court system. Peasant lives were limited and parochial and in spite of Dall's presumptions about the blessings of British rule, and also his understandings about the shortcomings of imperialism, he seemed to miss the mark in his justifications of such practices as a plantation court system. Dall had been appalled by the wretchedness of peasant living conditions, worse, he argued, than that of American slaves, and by the cheapness of the labor, one to three rupees a month.

> The immediate encouragement for Europeans to be planters here is that ryot-wary labor gives them the same rapidly acquired wealth and the most successful slave labor. Of course, very few of the planters are philanthropists. The good of the ryot is not their chief purpose. Now and then a planter here will tell you, that if he could make it for his own interest, he would drive the ryot even as the African slave is driven. Happily he cannot do this. Were he to attempt it, his ryots would soon leave him.[35]

Dall's trip to Dacca and East Bengal made him much more confident about the Bengali personality than he had previously been. Finding that Europeans of the interior spoke far more positively about Bengalis than did those in Calcutta, Dall was both pleased and surprised to hear a rural resident speak of "the innate fidelity of the Bengalee," indeed to speak of him as anything but "a sneak and a liar," the kind of derision Dall had heard so often in Calcutta. Suddenly he was realizing that many Europeans believed that Bengalis "learned rascality from contact with the whites." "Suffice it to say," Dall continued,

> that my faith in the Asiatic nature, which was very feeble, has been much strengthened by a month's experience of dealing directly with those Bengalis whom Thomas Babington Macaulay should have known better, before slandering them as he has done, as shirks, cowards, and deceivers beyond hope of mankind.[36]

The total British victory in quelling the mutiny nevertheless brought the realization of needed reforms in India. Thus, the control of the British East India Company was terminated. Control of government passed to the British Parliament and the Cabinet symbolized for most Indians by Queen Victoria herself. Dall, while suspicious that "great mischief" might arise when India's governance fell to political factions in England, saw this change as a great improvement. Yet somehow, for all his growing understanding of Bengalis and Indians, Dall viewed Britain's new role in India from a most paternal point of view. He did, however, anticipate well the approach of uncertain flexibility the British would take when he said,

> I have more fear . . . that England will be unwisely and weakly lenient and yielding, than that she will be over forceful and too steadily hard, stern and decided. Man in India, especially since this bloody quarrel with his overseers . . . must be treated like a naughty boy . . . I do not say that the master should 'beat the boy within an inch of his life. . .' but I see clearly that the fellow who fears not the true God . . . must be made to know that there is an arm which can hold him, and a reserved force, which, if he yield not to reason, can be effectively brought to bear on him.

Urging the British to forego their Company policy of "flattery and cunning" and replace it with "generosity and strength", Dall concluded the last of his political assertions to the American Unitarian Association with positive comments on the new charter for India but disbelief about the eighth clause which assured no governmental interference in religious matters. "I cannot think she has no 'desire' to Christianize India," he wrote of Queen Victoria, or

> to '*interfere*' with the foul practices of her devil worship, or to disquiet her from hugging her idols, and their necessary slavery and degradation . . . I hope I am mistaken in supposing that English bravery and honesty have in that eighth clause fallen a little short of their usual lofty aim and attainment.[37]

Though Charles Dall had high hopes for India under a new

political system in the years after the Mutiny, the effects of events in the late 1850s had driven many English and American merchants away from an increasing economic depression in Bengal. As Dall's congregation withered away, his interest in three Indians, two Hindu and one Muslim, and interest in organizing a school greatly increased.

Dall and His Proteges

Dall first met Jogut Chunder Ganguli when he visited the school at Bali where the twenty-year-old Ganguli served as a teacher. Of Brahmin origins, Ganguli fully intended to become a Hindu priest until he read some Christian tracts with the intention of writing a refutation of them. A tract on the "Sermon on the Mount" so impressed him that he then sought out the entire New Testament and other information on Christianity. Unable to accept the Trinity which he likened to the Trinity of Brahminism, and meeting Charles Dall, whose Unitarian message appealed to him, he urged Dall to baptize him and help him to become another Unitarian missionary.[38] On December 27, 1857, Dall baptized his first convert to Unitarianism and a year later, Ganguli departed for the United States, the first Brahmin to set foot in America. After two years of education and a major reception among the Unitarians which could not help but impress the young man, Ganguli, whose Christian name was "Philip," was ordained in Boston on June 10, 1860, in the presence of E. E. Hale and James Freeman Clarke. In his address to the congregation, Ganguli expressed deep emotion over his conversion experience and reception in America. Describing himself as a "fugitive slave from Brahminism" who had arrived in America weak and helpless, he now departed for India full of strength, not to return to his home from which he would be rejected, but to bring "the light of Christianity" to "the superstitions of the Hindoos."

Pointing to the shortcomings of missionary work in India and especially to the fact that most conversions were of low-caste people, Ganguli emphasized that such conversions could have no great influence. "You see that in India the high castes have all the knowledge about religion," he observed,

> and when these missionaries convert a low caste . . . who know nothing even of their own religion, they cannot open their mouth

> before the high castes. . . In India, if you convert one of the high castes, you convert ten of the low caste.[39]

Ganguli professed his desire to return to support Dall but not to live with him. He would translate Unitarian tracts into Bengali but live among the Hindus, for he feared they would in turn reject him if he were to eat and drink with an American Christian. On his return to India, Ganguli stopped off in London, where he was warmly received and supported. In London, particularly, he came to Dall's defense saying that Dall should be judged by quality rather than quantity in the success of his mission work.

Though all outward show by the British Unitarians excitedly supported Ganguli prior to his return to India, it appears that the convert had entered into illicit relations with a young woman while in America and had become engaged to an English woman whose parents objected. Later, he became engaged to another English woman. Dall, learning of this latter marriage plan, was deeply shocked and did all he could to counter it believing Ganguli's effectiveness among Hindus would be nullified were he to marry a European. Correspondence with English Unitarians indicates that their racial prejudices did not favor such a marriage either. Thus, while Philip Ganguli returned to India and directed the School of Useful Arts when Dall set out for England and America in 1861, the two had a serious falling-out just before Dall's departure for America in 1862 (the first trip having gotten him only to England).

Of equal interest to Dall and of equal difficulty was the Persian Muslim convert Abdul Masih introduced to him by Captain Edward Smyth Mercer. Masih, twenty-five when Dall encountered him, had been converted at age fifteen after reading the Persian translation of a book on Christianity. Arriving in Peshawer, in northwest India, with an uncle whose caravan had crossed Afghanistan with woolen goods, and troubled by the creeds and prayer book as presented to him by an American Presbyterian missionary there, Abdul Masih happened to encounter the Unitarian Captain Mercer and eventually Charles Dall during a visit to Calcutta in 1860. Mercer had arranged to take Masih and his wife to England, a plan with which Dall strongly concurred, for Dall believed that if Masih could learn English as well as Philip Ganguli had he could carry on a mission to Muslims in the Northwest of India.[40]

Letters to the American Unitarian Association in May of 1860 extolled the potential of Abdul Masih and the claims of Captain Mercer "that the whole country is ripe for us."[41] Within a few weeks, Abdul Masih preached in both Hindustani and English, the latter somewhat haltingly, to the congregation on Dhurumtollah Street. After Abdul Masih spent about a year in England in the care of Unitarians there, he developed an interest in polemics and tract writing rather than in religious organizing of the kind in which Dall was engaged. About the time that Dall and Rakhal Das Haldar arrived in England in May, 1861, Abdul Masih and his family departed for Madras to serve for a period of time with William Roberts, when the relationship with Abdul Masih quickly ended. Seizing the opportunity to take over the Madras operation by joining with several of Robert's opponents, Abdul Masih contrived charges of adultery against Roberts implicating Masih's own wife.[42] Sent to investigate the charges on his return to Calcutta from London in the fall of 1861, Dall absolved Roberts of all charges in the matter, thereby ending any confidence in the responsibility of Abdul Masih to serve as a leader for the Unitarian movement in India. This action, coupled with the censure of Philip Ganguli by the Executive Committee of the Calcutta mission in its support of Dall in 1862, effectively terminated Ganguli's role as well as the great hope that indigenous Indians could adequately serve the mission cause.

Anticipating Dall's visit to England of 1861 *The Christian Reformer* carried his "Ninth Semi-Annual Report." An account of his daily schedule included in this publication illuminates the way Dall spent his days in Calcutta during the thirty-one years he was there:

1. Writing or study from four to six a.m., and then refreshing bath.
2. A walk for health until sunrise, often with Bengallee gospel or Hindoostanee phrase book or Sanskrit pamphlet in hand.
3. The first hour after sunrise is given to visiting such public institutions as open with the day — like the mission houses, the School of Industrial Arts, the Government Ward's Institution for young Rajahs and Zemindars etc., conversing with and encouraging their native teachers and pupils.
4. Return to morning papers and breakfast.
5. Bible reading and family prayer.
6. Writing up journal of the previous day, reply to letters, etc.
7. From about ten a.m. the Bengali and Sanskrit pundit has the missionary's time until noon. . .

8. Writing till dinner at two or three o'clock, and preparing sermons, or tracts, or articles for the press. . .
9. Conversation, less important writing, proof-reading, copying or attending committees of schools, etc.
10. Receiving daily visits from young men between four and six p.m., as they are on their way home from office, answering their many questions chiefly bearing on religion, and giving or lending tracts and books. . .
11. A walk for fresh air out of rooms usually closed to exclude the heat between sun and sun.
12. Attending meetings and lectures, or addressing and lecturing to societies of young men (Hindoos for the most part).[43]

One month later, the same journal reported from *The Englishman* of Calcutta, what Dall himself was excitedly writing to Boston: that Dall's school of Useful Arts which had started with but seven pupils in May, 1860, now had an enrollment of 295 and an average attendance of 150 from age six to thirty-five, learning everything from English and Bengali poetry to stitchery and woolwork. Here too was a daily congregation for Dall which he felt was so well established that he could leave it in the charge of retired British Army Sergeant Major Charles Cress and Bengali Dwarkanath Sinha as well as with the returning Philip Ganguli when Dall and Haldar departed for England.

As with so much else in his mission ministry, Dall's 1861 visit among English Unitarians was also a source of controversy. A Diary written by Rakhal Das Haldar and published by his son in 1903[44] details Dall's argument with his Brahmo companion and the role played by Hodgson Pratt and other English Unitarians. Haldar's close relation with William Adam and his family, then living in London, also gave evidence of Adam's continuing interest in Bengali affairs, even in his old age. The diary gives details of his trip with Dall from Calcutta via Madras, Ceylon, Aden, Egypt, Malta, and France. The pair arrived in London on May 21, 1861, in time to attend the annual assembly of the British and Foreign Unitarians. In comments published by the *Christian Reformer* Dall made it clear that he found the meetings far too secular in tone. The overall reception he and Haldar had been given, while "generous and hearty," was overly demanding given their state of exhaustion after the forty-day journey.

After about a month in London, which included a period of illness, Haldar, accompanied by Dall, visited Professor Fredreich Max Mueller at his home in Oxford, and attended ceremonies at the university. Moving on to Bristol, Haldar and Dall visited the tomb of Rammohun Roy, and returned to London after visits to several other cities. On July 7, Haldar and Dall delivered three addresses before a working class congregation in Heywood. Two weeks later, a controversy with Dall broke open over the question of how Haldar's expenses would be paid. At a meeting held in the home of the Reverend Mr. Ham at Dall's request, in the presence of Pratt and others, Dall began to quiz Haldar with the result that Haldar was proven correct in claim to destitution and Dall incorrect in his claim that Haldar would convert to Christianity once in Europe. All the English Unitarians believed that Haldar was unprepared to become a Christian and simply should not be pushed on the point.[45] Dall and Haldar then separated, Dall departing for America on the ship Great Eastern which, when disabled in mid-September of 1861 off the English coast, compelled Dall to return to Calcutta and postpone the visit to America until 1862.

During the summer in England, however, *The Unitarian Herald* and *The Inquirer* continued to carry details of the issue between Dall and Haldar. After reporting the debate concerning Dall's responsibility for bringing Haldar to England and his promises of financial support, the Reverend Mr. Ham wrote,

> In respect to Mr. Haldar's religious position, it appears that Mr. Dall has never styled Mr. Haldar a Christian convert; but it cannot be denied that he had given the Unitarian public the impression that Mr. Haldar is a Christian believer.

The English Unitarians stressed their belief that Dall had pressured Haldar into using Christian terminology and into defending the positions of Rammohun as if Rammohun had himself been a Unitarian Christian. At the same time the committee of English Unitarians affirmed that

> Mr. Dall is incapable of intentional deception; but we feel bound to state our opinion that in the excess of his enthusiasm for the Indian mission — and certainly without any thought of personal interest — he has given both to Mr. Haldar and the Unitarian public of this country *impressions*, which are not strictly borne out by the facts of the case.[46]

Dall, of course, could not let the report go unanswered. In reply, he suggested that in the Indian context and over the past ten years, Haldar had moved "from the follies of Hindooism" toward "the steady advance of Christian labour and light." Haldar had several times indicated to Dall the significance of Christ for his life and had also questioned why Brahmos had moved steadily away from Rammohun's position. Dall likewise could not agree with Haldar's statement to the committee that "he now felt himself more of a Brahmo than a Christian" especially in light of the anti-Christian position Debendranath Tagore had taken, not to mention Debendranath's open hostility to Dall.[47] In a biting response appearing the following week, Haldar made it clear that Dall had long distorted Rammohun's religious position in relation to his total output, writing that

> If the Brahmos of Calcutta do not recognise me as a member on account of my reverence for Jesus, I must take no sectarian name whatever, until I find reason to change or improve in my opinions. Jesus wanted to make men — *men.* I stand assuredly on the same ground with Rammohun Roy, whose religious position, I suspect, is not distinctly understood in this country. A greater portion, if not the whole of his works should be read, in order to arrive at a correct conclusion regarding Rammohun Roy's religious position.[48]

Although Haldar and Dall did not see each other for a few years after this encounter because Dall was in America when Haldar returned to India in 1862, it turned out that they were not so far apart in their understanding as the above exchange, made under Haldar's financial duress, may have made it appear. During the year when Ganguli was largely involved in the mission during Dall's absence, the Indian convert wrote the American Unitarian Association that he had met and talked with "many" Brahmos who were reading Voltaire, Paine, Parker, Emerson, and Newton and that while they would not call themselves Unitarian Christian in public, he had every reason to feel that they were so in private.[49] Charles Cress also reported communication with Brahmos during Dall's absence. On his return from England, Dall commented that a new and increased vitality seemed to have come to the movement. Dall was pleased by the number of Brahmos reading liberal religious literature that he had personally brought to Calcutta. Writing to the American Unitarian Association in 1863, Dall summarized the greatest accomplishments of his first eight years in India:

(1) A quickening of the Unitheist churches of Bengal, mediators between Xty and Hinduism which were started by Ram Roy.
(2) A wide Hindoo Unitarian sympathy in the success of my own, your own mission: see how many of your books they have got, etc. . . . We are making Unitarians or say Unitheists, out of polytheists, by scores every year — and these are educating their wives out of the vile superstitions. Some of them are opening school at their own charges in their native villages. . . . They come to us for their manuals and hymn books.[50]

The continuing interest of young Brahmos in Christianity yet their continuing refusal to become Christian perplexed Dall. He laid the blame on the reputation of "Christians" among the Hindus while failing to understand somehow that there was a national sense and a feeling of social renaissance at work behind the Brahmo Samaj movement. The resurgence of a missionary program with the coming of Keshub Chunder Sen to new leadership in the Brahmo Samaj would bring Dall closer spiritually and intellectually to the Samaj but would also clarify for Samaj members new goals and aims for their institution.

KESHUB CHUNDER SEN

CHAPTER NINE

Keshub Chunder Sen and the Unitarians

Considered by many the true founder of the Brahmo Samaj organization, Keshub Chunder Sen was barely eighteen years old when Charles Dall arrived in Calcutta. It is no wonder then that his name did not appear among the impressive list of religious liberals with whom Dall came into contact during his first years.[1] By 1866, however, when Dall first referred to Keshub in official correspondence with the American Unitarian Association, Keshub, not yet thirty, was a celebrity in Calcutta. That year when he delivered one of his most famous lectures "Jesus Christ: Europe and Asia," he had already actively engaged in missionary journeys throughout India for the Brahmo Samaj and had published regularly in Tagore's newspaper, *The Indian Mirror*, one of the two English language newspapers then published by Indians. In 1866, he led the "progressive Brahmos" in their split from Debendranath Tagore's more conservative 'Adi Brahmo Samaj.

Keshub Chunder Sen was lucky in his biographer; his cousin and disciple Protap Chunder Mazumdar wrote a lively biography which, while partly hagiography, still gives us many vivid details of Keshub's life as well as the lives of his contemporaries such as Charles Dall. Born November 19, 1838, in Calcutta, his ancestors had come from a small village up the Hooghly river and were of the Vaidya caste, a caste second in rank to Brahmin (in Bengal). At the age of seven Keshub entered the Hindu College, a preparatory school for the well-to-do, where he excelled in both English and arithmetic. Actively interested in both theater and festive religious life practiced by Vaisnava Hindus, Keshub early showed a flair for the dramatic which would appear later in life when he lectured and led worship.

During his days as a student at Metropolitan College Keshub began the search for religious meaning and identity, and sought the company of three missionaries in Calcutta: the Reverend James Long, best known for his activism on behalf of indigo ryots and his trial in 1861; the Reverend T. H. Burn, domestic chaplain to Bishop Cotton; and "our old friend the Reverend C. H. A. Dall of the American Unitarian mission."[2] In one of Dall's later notebooks he remarks that he first met Keshub in 1856 when Keshub was eighteen.[3] More direct proof of their early contacts appears in the published report of Keshub's Colootolah Evening School for 1857 in which Dall is reported to have made "learned remarks" at the second prize day ceremony in December 1856.[4]

Among Dall's papers are the originals of two brief letters from Keshub inviting him, in January 1858, to participate in the British India Society. Keshub, one of the forty-six founders of this association who were mostly students from the Presidency College, urged Dall and James Long to participate. Dall pleaded the pressure of other duties but obviously came from time to time. Keshub's biographer describes how the society, which was primarily concerned with literary and scientific subjects, would get into religious debates from time to time:

> We all witnessed with a great deal of amusement the somewhat furious passages at arms between Mr. Long and Mr. Dall. . . Mr. Long who was a low-churchman, square-built, undersized, red-faced, and short-tempered, tried in a husky voice and brief nervous sentences, to silence his heretical opponent. Mr. Dall was a pale, lank, long-legged Yankee, who in disjointed nasal vocabulary, uttered sharp retorts, and irritated his antagonist by invariably styling him, 'Our Brother Long.'[5]

While Mazumdar's biography must be taken in part as hagiography, written in praise of Keshub, his remarks about Long and Dall give some idea of how the two were perceived and why it would be difficult for young liberal Hindus to convert to Christianity as presented by them. No doubt Long and Dall were effective teachers; however, their attitudes surely presented problems. Recounting an incident in a speech made in 1884, Dall told of how Keshub rose in a meeting chaired by Long to resolve that the British India Society cultivate the habit of prayer. "Why Keshub," Long replied,

> 'what do you mean, pray? You can't pray. You've no God. Unless you pray to the Father, Son and Holy Ghost — the Holy Trinity — your prayer is nothing. Move something more practicable.' There was a pause. A look of surprise and disappointment rested on Keshub's handsome face. He raised his eyes to the platform as if hardly believing that *that* was to be the end of his appeal for what seemed too natural, so elevating, so good to do.[6]

Dall, feeling the necessity to respond when Reverend Burn did not, rose, but before he could speak, Long said, "Now listen to

Brother Dall . . . he is only a Mahomedan, and can't hurt you." Dall then came to Keshub's support in an equally pious and paternalistic way. Calling on Keshub to be of good courage, Dall stressed that one God "made us all" and we "who love Jesus and want you all to love him as he deserves to be loved" should respond to such a resolution as Keshub had set forth. Dall then described how the matter was concluded:

> The desire to accomodate and please all parties which makes the Hindoos, at least of Bengal, the politest people in the world, moved Keshub to modify the form of his resolution, so that it should read — "Resolved that the members of this society cultivate habits of devotion." This was condemned by the good Padree Long as no better than the other; and the matter dropped.[7]

One cannot help but wonder how such inter-Christian polemics affected the attitudes of so bright and sensitive a young man as Keshub Chunder Sen. Keshub did come to the mission house to read and talk with Dall, for Dall notes how religiously compatible they were. The young Hindu read avidly the works of Channing, Hedge, and Theodore Parker and "was indefatigible in distributing such books as Channing's 'Perfect Life,' Hedge's 'Reason in Religion,' and 'The Discourse of Religion' " to be used as manuals among the samajes.[8] In addition, Keshub appears to have borrowed Rakhal Das Haldar's copy of Rammohun Roy's *Precepts of Jesus* from the mission library in 1859.[9]

In his 1874 lecture on the Brahmo Samaj and Keshub, Dall took direct credit for formulating Keshub's thought while also tracing how he, Dall, had decided to become a Brahmo under Keshub's leadership in 1872. "I have told him and he had published over India, that 'Life is one continued growth of heaven-ward enterprise' "; that all religions must either accept "fresh inspiration . . . the proper Christ of Love, Faith, Wisdom and Power" or die out, "perish." Dall continued,

> I have often given him such thoughts as these, which come to me out of the Bible of Hebrew Theism, and its last distillation, in the theism of Jesus. Keshub Baboo gratefully encouraged me to bring him my best thoughts and principles, — with manly freedom from prejudice against the person, or the record, through which our Father sent them from heaven into the world.[10]

Dall, twenty-two years Keshub's senior, looked upon the young man as his pupil and wrote to the American Unitarian Association shortly after Keshub's death in 1884, "The newspapers call Mr. Dall K. C. Sen's '*teacher*' and 'tis *true.*"[11]

Whatever credit Dall may have wished to take for helping to shape Keshub's mind and religious orientation, it is clear that Brahmo and Indian nationalist-oriented historians have simply ignored his role even if Dall himself may have overstated it. Nevertheless, P. C. Mazumdar relates how, at the Goodwill Fraternity, an organization with both a devotional and theological orientation, Keshub read, during 1857 or 1858, Dr. Chalmer's "Discourse on Enthusiasm" and Theodore Parker's "Sermon on Inspiration" to the young men present.[12] While Keshub's biographer has attempted to minimize the influence of any missionary on his thought, almost all other writings about Keshub constantly compare him to Theodore Parker, the controversial Boston transcendentalist and abolitionist minister who died in Italy in 1860. While Dall must have been the channel through which Keshub received Parker's works, Dall never mentions Parker as one of those whose works he was distributing in Calcutta during his first decade. From published correspondence between Mrs. Dall and Parker, it appears that the Dalls had much to disagree about with the great Boston preacher who was, after all, roughly a contemporary and not in the least to be considered with the awe that one of the Dall generation would look upon Channing, Ware, or Dewey.

Dall wrote the American Unitarian Association during the fifties that many bookstores would not even carry his own *Gospel Principles* nor the works of other Unitarians and that he himself was chief distributor of these. It was not until 1863, however, after his return to India from America, perhaps newly aware of the impact the deceased Parker now had on American Unitarianism, that he noted, perhaps sarcastically, in requesting thirty sets of the complete works of Parker recently ordered by Bengalis, that Parker's books "well meet a transition state of mind between Hindooism and Xty."[13]

Many contemporaries, both Indian and Western, Unitarian and non-Unitarian, while ignoring Dall entirely, have stressed the impact of Unitarian thought in shaping Keshub. *The Unitarian Herald*, reporting in 1866 on the famous "Jesus Christ: Europe and Asia" lecture, wrote that Keshub used "language like that of Channing and the better class of Unitarians."[14] *The Inquirer*, anticipating Keshub's arrival in London later in

1870, wrote that in Keshub's early tracts, those from 1860 and 1861, and in his various public lectures, his Brahmoism "greatly resembles the spiritual theism of England and America, as represented by F. W. Newman, Theodore Parker, and Miss Cobbe, all of whom have evidently exercised no slight influence on the leading minds of the Brahmo Samaj."[15] The Reverend C. N. Banerji, writing in an early volume of the *Indian Evangelical Review* in 1875, as a Trinitarian Christian, stated that "the writings of Francis Newman and of the late Theodore Parker have done much for intuition or *intertuition* in Calcutta. For a time, Keshub Babu's success was remarkable — for every Brahmo talked of intuition."[16] Dwijadas Dutta, a later apologist for Keshub, reflecting on his youth, wrote that Keshub made Theodore Parker "familiar to every Brahmo in these early days."[17]

A New Brahmo Leader

During the period of his university studies, his interaction with the missionaries, and his involvement in organizations such as the Goodwill Fraternity, Keshub began a search for religious meaning through devotionalism and a moderately ascetic life. Although married in 1856 at the age of eighteen, it appears that by 1857 Keshub had made a conscious decision "not to be overly fond of wife or world."[18] Conversion to Brahmoism came after reading Raj Narain Bose's pamphlet, "What is Brahmoism," and after both Keshub and Protap Mazumdar saw Debendranath Tagore for the first time.

> He was tall, princely, in the full glory of his health and manhood; he came attended by liveried servants, and surrounded by massive stalwart Brahmos, who wore long gold chains and impenetrable countenances. We, who were very young men, . . . were highly elated and encouraged by such company, and it was an inducement to us to follow with zeal our religious career.[19]

Keshub, after reading the Bose tract, wrote:

> I found that it corresponded exactly with the inner conviction of my heart, the voice of God in the soul. I always felt that every outward book must be subordinated to the teachings of the Inner Spirit, — that where God speaks through the Spirit in man all earthly teachers must be silent, and every man must bow down and accept

> in reverence what God thus revealed in the soul. I at once determined that I would join the Brahmo Samaj, or Indian Theistic Church.[20]

The basis of Keshub's rise to leadership in the Brahmo movement was clearly religious. As early as 1860 in his speech to "Young Bengal" there were overtones of social and political reform, such as those Dall also believed were necessary to regenerate India. Neither Dall nor Keshub was very original in anything he had to say. Progressive ideas had been in the air since the time of Rammohun Roy and had certainly dominated opposition movements to the Christian missionaries. Many saw the need for a religious faith which would raise the Hindu personality out of the social and religious predicament in which it found itself. But Dall and Keshub, particularly the latter, were capable of reshaping ideas in the air and using them to make an impact on the Bengali Hindu community. Keshub agreed with Dall and with Parker that religiousness was to be found in social action for human betterment and not just in doctrine and creed. His biographer has written that

> From the moment he had entered the Brahmo Samaj, he had taken the vow of finding in it "a Religion of Life"; as opposed to a religion of theories. Every principle that he developed, every reform that he undertook, was the result of that vow.[21]

In Keshub's 1863 lecture, "Social Transformation in India," he asserted that once all people came under one church and one God, all caste distinctions would "naturally perish in the uncongenial atmosphere of religious brotherhood."[22] It was this kind of idea, drawn from things Dall had said, that was the basis of the Goodwill Fraternity of Sangat Sabha whose members in 1861 voted an end to caste distinctions in the organization, and pledged to educate their wives and abstain from alcohol.[23] Throughout the early 1860s young Brahmos, under the influence of Keshub's personality and his teachings on social and religious reform, began publication of the *Indian Mirror* and convened public meetings to draw Government attention to the need for educational reform and programs to alleviate poverty.

The model Keshub developed for Indians to follow in his reform message was not one normally to be expected in Calcutta. It was Jesus, the center of Christian salvation, whom Keshub adopted in an Asiatic context, the reformer who was "meek" like an Indian, and not "rough, stern, impulsive and fiery" as Europeans were.[24] Jesus, the Asiatic, was the force making for civilization both West and East. It was not the British but the spirit of Christ ultimately at the root of British rule, responsible for progressive changes that had occurred in India. Jesus's life was the ultimate symbol of selflessness which, when considered in the Indian context, meant an end to caste distinctions and willingness to work for the greater good of all mankind.[25]

For Keshub, Brahmoism was to be sharply differentiated from Christian sectarianism. Even Unitarian Christianity was not "Absolute Religion." The essence of Brahmoism, as Keshub articulated it in his 1860 essay "Religion of Love," was "Love God as thy Father and man as thy brother," certainly a late-nineteenth-century American and English Unitarian cry.[26] Keshub had been swept away by the concept of Christ, revering him above all prophets and teachers, even so important a one to Bengalis as Chaitanya. But Jesus, like Chaitanya, could not be for Keshub a mediator between God and man, for Brahmoism, out of its Vedantic tradition, was a faith based on belief in God as Brahman, the One without a Second. "Christianity," he argued in a lecture in 1863, defending Brahmoism, "has prepared the world for the Brahmo Samaj, but has not given birth to Brahmoism," for God, not the Bible, was the source and inspiration of Brahmo ideas.[27]

Throughout the 1860s, Keshub and the other Brahmos engaged in polemics and controversy with Christian missionaries other than Charles Dall. Keshub directly answered charges when attacked both by a Reverend Dyson of Krishnagar, by the native preacher Lal Behari Day, and also by a Scottish merchant R. Scott Moncrief who deliberately insulted the Indian character. The impact of Keshub's work resulted in figures showing that 105 members (10 percent) of the entering class at the University of Calcutta in 1862 declared themselves Universalists, Brahmos, pantheists, deists, atheists, or "etc."[28]

The attacks on or rebuttals against the missionaries were but one stage in Keshub's quest to articulate a sense of identity for young liberal religious Hindus. A sense of patriotism comes through in words spoken in 1860 when Keshub was only twenty-two years old:

> Rest assured, my friend, that if in our country intellectual progress went hand in hand with religious development, if our educated

countrymen had initiated themselves in the living truths of religion, patriotism would not have been a mere matter of oration and essay, but a reality in practice; and native society would have grown in health and prosperity . . . and effectually surmounted many of those difficulties in the way of social reforms which are now considered insuperable.[29]

In "Jesus Christ: Europe and Asia" Keshub exhorted the new generation of Indians to reject the selfishness he believed to be the principal negative characteristic of Indians so long a "subject race."

We have too long been under foreign sway to be able to feel anything like independence in our hearts. Socially and religiously we are little better than slaves. From infancy up we have been trained to believe that we are Hindoos only so far as we offer slavish obedience to the authority of the Shasters and the priests, and that any want of disobedience would be so much a want of our nationality.[30]

In 1866, Keshub Chunder Sen stood at the turning point of his career. He had taken a stand for Christ, but for Christ in a universal sense; he had cried out for needed social reform which also implied political reform. All this would require a major change in attitude and a religious revolution among the Hindus. It would not be enough to speak of reform; significant action was required. Keshub's stance against caste was especially controversial. Debendranath Tagore was not prepared to give up the sacred thread of Brahminism in favor of a true democracy for Brahmoism. In 1865, Keshub and his supporters had taken control of the Brahmo newspaper, *The Indian Mirror*, while also beginning a far more dynamic program of missionary expansion for the Brahmo Samaj.[31] His two strongly articulated lectures, "Jesus Christ: Europe and Asia" and another, "Great Men,"[32] in which he quoted from Christian history almost directly refuted the traditional non-historical emphasis of Hinduism. Keshub led a split in the Samaj in November 1866, establishing the Brahmo Samaj of India.

The split between Keshub and Debenranath's Adi Brahmo Samaj also had its roots in Keshub's decision in 1864 to carry out a major missionary journey throughout India. By this time the Brahmo Samaj and its opposition to the efforts of Christian missionaries in Bengal was well enough known for him to want to pursue a more broadly based Samaj. Well received in Madras, Bombay and Poona, it was only a matter of time before active chapters would exist there. Debendranath, while concerned with social service in needy areas of India, did not have a vision through which the Samaj would be carried into non-Bengali areas. Neither could he accept the social reform which would mean pressing for legal status for Brahmos to conduct their own inter-religious marriages, widow remarriage, and inter-caste marriage. Perhaps the greatest difference and that which eventually split the two men was Keshub's "Christian training" and his desire to integrate the best of Christ into his religious movement.

That Keshub was affected by the teachings of Jesus, and by the spiritualized person of Christ to the extent that he had to lead the younger, missionary-oriented Brahmos away from the Hindu-oriented Tagore section is a clear indication that he was a product of an acculturated environment. The impact of William Ellery Channing as well as American transcendentalists such as Emerson and Parker on Keshub is apparent from what he and his biographers have reported. It appears, in fact, that Keshub became familiar with Jesus through the writings of modern theologians first, and only later through a study of Christian scriptures. While he quotes famous scriptural passages in many of his religious lectures, he never seems to have carried on systematic exegesis as Rammohun had.

Keshub did not, however, accept Dall's or James Long's Christianity wholesale. He spoke as the representative of a new India to which his earliest published address, "Young Bengal, this is for You," testified. While some could dismiss Keshub as an assimilationist or eclectic mystic, his organizational abilities and his social reform program developed prior to his later strongly mystical stage give evidence of a highly integrated approach to his religiousness. While M. M. Thomas and most writers on Keshub have cited his "Jesus Christ: Europe and Asia" lecture of 1866 as his opening on the subject, Keshub's published theological essays indicate writings earlier than 1866, notably an essay, "The Spirit of Christ," which seems to have preceded it.[33] Pointing out that Christ was a subject of controversy among Christians and non-Christians, he wrote in order to make clear his own position.

> We Theists must take it to be foreign to our purpose to canvass the thousand theories which have been propounded about him and his creed; but surely, it is our interest and duty to receive from him

> that healthy moral influence which he is appointed in God's economy to exercise on the world, to love him and revere him and follow his teachings and example.[34]

Keshub then juxtaposed the particular and the universal with respect to Christ intimating that it was the spiritual dimension, not the "body," the "son of God," not the "son of man" that is needed for human salvation. Though not an avowed Vedantist in the sense that Rammohun had been, Keshub, in this earlier essay, reflected a vision of ultimate reality that divorced the transcendent from the particular. He asserted that

> In the purely human Christ we can hardly feel any interest; but the divine elements of his character come home to every "man's bosom and business," and are of the highest importance to our redemption as involving the eternal and universal principles of ethics.[35]

Although his lecture "Jesus Christ: Europe and Asia" had as its fundamental purpose the assertion that Christ was an Asiatic, not a European, and his second major 1866 lecture, "Great Men," had the fundamental purpose of using Christ as one example of how God sends "great men" to serve and save mankind, Keshub's familiarity with Biblical literature and teaching stands out. In the lectures "Regenerating Faith" (1868), "The Future Church" (1869), and "The Kingdom of Heaven" (1874), Keshub was utilizing Christ's concept of an ideal religious situation to set an ideal before his Indian audience.[36] He was describing "an invisible reality which must be sought in the domain of the spirit, and not in the world of matter."[37] The contrast between Keshub's approach to Christ and Rammohun's approach to Jesus is clear. Where the latter came to Jesus because of his sense of the inadequacy of Hindu spiritual life in his time (the 1820s), the former came to Christ (not the human Jesus) for the opposite reason: to spiritualize a generation of Young Bengal which had fallen from faith, albeit a corrupted faith. This is not to say that Keshub did not have a socio-ethical dimension. Keshub tried to synthesize aspects of Hindu devotionalism and festivals in an attempt to formulate a non-Western but also anti-traditional, anti-caste religious community. Debendranath Tagore had turned Rammohun Roy's ideals around by limiting the Samaj to Brahmin membership. But Keshub Brahmoism was not some variation or reformation of Hinduism but "catholic" religion, a religion in which all the various sects and peoples of India could be reconciled to each other and live in peace.

The Visits of Mary Carpenter and Dall's Later Ministry

1866 represents something of a turning point for Charles Dall in his relations with the Brahmos and his renewed hostilities with English Unitarians. On May 21, in a letter to the American Unitarian Association, he enclosed a photograph of Sayyid Ahmad Khan, leading liberal of the north Indian Muslim community, "an able man . . . whom I have not yet seen, but who as I learn from his letters, is willing and even eager to translate and scatter our publications."[38] Though none of Sayyid Ahmad Khan's letters is extant, the revelation of his communications with Dall and Dall's interaction with six or eight liberal Muslims in Calcutta was significant because this took Dall, however briefly, into another direction beyond his continuing involvement with Brahmo-oriented Hindus.

One month later Dall's first reference to Keshub appeared in a letter to the American Unitarian Association. Writing of "two quite able men, born Hindoos, now before the public here, who, with much enthusiasm are advocating this free indigenous growth of the Gospel seed," he referred both to Keshub and to Debendranath Tagore's nephew, Ganendro Mohun Tagore, already a professor of Hindu law in London. Of Keshub, Dall commented, "I never met in Europe a man, not calling English his mother tongue; who was so perfect a master of it in tone and idiom as is either of these gentlemen."[39]

Although Dall had several American Unitarian Association visitors during the first dozen years of his ministry in Calcutta, it was not until 1866 that a major figure arrived. This was an English Unitarian, Mary Carpenter (1807-1877), who as a young woman had met and been strongly impressed by Rammohun Roy. Her father, the Reverend Lant Carpenter, had eulogized Rammohun at the time of the Brahmo's death and burial in Bristol. In the context of Unitarians and India, Mary Carpenter was already known for her editorship of the recent book, *The Last Days in England of Rammohun Roy.* To many others in England, she was best known as a diligent worker for women's education and general social reform. In her early twenties at the time she met Rammohun, Mary Carpenter also encountered the Reverend Joseph Tuckerman at the time the American minister to the poor visited with Rammohun in England.

At the age of fifty-nine, Mary Carpenter decided to visit India in order to explore the possibilities of establishing educational facilities for women there. Arriving in Bombay with numerous important high-level contacts in the British colonial government, Mary Carpenter pressed her way through the country, both visiting and establishing a number of reform institutions. Staying in Calcutta in the home of Dr. Chuckerbutty (Chakravarti), her first visitor was Keshub to whom she gave an engraving of Reubens's "Descent from the Cross," declaring at that time that she had not yet made up her mind about whether to support the Keshub or the Debendranath faction in the Brahmo split.[40] Visiting a Brahmo service, she regretted not seeing Debendranath who was out of Calcutta but even more strongly regretted being unable to locate Rammohun Roy's house or the Unitarian press. In fact, she wrote, there was no trace of his works or person. "I found among the Brahmos an extreme prejudice against Christianity . . . that even the *Precepts of Jesus* with its various translations is out of print and its very existence appears generally unknown."[41] This observation seems clearly to refute Dall's assertion that he had republished and circulated the *Precepts*, or may perhaps imply that he was ineffective in his efforts.

Commenting on the various mission enterprises in Calcutta, Mary Carpenter wrote, "Dr. Duff's girls' school is the best I saw in this city except the Bethune School.[42] Meeting the Reverend James Long, she wrote, that "among the enlightened natives he is regarded as a martyr to his anxiety to protect the weak in the indigo troubles, which led to his imprisonment for libel." Long took Carpenter to the mufossul, rural areas, that she might see the extremes of poverty for herself and also arranged a canoe ride on one of the canals and a "horrifying" visit to the Kali temple.[43] Charles Dall she left for the last, not even indicating that he was a Unitarian when writing that the School of Useful Arts in Dhurumtollah deserved special mention for its training in the manual skills. She spent Christmas with Dall and the schoolchildren in 1866, however. Calcutta newspapers recorded in detail her address to friends at Howrah on female education and a speech to the Asiatic Society on "Social Science in India," attended by the Reverend James Long, Dr. Farquhar, the noted scholar of Indian religions,

Keshub Chunder Sen, Debendranath Tagore, Peary Chund Mittra, and Ram Chunder Mittra.[44] A few weeks later, on January 24, 1867, Dall was present when Mary Carpenter spoke at the Social Science Association. Though Dall seemed resentful that one visit by this English Unitarian woman, or one by Keshub in England in 1870, could make such a startling impression when years of his own plodding work did not, Mary Carpenter's presence in Calcutta led Dall to request the American Unitarian Association to support his selection of Mary Chamberlain, who had come to India with Carpenter, to be director of a Unitarian-run school for girls. While extolling Mary Chamberlain's virtues, Dall commented that he had heard that,

> Miss Carpenter has been very cooly received on her return to Bombay, the mischief being, in the one hand, that she walks roughshod over everybody and meets her best advisers with rebuke, saying, 'she knows better.' This style of hers has become so inveterate that the old lady has hardly a friend left. If she could but begin to see how little she knows of India.[45]

Dall's initial impressions of Mary Carpenter were positive compared to those he expressed following her visits of 1868, 1869, and 1872. Throughout her first visit, Mary Carpenter had done all she could to gain support from the Government for women's schools. This would not seem such a radical idea except that she wanted schools which both Christian and Hindu girls would attend. The idea was not well received either by orthodox Christians or by Hindus who considered Christian converts as low-caste. In correspondence with Theodore Parker a decade earlier she had made her ideals clear:

> Perhaps you feel as I do that the doctrines of religion ought not be separated from the work of religion in the world. I believe "Evangelical Unitarianism" . . . to be "the doctrine of the gospel," i.e. simple Christianity, and as such I desire its extension. . . I should not care much to convert anyone to it *intellectually* only, nor do I value it except as a *living reality*. . .[46]

During their earlier visits in England, Mary Carpenter had met Jogut (Philip) Ganguli, Dall's Unitarian convert and Rakhal Das Haldar, Dall's friend and colleague. The American had, as with so many others, come into conflict with these two supporters because they had overstepped the bounds he had set for them.

When in India, Mary Carpenter re-established her ties with these old acquaintances and when, during her second visit, she felt certain that a school would be established in Calcutta following her model, she turned over a considerable amount of money to Ganguli.

The Indian Mirror, the Brahmo newspaper, had given her first trip detailed coverage and had supported her program for non-sectarian women's education while ignoring Dall's efforts entirely. Letters to the editor continued to support Carpenter's ideas but in practice, except for the formation of a non-functioning committee, Brahmos never carried out any practical plan to aid her. At the outset, Debendranath Tagore and the Adi Brahmos were opposed to her activities. Keshub would have been sympathetic in ways more helpful than those idealistically editorialized in the *Mirror*, except that Carpenter wished her school to be associated with the Bethune school and its English committee. Keshub and Mary Carpenter also had differing visions for women in Indian society. For Keshub emancipation meant an end to illiteracy within the framework of home, school, and family. In conversations with Sivanath Sastri and later with another English Unitarian woman teacher Annette Akroyd, Keshub indicated his strong opposition to teaching women sciences, geometry, and metaphysics. Keshub's concern in female education was the teaching of English and practical skills such as needlework.[47]

With little support even from the Brahmos, Mary Carpenter's last real hope for non-governmental support was with Charles Dall. On returning to England after her first visit she promised to seek English Unitarian support for his mission to add to what Dall was receiving from America. During a stay in Madras in January 1867, she visited Roberts's congregation and also promised English support. Nothing major was ever forthcoming as a result of these promises, nor was the promise of a school for female education developed along the lines Mary Carpenter had wished ever to come to any meaningful existence. What brief approval she had had from the Government was terminated in 1872. Her efforts in India proved a sharp disappointment. The next stage in the inter-relationships among Brahmos, English and American Unitarians was to come with Keshub's spectacular visit to England in 1870.

Keshub in England and Dall's Reaction

On February 16, 1870, Keshub Chunder Sen departed for England via Madras and the Middle East, arriving early in April and remaining through September. Of more than fifty lectures, speeches, and sermons that he delivered, mostly among English Unitarians, a large number were immediately published by a new Brahmo supporter and enthusiast, Sophie Dobson Collet, herself an Anglican. The morning after Keshub's arrival in London on March 21 he called first on Collet whom he described as having a "mind . . . of an eminently historical or rather statistical type; she is ever gathering facts and eliciting information."[48] Sophie Collet, sickly and crippled, later the author of the first definitive biography of Rammohun Roy, was truly statistical in her orientation. From 1876 to 1883 she prepared her *Brahmo Year Book*, an almanac of details, statistics, and commentary on the Brahmo Samaj during those years.

Keshub's second visit was with Frances Cobbe who had published an essay on the Brahmo Samaj in 1867[49] At that time Cobbe had written that "If Brahmanism be surely though slowly sinking, and chance exists for its revival, is there a chance of acceptance for Christianity in India?. . . Very small as yet seem the indications that such a thing may be."[50] The religious future and ultimately the social and political welfare of India lay with the Brahmo Samaj, she asserted. Tracing the origins of the Samaj in the writings and work of Rammohun Roy and its development through Debendranath Tagore, Mrs. Cobbe finished her supportive article by relating Keshub's conversion to the Samaj and quoting at length from his 1860 speech to "Young Bengal." Detailing the split of 1866 but emphasizing the respect Keshub had continued to show for Debendranath, the English critic pointed to the kinds of social and religious reforms which the Brahmos were undertaking. She had thus presented the first full picture of Brahmo history to an English audience.[51] Within a few days, Keshub met with Unitarians and important government figures such as Lord Lawrence and Sir Charles Trevellyan and such religious and academic leaders as the Dean of Westminster and Max Mueller. Everywhere Keshub was well received, though once insulted by the conversion attempts of a zealous Christian woman. The first of his numerous speeches and sermons took place at James Martineau's chapel on the text from Acts, "In Him, we live and move and have our being."[52]

Two nights later a major soiree sponsored by the Unitarian Association brought together members of parliament, leading clergy of several denominations, and even one rabbi to honor Keshub.

The Dean of Westminster, in introducing the meeting, welcomed Keshub, and set the tone by praising Keshub "and his fellow labourers" for their work of "abolishing idolatry, breaking down caste, and diffusing a higher moral and intellectual life" among the people of "that vast empire."[53] Speeches by Lord Lawrence, James Martineau, and Rabbi Marks preceeding those of Keshub, while not platitudinous, took the same moralistic stance about Keshub's contribution and progressivism in India. Keshub, in reply, expressed gratitude for the tremendous public welcome he had received. "A sacred duty brings me here," he continued,

> I have an important mission to fulfill. I come from India to tell you, Englishmen and women, what you have done in my country. I bring you the heartfelt thanks of one hundred and eighty millions of my countrymen for the great work which you have commenced there. . . It is not only the opening of railways, nor the conversion of forests into smiling fields to which I allude. . . The great work . . . of the British Government, is a work of revolutionary reform . . . you are carrying on a crusade against all the evils from which India has been suffering for many centuries.[54]

Tracing how the presence of the British in India had precipitated the Indian renaissance under Rammohun Roy, David Hare, and others, and the role Brahmos had played in bringing reforms to Hinduism, Keshub then proceeded to explain how Christ, but not Christianity as practiced by the missionaries, could help India to reshape itself in the coming decades. "I do not come to study the doctrines of Christianity," Keshub continued, "but truly Christian life as displayed and illustrated in England." "We Indians attach far greater importance to righteous life than to pure doctrines," Keshub told his responsive Victorian audience, concluding with no statements of criticism or of national feeling which he had expressed to his supporters throughout the previous decade.[55]

In later speeches, Keshub would attack Christians who beat Hindus and enslaved them, and would speak out against the English propagation of liquor and opium in India. He would call for much more significant roles for educated Indians in government, and improved education and life-style for Indian women.[56] In his lecture of May 28, Keshub spoke as a Hindu theist about the significance of Christ for his life and why he did not become a Christian. Reporting that he had studied Christianity but never through polemical writings that were anti-Christian or apologetic, Keshub explained,

> I studied Christ ethically, nay spiritually — and I studied the Bible also in that spirit and must tonight acknowledge candidly and sincerely that I owe a great deal to Christ, and to the Gospel of Christ.[57]

He further asserted that,

> Jesus is not a proposition to be believed, nor an outward figure to be seen and adored but simply a spirit to be loved, a spirit of obedience to God that must be incorporated into our spiritual being.[58]

In Calcutta, Charles Dall quickly learned of Keshub's success in London and of the extensive press coverage he had received in Europe and America. In an article published on May 19, in response to the report of the Unitarian-sponsored soiree, Dall editorialized cryptically that the *Pertshire Advertiser* had overstated its case when saying that Keshub "Stands to his countrymen, in this nineteenth century, as Mohamed stood to his in the seventh, or Luther, to Christendom, generally, in the sixteenth." Judging Keshub by his "birth-gifts and his opportunities" and expressing appreciation for his good fortune in public appearances abroad and his joy that representatives of ten denominations could come together in "creed-riden London" to honor Keshub, Dall still feared that Keshub was throwing out Christianity because he could not separate good doctrine from bad dogma. Calling Keshub to speak far more in the spirit of Rammohun Roy who, according to Dall, had taken the wheat from the missionaries while discarding the chaff, Dall urged that Keshub not merely say "Let us alone you missionaries . . . what have we to do with you?. . . Leave us to ourselves and let us study the Bible ourselves."[59] From his isolated viewpoint as Calcutta's Unitarian missionary, Dall could point critically to the shortcoming of Keshub's assertions. However, he could perceive the glibness and lack of understanding that the Dean of Westminster or James Martineau could express in encouraging Keshub in London. And Dall could deeply resent this young man for being so well received and overly appreciated when few if any paid much attention to his fifteen years of work in Calcutta. Through the rest of his ministry in Calcutta, Charles Dall would play out this theme: Brahmos must not foreswear the Christian label though they would claim the teachings and spirit of Christ alone essential for them.

Dall's despair with the English and American Unitarian love affair with Keshub came clear in letters written to the American Unitarian Association in the autumn of 1871. Noting how much had been written of Keshub in Unitarian publications and the extent to which the British Unitarian Association had voted funds to support Keshub's Brahmo Samaj of India, following the 1870 English tour, and while lamenting the lack of American Unitarian Association equivalent support, Dall again stressed that Keshub was not now nor would he ever be a Christian. Dall could not accept the trend among British Unitarians, in response to Keshub's visit, that all Unitarians would declare themselves theists and thereby join with Frances Cobbe and some others to disavow the centrality of Christ. Shocked at the thought that English and possibly American Unitarians might be ready to forsake their Christian mission, Dall asked how this could be done "when Brahmos now even refused to publish the Christian works of Rammohun Roy?"[60]

Dall Becomes a Brahmo

While Dall understood what motivated the Brahmos to keep away from the Christian label as well as from mainstream Hinduism, he could not understand how Keshub could use Christ so freely in his theology and ethical teachings while refusing to identify himself with Unitarian Christianity. Perhaps the only way to get Keshub to understand and accept his point of view was to do something radical — to join the Brahmo Samaj itself and to work at the problem from the inside.

To prepare himself and his American Unitarian supporters for this unusual step, Dall had begun writing Boston about his deeply personal relations with many Brahmos, a relation he came to describe as "more intimate day by day."

He was meeting regularly with many Brahmos present to discuss "the claims of Jesus to lead men in the way to God." Quoting a letter from Okhoy Chunder Kamoker, Dall excitedly wrote that the former had asked Keshub about Dall's joining the Brahmo Samaj. Keshub had replied that anyone could join "if he will only worship Him whom Jesus directed to worship."[61] Dall, stating that he would do nothing in haste, continued reporting a conversation with Keshub, who was about to depart for England. Finding Keshub receptive to having Dall join, and Dall, finding no stumbling block in the Brahmo statement of faith, expressed the hope that Keshub would also visit America and that he would so impress American Unitarians that Boston Unitarians would support his membership as a Brahmo. The step of membership was made official on November 7, 1871.

Feeling it necessary to apologize for the radical act he had undertaken as the first Christian and Caucasian to join a progressive, reforming, and nationalist-oriented "Hindu" movement, Dall wrote *The Indian Mirror* his reasons:

> (1) My faith in the pure theism of Jesus, and hope that I may do something to keep men true to it.
> (2) My faith in the Brahmo movement as sincere, beneficent, and stirred by the spirit of God.
> (3) My confidence in its present leadership and the good I may get from a closer companionship and cooperation with them.
> (4) Their cordial acceptance of Rammohun Roy's affirmation (repeated by one of their leaders at the hour of my joining them, in the words, "We are all followers of Christ"). If any one man more than another brought me to the honored founder of the Brahmo Samaj.[62]

That all Brahmos were not pleased that Keshub had welcomed Dall was clear from the editorial comments following Dall's postscript in which he added that the words of his membership vow were simply, "I do hereby avow my faith in theism and become a member of the Brahmo Samaj of India."

> As this letter requires elucidation we make some remarks thereon, and number them according to the number of reasons given above by Mr. Dall.
>
> 1. Had Mr. Dall no faith before in the "theism of Jesus," how then can that be a motive of his entering the Brahmo fraternity? Mr. Dall was told and ought to remember that the Brahmo Samaj recognize no denominational kind of Theism, such as he or any other person may imagine was held by Jesus or any other religious teacher. We hold, and Mr. Dall by signing the theistic declaration has pledged himself to hold, directly or indirectly, privately or publicly, no sectarian creed, but that broad universal faith, which has opposed every existing form of Christianity, is known in England, and America by the name of Theism. If Mr. Dall thinks that by for-

mally entering the Brahmo Samaj he will succeed to help men into Unitarian Christianity, which he miscalls or conceals by the name of "the Theism of Jesus," we are afraid he will find himself mistaken. We believe Mr. Dall still unconscious of the responsibility he has incurred by signing the Brahmo covenant.

2. We know there are many orthodox Trinitarian Christians who, though they do not join it, think of the Brahmo Samaj as a movement stirred up by the spirit of God. Mr. Dall now being a member of the institution ought to identify himself with it completely, and not merely extend to it his patronage.

3. Many thanks for Mr. Dall's confidence, though we are sorry he has not been speaking at all favorably of these readers in England, as his professed confidence would lead us to expect.

4. Did he ask the Brahmo in question whether the latter called himself a follower of Christ exclusively, or whether he did not as well call himself a follower of Nanuk, Chaitanya, Mahomed, and Confucius? The fact is that the Brahmos profess themselves, as did Rajah Ram Mohun Roy, to be the followers of all great men and prophets. And Jesus Christ is one of them.

5. We cannot possibly undertake to keep and sell these books. And, we further beg Mr. Dall will be good enough not to send us any more letters of this kind for publication, because we think they are neither pleasant nor interesting to the public.[63]

Dall's lengthy and friendly response to these charges did not seem to help much for on November 30 another Brahmo charged Dall with changing his identification rather frequently.

He announces himself on one occasion a Brahmo follower of Christ, on the next a Rammohun Roy Brahmo and on the latest occasion advertised he announces his intentions of proving that the founder of the Brahmo Samaj was a Christian. In one of his lectures just published, he attempts to show that both the present leader of the Brahmo Samaj as well as the founder of that institution view Christ in the same light as Mr. Dall himself. If Mr. Dall intends to preach Unitarian Christianity under the assumed name of theist or Brahmo let him do so on his own account and not on that of Baboo Keshub Chunder Sen or Rajah Ram Mohun Roy. We again warn Mr. Dall that his course of conduct is improper.[64]

Dall was not only in trouble with the Brahmo establishment and *The Indian Mirror* for joining the Brahmo Samaj but also he came under fire in various American Unitarian publications, one going so far as to publish a note that they could not believe that he had joined. In Calcutta, Dall felt the need to defend himself again in April 1872, and, feeling forced to say whether he gave his top priority to Christianity or to Brahmoism, took his stand with Christianity, justifying his position with the claims that both Rammohun and Keshub had also followed Jesus Christ.[65]

Keshub in Controversy

The Brahmo Samaj reform program developed during the late 1860s and 1870s under Keshub's leadership was impressive. The Brahmo Marriage Act passed in 1872 after four years of education and lobbying. In spite of opposition from the Adi Brahmos it reformed the practice of child marriage and ignored the old practices of caste associated with marriage. The liberalizing and simplification of other life-oriented religious ceremonies accompanied the marriage reforms in the Samaj. Keshub and his followers were also instrumental in founding the Indian Reform Association, a Normal School for girls and the promotion of temperance.[66]

By 1876 and 1877, Keshub Chunder Sen had taken the Brahmo Samaj of India into a new direction. He felt an increasing pull towards *bhakti* or traditional Hindu devotionalism while drawing his closest followers into an increasingly ascetic community which developed logic and meditative disciplines over and above those which had usually been practiced in the Brahmo Samaj. But a new crisis arose for the Brahmo Samaj when, in 1878, Keshub announced that he had arranged for his daughter, very much underage, to marry the youthful Maharajah of Kuch Behar. Great criticism arose immediately on three counts: (1) that this was a breach of the Brahmo Marriage Act in regard to age, (2) that the marriage could not be performed without idolatrous ceremonies taking place, and (3) Keshub had arranged the marriage because of the material benefits that would come to the family. Keshub, on the other hand, justified the decision and followed through on it on the basis of revelation. Protap Chunder Mazumdar and Gour Gobind Roy wrote defending Keshub's action but the opposition was adamant. Many of Keshub's earlier followers withdrew to found the Sadharan Brahmo Samaj, the active Samaj to the present day. Keshub continued as leader of the Brahmo Samaj of India but by 1881 his group called itself the "Church of the New Dispensation."

In England, Sophie Dobson Collet, publishing annual reports on Brahmo happenings, made her opposition to Keshub's change of policy and religious style completely clear. She was fair in publishing a full record of the controversy, but extremely one-sided in her editorializing against Keshub. In 1879, he had preached in the Calcutta Town Hall, "Am I an Inspired Prophet?" in which he asserted that he would not justify his conduct for "judgment belongeth to the Lord." While confessing to be a sinner and not a saint, Keshub stated that he was "commissioned by God to preach certain truths."[67]

Keshub's claims to revelation offended most Unitarians, not the least of whom was Charles Dall. Shocked at his actions in the Kuch Bihar marriage, Dall found Keshub's rejection of the practical and intellectual in favor of devotionalism and asceticism totally out of keeping with the spirit of Christ which Keshub had preached for nearly twenty years. Keshub had dwelt too long on Jesus's words, "Take no thought for what ye shall eat," and "Take no thought for the morrow," Dall wrote in *Brahmo Public Opinion.* "India needs other words of Jesus now," he continued,

> and among them these: 'whosoever doeth the will and work of the Infinite and Constant worker doth the will of my Father, the same is my brother.' Labor, practical godliness is worship now. It is coordinate with devotion. Service to man is the best consecration to God.[68]

Yet when Dr. Murray Mitchell, a missionary with whom Dall had often conflicted, attacked Keshub and predicted the total downfall of the Brahmo movement, Dall condemned him as "the voice of Esau" and defended Keshub's new Samaj as a Protestant movement breaking with the Catholic church. Dall stated clearly, however, that he did not believe The New Dispensation Church any longer to be the Brahmo Samaj itself, but merely a branch.[69]

In his later years in Calcutta, Dall's impact was no longer as a Unitarian Sunday preacher nor as the tutor to hundreds of young men, who came seeking advice or ways to emancipate themselves from the bonds of Hinduism. The three alternatives of the Brahmo movement and the emergent Ramakrishna and Arya Samaj movements served political and social as well as religious of young Hindus. Dall's impact came in the area of education. By 1877, he was manager of four schools. The Rover's School for Poor Boys began in 1866 teaching in Bengali only with Hindu boys learning knitting trades and Muslims learning bookbinding. Some went on to the School of Useful Arts to study English, Sanskrit, and mathematics. The American Unitarian Association Hindu Girls' School opened in September 1866 and from 1870 on had been managed by Mary Chamberlain, Dall's steadfast supporter, until she was succeeded by Helen Tompkins in 1878. In 1877, ninety-six pupils were enrolled with a daily average attendance of sixty-two. The Hayward School for Girls was started as an experiment with American money in 1874 and it received continuing private support from Americans and Europeans in Calcutta while the other three schools continued to receive government aid. Most successful for the last twenty-six years of Dall's ministry was the School of Useful Arts which had 246 regular pupils in 1877 and through whose classes thousands of Calcuttans must have passed during Dall's tenure there.[70]

By 1880, when Dall published a short report on twenty-five years of missionary work, it was the schools, his travels and speeches throughout India, and the 117 publications, ninety-four of which had come from Dall himself, that Dall wished to emphasize to his diminishing audience in America and England. The last years of Charles Dall in Calcutta could only have been years of bitter struggle and determination not to give up. Even returning to Boston in 1881 at the age of sixty-five, he would not retire for fear that the mission and the schools could not continue without his leadership.

During the more than thirty years he was in India, Dall's wife, Caroline Healey Dall, became known in her own right. Taking an active role in the early stages of the feminist movement, she wrote books on education, travel, literature, and justice. Although she never travelled to Calcutta to visit the mission, she maintained a lively interest in Indian affairs. Two years after Dall's death, Caroline Dall wrote a book on the life of Dr. Anandibai Joshee, the first Indian woman to travel to America and to receive a medical degree. Dr. Joshee's untimely death at the age of twenty-two on her return to India to take up her first medical appointment so moved Mrs. Dall both as a feminist and as a person deeply interested in India that she published the book of 197 pages memorializing the unusual young woman.[71] Although Dr. Joshee had never met Charles Dall during her time in Calcutta, her life was of more than passing interest to Unitarians for by some chance she had attended meetings of the Free Religious Association in Boston during May of 1886 where she had met Mrs. Dall, and was therefore known to American Unitarians.

The End of An Era

The attitude of English and American Unitarians toward Keshub Chunder Sen changed remarkably after the events of 1878 and 1879. While the American Unitarian Association remained a continuing but silent supporter of Charles Dall up to his death in 1886, the British and Foreign Unitarian Association opted to support the Brahmo movement believing that an indigenous reform program was a more sensible approach. They had in fact held this attitude from the time in 1818 when Thomas Belsham had written the Madras Unitarians that their own men, well-trained, would be far superior to any English missionary. Low-caste Madrasis wanted a foreign missionary to provide them status and give them a ground for competition. But the elite of Young Bengal under its increasingly dynamic leadership came to feel quite the opposite. It was not that they did not appreciate what a James Long, an Alexander Duff, or a Charles Dall had done or could offer them. But, between 1855 and 1886, the duration of Dall's tenure in Calcutta, Bengali Hindu leadership had developed a clear sense of political and social reform. That the religious identity of the liberal "Brahmos" was a matter of debate following the second split of 1879 was a source of disillusionment more to Unitarians in England and America than it was to the Brahmos struggling in defense of their own positions.

Sophie Dobson Collet, the primary source of information about Brahmo affairs for the Unitarian public, had made her opposition to Keshub clear at the time of the Kuch Behar marriage. In June 1879. *The Inquirer*, in a lead story, picked up the criticism in its article, "The Latest Mystic."[72] English Unitarians looked with disbelief upon Keshub whom they had admired so much during his visit in 1870. How could a man so articulate and rational, one so much the ideal religious and social reformer, have deteriorated into "superstition"[73] and "mysticism"? Although *The Inquirer* made it clear that its sympathies and those of most Unitarians lay with the rationally-oriented Sadharan Brahmo Samaj (which now stood in the middle between Tagore's Adi Brahmo Samaj and Keshub's coming Church of the New Dispensation), it openly published responses from Keshub and his colleague Protap Chunder Mazumdar who had visited England in 1874.

The Brahmo response to Unitarianism also differed before and after 1878. An article in *The Indian Mirror* of 1875, "Thoughts on Unitarianism,"[74] struggled with the difficulties of defining a Unitarian. Likening it to other heresies of Christianity, the article stressed that it was far better organized and had never been "reactionary." "Their system is more a development than a reaction," *The Mirror* wrote. Causes of Unitarian success were attributed to "the strict purity of character" maintained by the committed membership and the "remarkable erudition and intellectual power which some of its leaders have shown." Putting his finger on the difficulties Unitarianism faced in pointing to the problem of authority versus independent judgment, one is able to discern how some Brahmos were drawn to the kind of authoritarian leadership which had typified Hindu religious movements throughout the centuries. The differences among Unitarians would always be inevitable, the author concluded, but if Unitarians could live with them, then differences were a sign of progress.[75]

In 1877, the progressive Brahmos, under Keshub, directly attacked Dall through an article by Keshub's brother, Krishna Bihari Sen, editor of *The Indian Mirror.* The confusion about whether Dall was a Christian or a Brahmo, emerged once again. For five years relations between Dall and Keshub had been relatively cordial until Keshub preached on the topic, "The Disease and the Remedy,"[76] a lecture in which he articulated what Dall believed to be a "Calvinistic" concept of sin and natural depravity. Dall saw here the first signs of a "back-sliding" to which Krishna Bihari Sen replied:

> We have never been able to persuade Mr. Dall that he cannot be a Brahmo and a Christian at the same time, and that his views of Christ are different from what the Brahmo Samaj holds. . . All Brahmos in whatever presidency, ought to know that Mr. Dall is a Unitarian Christian missionary, pure and simple, and we dispute his right to preach Christianity under the cover of the Brahmo name.[77]

In May 1883 *The Inquirer* published an assessment taken from another perspective: a speech by an orthodox Christian minister based on a recent interview with Keshub.[78] In making it clear again that English Unitarians felt a shift in sympathy from Keshub to the Sadharan Brahmo Samaj, this article reported the missionary Joseph Cook quoting Keshub as having said that Martineau and Parker were "cold."

> He cannot tolerate Unitarianism, although it has treated him with the utmost courtesy. There was a time when it was supposed that Mr. Sen would be the leader of a reform of religion in India, and make that reform substantially Unitarianism; but I asked Mr. Sen point blank, 'What do you think of Unitarianism?' His answer was, 'Its representative in Calcutta has made it ridiculous here: it is an icicle. I take pains to call myself not a Unitarian but a Unitrinitarian.[79]

Both Cook and the editor of *The Inquirer* were most concerned about how Keshub could distinguish the truth of God from his own personal and subjective insights. To this, Protap Mazumdar had responded, "That is one of the secrets of religious genius." Cook and the English Unitarians answered that "precisely here is the weakest and most dangerous, and yet to the Hindoo mind the most fascinating part of Chunder Sen's claims and inculcations."[80]

In this instance, it appears that the Unitarians had depended too much on the orthodox Christian assessment of Keshub and particularly on hostile quotations about Dall. These charges and counter-charges were promptly refuted by Gour Govind Roy, "Apostolic Durbar of the Brahmo Samaj of India" (i.e., a supporter of Keshub's Church of the New Dispensation), who sought to remove "misconceptions and unfriendliness."[81] Expressing great gratitude to the English Unitarians for their earlier support of Keshub and Protap Mazumdar while testifying about how Brahmos had circulated the works of Channing and other Unitarians in India, Govind Roy likened Brahmo work among the Hindus to that which Unitarians had done in England and America. Thoroughly disclaiming "anything like antagonism or rupture, ingratitude or disrespect," Govinda stressed that none the less, "unity is not uniformity."[82] He quoted a Unitarian minister who had recently suggested that the mystic life was very much missing from rational Unitarianism.

An earlier issue of *The Inquirer* had also republished an article from *The Liberal* of Calcutta in which Cook's charges that Parker and Martineau were "cold" and Keshub's remarks against Dall were refuted. Of Dall's ministry, the new Dispensation newspaper had written, "What the minister urged was perhaps the failure of Unitarianism in India as a proselytizing church. Mr. Dall has hardly made any converts here, and for this not he, but his church, is responsible. The Brahmo Samaj does all its work and more."[83] The old hostilities with Dall were still very much in the air though the language in which they were now expressed had been toned down.

Despite hostilities and misunderstandings between Unitarians and the Brahmo Samaj, the unexpected deaths of both Keshub Chunder Sen at the age of forty-six and Charles Dall came as a shock to the two communities. *The Indian Messenger*, now the publication of the Sadharan Brahmos, reported and rejoiced that students in Calcutta were organizing a memorial for Keshub shortly after his death. Among those present at a meeting to plan the memorial, as he had also been present as the only non-Hindu at Keshub's deathbed, was Charles Dall.[84] Following a trip to Assam in July 1886, Dall died suddenly at the age of seventy following a gall bladder attack and subsequent emergency operation.

The Messenger and *The Indian Mirror* both reported Dall's death and funeral in late July 1886. While the service was conducted by an orthodox minister, such notable Brahmos as Narendran Nath Sen, Krishna Bihari Sen, and the politician Surrendra Nath Banerji attended. Umesh Chandra Datta, one of the ministers of the Sadharan Brahmo Samaj, also performed a service, thus bringing together with boys from his schools the three major forces with which Dall had worked for thirty-one years in Calcutta. With the death of these two men, three decades of liberal religious leadership in Bengal came to an end. What began in excitement and idealism ended for both in controversy, pettiness, and much disillusionment. Yet the impact of both men was significant in the context of the lives of those whom they served.

CHAPTER TEN

From Mission to World Parliament: Protap Chunder Mazumdar and Moncure Daniel Conway

The most significant impact of the Brahmo Samaj on American Unitarianism surprisingly occurred after the death of both Keshub Chunder Sen and Charles Dall. The important transitional figure was Keshub's associate, Protap Chunder Mazumdar, who made a far less heralded visit to England in 1874 and a trip around the world in 1884. Only two years younger than Keshub, he remained in the latter's shadow, only to be overshadowed after Keshub's death by two new and unexpected forces. The first of these was the predominance of neo-Vaisnava and bhakti-oriented followers of Keshub who prevented the Westernized, well-travelled Mazumdar from succeeding to Keshub's pulpit in 1884. The second factor was the meteoric rise of Swami Vivekananda, once a Brahmo himself, to dominate the public eye despite Protap's presence as the representative of Hinduism at the World Parliament of Religions in Chicago in 1893. Where Keshub turned inward in his later years, listening primarily to the ascetic-oriented membership of the "New Dispensation," Mazumdar remained loyal while speaking to Keshub about the more rational and Christian-oriented side of Brahmo faith. There is little if any remaining evidence to show a relationship between Protap and Charles Dall. It is clear, however, that Mazumdar, following in Keshub's footsteps as early as 1859 or 1860, as a young man, orphaned, without immediate family, and in search of a religious identity, studied the works of Channing and Parker in Dall's mission rooms. Dall's support of Keshub as against Debendranath Tagore in 1866 and his membership in the Brahmo Samaj in 1871 lend further evidence that the two must have known each other.

Some of Keshub's followers such as Bijoy Krishna Goswami wanted to propagate Brahmoism among rural and less well educated peoples, while Protap Mazumdar, himself urbane, Western-oriented, and deeply influenced by Christian Unitarianism (this is evident from his numerous writings), preferred to travel throughout India by train joining Keshub on missionary journeys to Madras and Punjab, as well as other parts of the country. While the Brahmo Samaj might be spread in the

Bengali language in the environs of Calcutta or Dacca, English, rather than Tamil, Urdu, or Marathi could be used in other areas.[1] Throughout his travels in India, Mazumdar appears to have been a major factor in organizing chapters, keeping them alive, and moving them toward social and political reform.

During the 1860s and early 1870s Charles Dall had made extensive tours throughout India, often speaking to Brahmo or potential Brahmo audiences, invoking the Christian message of Rammohun Roy, and relating Brahmoism and Unitarianism whenever he could. Dall's trips as well as Keshub's offered Protap a model for his own travels. Lectures and speeches on his trip to England recorded primarily in *The Inquirer* show his open support of Unitarianism, Charles Dall, and his effective communication with Westerners.[2] Protap's first book, *The Faith and Progress of the Brahmo Samaj*, published in Calcutta in 1882, written in defense of Keshub's "spiritual universalism," was dedicated to Rammohun Roy, not as Dall would have had him known, but as one "who first cast on the wild waters of Hindu Society, the bread, which, in the writer and others, has been returned a hundredfold."[3] The image was biblical if the reference to Rammohun was not.

Protap Mazumdar's letters to Oxford professor F. Max Mueller, written in 1881 and printed in part in Mueller's *Biographical Essays*, indicate the extent to which Protap Mazumdar was disturbed by Keshub's move away from Unitarian-oriented Brahmoism. Impressed by Mueller's comparative method in the study of religion, Protap sought to see it applied to faith and devotion in the context of the Brahmo Samaj.

> The Fatherhood of God is a meaningless abstraction unless the unity of truth in all lands and all nations is admitted. And the brotherhood of man is impossible if there is no recognition of the services which the great people of the earth have rendered into each other.[4]

Protap Mazumdar's book, *The Oriental Christ*, ingratiated him to American Unitarians in particular. In *The Oriental Christ*, Mazumdar developed, somewhat as an outgrowth of what he had said to Max Mueller, the earlier Keshubite doctrine of Christ the Asiatic. Careful not to present Christ in an uncritically universalist manner Protap wrote that he came to Jesus out of a secular vacuum. He was awakened, as he says, to "a sense of deep inner unworthiness" and a "strong sense of sin."[5] The influence of Jesus upon him he did not attribute to any direct contact with Christianity but rather from indirect contact through Keshub and perhaps the influence of Christianity in the Indian environment of his time. Protap's experience of Christ combined elements of Rammohun's and Keshub's. On the one hand, he encountered Jesus during a period of meditation but it was Jesus in human terms as well as Christ in ideal terms that held meaning for Protap. He explained that

> It was an impulse then, a flood of light, love and consolation. It is no longer an impulse now. It is a faith and principle; it is an experience verified by a thousand trials. . . My aspiration has been not to speculate on Christ, but to be what Jesus tells us all to be.[6]

Building on Keshub's image of the Asiatic Christ called to serve and be served by Asians, Protap cited Keshub's lectures, "Jesus Christ: Europe and Asia" and "That Marvellous Mystery, the Trinity," as the two substantial lectures in which Keshub set forth his teachings on Christ. Denying a position of pantheism for himself or for the Brahmo Samaj, he too appeared something of a Vedantist when he wrote of the experience of *samadhi.* The experience, as understood in the Hindu tradition, could give one a different apprehension of Christ than he would receive from the European dogmatic tradition. Like Keshub, Mazumdar offered in his 1893 book, *The Spirit of God*, a comparative evolutionary principle between Hinduism and Christianity.

> Thus the presence of God in creation (Vedas) in the soul of man (upanishads) and in his dealings with the types of the race, through religious and national dispensations (Puranas) discloses the marvellous analogy that there is between spiritual Hinduism and the characteristic doctrine of Christianity. The Spirit of God is the source and substance of all things, the evolving principle in all matter, and bears forth all souls. . . The Hindu conception of the Spirit is a pervasive presence.
>
> Generally speaking, the Old Testament corresponds to the Vedas, the Gospel to the Puranas, and the Epistles of St. Paul to the Upanishads. But Christianity in the Old and New Testaments has mainly the dispensation of the Father and the dispensation of the Son, scarcely anything that can be called the dispensation of the Spirit. When the last finds adequate record, the analogy between the Hindu and Christian schemes will become complete.[7]

In this same work, Protap stresses that Christ is unique, "not because he was born of a virgin but because he was the unity of all those who preceded him in the divine order of humanity." Christ was also unique because he "perfectly embodies the true and universal relation between God and man." Christ was the most perfect manifestation possible of "the eternal reason."[8] Such statements might lead one to regard Mazumdar as a Christian, rather than a Hindu. For Mazumdar, Christianity was not the issue; rather, it was the universal spirit of Jesus Christ, a spirit which could harmonize religions, a harmony already at work in the Brahmo Samaj, because for it "the Spirit of God is all in all, both for worship and the sanctity of personal character." The Brahmo Samaj, therefore, was one religious organization in which one could see the end toward which the Spirit of God was drawing all religions. His criticism of most Christian doctrine and culture came at the point where he asserted that European Christianity had taken Christ out of context. But for Protap, the contextual argument applied limitations on other prophets and teachers. Thus, according to the recent study of Indian doctrines of Christ by M. M. Thomas,

> Socrates is for the Greeks, Moses is for the Hebrews, Confucius for the Chinese, Krishna for the Hindus. (But there is need for a) central figure, a universal model, one who includes himself, all these various embodiments of God's self-manifestations.[9]

For Protap Mazumdar, Christ was the best representative to unite humanity and bring brotherhood. This approach to comparative religion and personal religiousness was very much in keeping with that developed by the American Unitarian James Freeman Clarke, and while debatable among some of the more radical late nineteenth-century Unitarians of the Free Religious Association, was essentially well received when Protap arrived in America on his "tour 'round the world" in 1883-1884.

On returning from this second major foreign journey, Protap published his diary including extensive comments on life in America: his visit to President Chester Arthur, the condition of Negroes and Indians, the vastness of the country, a trip to Concord to the Emerson manse.[10] But on returning to Madras in January 1884, Protap was struck with the news that Keshub had died. Of this he wrote,

> My head, heart and liver on fire. My throat and mouth as dust. What strange unearthly sounds are these, what abnormal thought? Keshub dead!!!. . . How can this be? Anticipation of glad welcome after ten months separation turn into the wilderness of despair.[11]

Keshub's death did not lead Protap into a retreat from his commitments, however. Rather, it led him to take command of those of Keshub's followers who would advance the causes of social and religious reform Keshub had espoused prior to his final ascetic period. Ten years later, Protap Babu returned to America for the most important moments of his public career. A glowing review of *The Oriental Christ* coupled with a moving personal obituary from Charles Dall on Keshub Chunder Sen[12] had laid the groundwork for Mazumdar's superb reception in 1893. Appointed at the suggestion of American Unitarian Association leaders to be a member of the Advisory Council Selection Committee for the World Parliament in Chicago, he was overshadowed there, in the general public eye, by Swami Vivekenanda. For Unitarians, however, Protap was still a man to be deeply respected for his intellectual ability and dearly cherished for his sound religious faith.

Not long after his 1883 visit to America, the editor of the monthly journal *Unitarian Review*, highly impressed with Protap Mazumdar's visit, claimed that he had already "won wide sympathy and recognition as his earnest and rational devoutness have kindled anew the sense of universal religious fellowship." His recent addresses, the reviewer continued, had shown the assimilation of "Christian faith and ethics by intelligent Hinduism and the ample common ground of conviction and aims between the Brahmo Samaj and liberal Christianity of England and America."[13] Writing in sharp contrast to Sophie Collet and the English Unitarians, the American Unitarian editor remarked in the context of his strong interest in Protap, that the activities of Keshub Sen, his mysticism, and the Kuch Bihar marriage did not indicate "any serious inconsistency of the Brahmo leader." Surely there was nothing in Keshub's doctrine of inspiration to which George Fox, Jonathan Edwards, or Theodore Parker would have objected. Reflecting on the positive values of Keshub's 1870 visit to England the editor concluded,

> Nor is it difficult for us who have read his impassioned and masterly sermons and addresses, and listened to the broad and clear, yet fervid expositions of his disciple and relative Mr. Mazumdar, to understand the secret of his influence and leadership and we share the deep sorrow which all intelligent theists in India must feel in his untimely death.[14]

Moncure Daniel Conway

Present with Protap Mazumdar when he arrived in Calcutta from Madras to learn of the death of Keshub Chunder Sen was an enigmatic and dynamic southern American Unitarian minister, Moncure Daniel Conway.[15] Conway deserves attention in this study because he bridges the gap between those American and English Unitarians interested in Orientalism for its own sake and those who went out to be missionaries. Born a Virginia Methodist in 1832, Conway had his first exposure to liberal religious ideas and particularly Unitarianism while attending a lecture by Dr. G. W. Burnap, minister of the Baltimore church, given at Dickinson College in Pennsylvania. Through a growing friendship with Burnap and against the wishes of his family, Conway attended Harvard Divinity School in 1853 where he was befriended by Harvard President Jared Sparks, former minister of the Baltimore church.

In New England, Conway the southerner came under the spell of transcendentalism and the anti-slavery movement. He began a personal study with Emerson of the *Bhagavad Gita* and the *Gulistan* of the Persian poet Sadi, about which the Concord lecturer had written essays. Called to a Washington, D.C., Unitarian pulpit upon graduation, he was quickly fired due to his radical abolitionist views. In 1858 Conway moved to Cincinnati where he married Ellen Dana, the daughter of one of his parishioners. Throughout his ministry in Cincinnati and after his departure to serve Unitarianism in England during the Civil War, Conway wrote and published avidly. Conway's *The Sacred Anthology* published simultaneously in London and New York in 1873, was very popular. Reviewed by both Professor Max Mueller and the German scholar Max Weber, it was declared unscholarly but recognized as a useful way to familiarize the public with the scholarly translations and studies scholars were carrying on in the field of Oriental religions.

A trip to lecture in Australia in 1883 included Conway's only journey to India, a visit covered in some detail in his book *My Pilgrimage to the Wise Men of the East.* Following a chapter in which Conway detailed his visit in South India with Madame Blavatsky of the Theosophical movement, a personality and organization for which Conway, despite his universalism, had little sympathy, he turned to a discussion of Keshub Sen, Protap Mazumdar and the Brahmo movement in Calcutta.

Conway was clearly not sympathetic with the devotional turn of Keshub's religiousness. He reported Charles Dall's anxiety when present at Keshub's death bed and his testimony that one of Keshub's devotees had cried out the name of "Hari, Hari," a Vaisnava name for Krishna (but called by Conway, "Chaitanya's Salvation Army god"). Conway had difficulty in understanding why "Unitarian" Brahmos should also call out to the Divine Mother as Keshub did. It smacked too much of traditional Kali devotionalism and Kali worship still implied sacrifice to the terrible demonic goddess.

Conway was critical also of the upper-class pretensions he found in much of the Brahmo movement. He likened this discovery to the surprise which he as a rural Virginia Methodist had found on his first encounter with Boston Unitarian Christianity. Of Protap Mazumdar, whom he considered a friend, he reported, "He was really in spirit no Hindu at all, but a preacher of average English Unitarianism."[16] The two men had met during Mazumdar's first visit to England in 1874 when he preached at Conway's Finsbury Street Chapel in London as Keshub had before him. In 1884 on the trip from Madras to Calcutta, they debated the nature of the deity, Protap demanding "a demonstrably working" deity and Conway a "lovable" one. Conway's defensiveness and lack of understanding were evidenced in his statement,

> And what was his own one Brahmo deity but all of those nature gods consolidated into — that one responsible for all cruel and destructive forces represented by Siva and Kali? Once he said to me, 'Is there anything at all that you reverence?' 'Yes,' I replied, 'a lovely and lovable woman, a sweet child, a man of wisdom, a mind consecrated to pure reason, a true and loving heart.' Mozoomdar tried to persuade me that all these beautiful qualities were deep in the heart of this dynamic, universal, omnipotent deity; I could not see love in cancers, Indian famines, etc., but was as tender as I could be with the faith of this Hindu so pathetically anxious to build up a new religion for his race.[17]

Of particular significance was Conway's friendship with the noted Islamic scholar Sir William Hunter, the man in charge of publishing the *Gazetteer of India.* Hunter took Conway to many places he would not otherwise have visited and arranged "an assembly of learned Brahmans, Brahmos, Moslems and Parsis" to meet Conway for a discussion of religious and philosophical subjects. While the nature of the discussion seems not to have been too important, Conway was especially arrogant in dismissing the contributions of the Hindu pundits and Muslims on religious matters. He was impressed, however, by the familiarity of the Brahmins on issues of concern to him (he saw these as issues of concern to the West) and seems to have given credit to the Hindu encounter with the West for making these pundits so articulate.

Conway was highly stimulated by private meetings he had with the Hindu scholar Dr. Rajendralal Mittra, who had been librarian of the Asiatic Society when Charles Dall first began his ministry in Calcutta and also with the noted Muslim jurist Sayyid Ameer Ali. Conway and his wife had known Ali when he was a law student in London. "He was often at our house; we loved him, and his beautiful spirit seemed to transfuse his face, form, voice and manner, — his entire being." Conway had been inspired by Ameer Ali's famous book on Muhammad:[18] "It raised all Islam — which I had deemed a hard eastern Calvinism — in my esteem that such a man could love it, and draw so much truth and beauty out of it." Of course, Ameer Ali wrote the book to sell Islam to the West, presenting Muhammad in a manner that would impress persons such as Conway. He did not misrepresent Muhammad so much as he attempted to make him palatable and understandable to Western taste, much as others have described Jesus in terms more meaningful to their time and place.

Such was Moncure Daniel Conway's encounter with the religious life of India, a fitting prelude to the next stage of Unitarian involvement, the World Parliament of Religions. Conway himself moved away from Unitarianism, further to the left. During the years before his death in 1907, he had joined a Congress of Free-thinkers and worked in pacifist causes while devoting most of the last decade of his life to writing and travel.

The World Parliament of Religions: 1893

One decade after the first visit of Protap Mazumdar to America and Moncure Conway to India, interest in the non-Christian religions of the world had developed broadly in intellectual and drawing room circles of America. During the years after Keshub Chunder Sen's death numerous religious and social reform organizations had developed in India. One, the Theosophical Society, founded by the mysterious Madame

Blavatsky and later developed by Annie Besant, an English woman with both a mystical and political bent, drew considerable attention and served as a bridge to Indian religious ideas for Europeans and Americans.

In America, the 1890's signified an era of expansion and development. The new century was at hand. The great Chicago exposition and world's fair of 1893 was conceived as a response to the great new age of technology. As a humanistic part of the exposition, the World Parliament of Religions idea was developed primarily by religious liberals seeking a world in which they dreamed of inter-religious understanding that would stand side by side with the new technologies.

A complete record of the World Parliament has been captured in the two volumes published by the Reverend John Henry Barrows, minister of the First Presbyterian Church of Chicago and a major organizer of the conference. Barrows along with Charles C. Bonney, President of the overall Parliament activities and the noted Reverend Jenkin Lloyd Jones were among the prime movers bringing the two week colloquy to reality.[19] Jabez T. Sunderland, editor of *The Unitarian,* minister of the Ann Arbor, Michigan church and long a staunch supporter of the Parliament idea, wrote in the October 1893 issue of the significance of the event, describing it as a movement "looking exactly in the direction of that breath, liberty and increasing unity in religions" for which his publication had been working so earnestly. Most significant, he felt, was that never before had representatives of so many countries, races, and religions come together. The parliament preceded by a number of American church conventions, ran from September 11 to 28.[20] 172 major addresses by representatives of dozens of religious groups were heard. Sunderland, two years later to be the next Unitarian representative to India, showed how far he had already moved beyond Charles Dall and how appreciative he was of the spirit which Protap Mazumdar expressed in his two major addresses to the Congress. This he demonstrated when he set forth four points concerning the future of religion in the context of the congress.

> First, it clearly means the great religions of mankind, notwithstanding their differences, yet have much *in common,* and that the more enlightened leaders of those religions are coming to recognize the fact of their common elements. Second, it means a growing conviction that the things which they hold in common are *more important* than those about which they *disagree.* Third, it means a deepening and widening consciousness that *tolerance* and *charity* are *essential*

qualities in all noble religion... Fourth and perhaps most important of all...this means an increasing recognition among the world's religious teachers and thinkers that *the heart and conscience of man can never* be coerced, and consequently that true religion...can in the nature of things be *promoted* only by reason and persuasion and love.[21]

Protap's two speeches to the World Parliament, "The Brahmo Samaj" and "The World's Religious Debt to Asia,"[22] were both profound, intellectual, and intelligible. They were the kinds of talks fully appreciated by Unitarians and Universalists. The speech on the Brahmos emphasized both history and social reform, while the second and longer lecture stressed the sense of immanence, mysticism, and spiritualism so much a part of the Asiatic traditions. Protap made clear his broad knowledge of Asian religiousness, presenting something of universalism but little of nationalism in his speeches. The time was not yet ripe for the nationalist appeals to which Sunderland would so strongly respond in the next decade.

Protap so impressed the Unitarians at Chicago that he was afterwards invited to tour the country, a tour highlighted by his delivering the four Lowell Lectures while in Cambridge, Massachusetts during October and November, 1893. A committee of American Unitarian Association members headed by Edward Everett Hale raised funds to provide Protap with an annual stipend which carried on until his death in 1905. He also received an all-expense-paid third visit to America in 1900 to join in the seventy-fifth anniversary celebrations of the American Unitarian Association.

Writing from Boston in November 1893 to the Brahmo Samaj, Protap stressed the spirit which had prevailed at the three-week-long international congress. Reflecting on how frequently Brahmos had quarrelled over "unessential differences" but how at Chicago a "high level of common faith" had brought "a harmony and reconciliation in this land (America) of hard animosities and traditional differences," Protap called upon his fellow Brahmos to make a common cause for the future of their own movement[23]. Overwhelmed by the spectacular size, scope, and cost of the exposition itself, Protap wrote appreciatively of the Parliament theme, "Not Things but Men." Christianity had deeply affected his life and ministry as this paragraph makes clear:

I am not reproachful of Hinduism, I am not reproachful of Christianity in my public utterances. I have done my best to acknowledge my indebtedness to both of these great religions which divide the interests of our country (India). These two must be fully reconciled in our hearts and in the heart of the Brahmo Samaj before we can worthily claim the sympathy and cooperation of the world for the welfare of our land and people.[24]

Somehow, however, Protap had left Unitarians at the World Parliament with a far different impression than Swami Vivekenanda had. The latter was clearly a disciple of spiritual Hinduism who was already advocating a nationalist ideology distasteful to Protap. One year later, John Henry Barrows, President of the World Parliament, wrote Protap from just the opposite perspective asking whether he thought that if Christianity were presented to India in a simpler form, without all the trappings of "theology and ecclesiasticism," it would not find a great acceptance among the educated. "I have sometimes felt," he wrote,

> that the mission of the Brahmo Samaj might be to furnish a type of Christian thought and life which India will receive. Your position, I think, I understand. A mediating course does not satisy either extreme. Is there not a theism such as Christ taught, which, made personal and mighty through the preachings of Christ as the Son of God, will accomplish more than the theism of the Vedas?[25]

This was not total Presbyterian or missionary paternalism for Protap. He felt that he could walk in both worlds, and continued for the rest of his career to interact with both. Barrows's interests were essentially comparativist despite his comments to Protap for in the same letter he informed the Brahmo of a $20,000 endowment of a Barrows Lecture Series in Comparative Religion to be administered through the University of Chicago. The lectures would be given both in India and America. Within a few years, Barrows would visit Protap in Calcuta while delivering the lectures there. While we do not know whether the Chicago-based Barrows ever read the farewell address of Protap Mazumdar preached at Arlington Street Church in Boston, after four months of travels and lectures in America, the address would surely have endeared him as much to the Presbyterians as it did to Unitarians. Protap was so thoroughly Christian and biblical in his imagery as he spoke of his indebtedness to "Jesus Christ, Son of God," and "Christ, the summing up of all those great and good men who have blessed the various nations on earth."[26] Stressing how centuries of Christian organization had buried the spirit of Jesus, Protap concluded that Christ was for him the very essence of a spritiual universalism.

In conclusion, Mazumdar told his listeners how much American Unitarianism had contributed to India.

> The best of your land have gone to my land. Your Emerson is there, your Longfellow is there telling my people that life is not vanity, but that it is earnest. Your Theodore Parker is there, and has done for the Brahmo Samaj greater good than you know...And some of our great men are here too. Rammohun Roy before I was born sent his spirit to the liberal thinkers of America; and if today, Keshub Chundr Sen had been living, he would have stood here before you as a glorious figure, a transcendent spirit, a true child of God.[27]

The spirit of interchange and dialogue, though it had reached somewhat sentimental proportions, had also reached its high-water mark. Protap's presence in 1893 had brought out the universalist strain in Unitarianism, while at home in India the first rumblings of national thinking were emerging in the Indian National Congress, largely Bengali and Brahmo in its initial makeup. Jabez T. Sunderland, the Ann Arbor, Michigan Unitarian minister was the next to reach out to join forces with those urging religious and political reform and renewal in India.

CHAPTER ELEVEN

Unitarianism and Nationalism: Jabez T. Sunderland in India

Two years after the World Parliament of Religions and Protap Mazumdar's second journey to America, Unitarian succession returned to India in the person of a new kind of missionary, the Reverend Jabez Thomas Sunderland of Ann Arbor, Michigan. Just as Charles Dall had grown in his Unitarianism at Harvard by reading about Rammohun Roy, William Adam, and Joseph Tuckerman, so also did Jabez Sunderland grow in his Unitarianism, a "convert" like Adam from the Baptist faith, by following the experiences of Charles Dall in Calcutta, and in the 1880s, through the development of the Khasi Hills Unitarian movement about which he regularly reported in the Chicago-based publication, *The Unitarian*, which he edited.

Jabez T. Sunderland's significance for American Unitarianism has never been adequately explored.[1] Born in 1842 in Yorkshire, England, his family moved to the United States when he was a young child. He remained active into his ninety-fourth year, continuing his extensive writing to the end of his life. Even in 1936, his death came not as the result of illness but from injuries sustained in a fall at his home in Ann Arbor, to which he had returned after retiring from his last pastorate in Poughkeepsie, New York, at the age of eighty-eight. His extant correspondence spans great Unitarians of two distant periods: James Freeman Clarke (1810-1888) on the one side, and John Haynes Holmes (1879-1964) on the other.[2]

Sunderland was clearly the earliest American public supporter of the Indian nationalist movement. He attended meetings of the Indian National Congress during the sessions held at Poona in 1895. By so doing, he was not only the first American ever to attend such meetings but also he was the first American to speak to that organization. Very much the Midwesterner, Sunderland was a Unitarian of theistic orientation, not explicitly the Christian Unitarian Charles Dall had been, but neither of the more radical bent of the Free Religious Association Unitarians who represented the ethically but not theistically-oriented Western Unitarian Conference.

Sunderland was educated at the old University of Chicago (1858-1886), receiving his B.A. in 1867 and his M.A. in 1869.

One year later, he also received a B.D. degree from the Baptist Theological Union, having already served at a church in Omaha. After he was ordained, he served at another Baptist pulpit in Milwaukee from 1871 to 1872. His switch to Unitarianism occurred at this point. As with so many other "converted" clergy, Sunderland's first four-year Unitarian pastorate was in a small New England parish, in the small western Massachusetts town of Northfield. After two additional years of service in a small Chicago church he began two decades of editorial service to *The Unitarian*, a conservative competitor to the emerging radical Unitarian journal of Jenkin Lloyd Jones, *Unity*. Sunderland became a frequent contributor to *Unity* during the 1920s when John Haynes Holmes was its editor.

Sunderland's Unitarian ministerial career, which spanned fifty years and some ten churches, also included a twenty-year ministry at Ann Arbor, Michigan. This period, 1878-1898, included his service as Secretary to the Western Unitarian Conference as well as a year spent in Europe, the Middle East, and India. Sunderland's sympathy with the Brahmo Samaj Movement and social reform in India was first articulated when he represented the interests of the American Unitarian Association in the West during the 1886 controversy. In a pamphlet written that year, Sunderland urged Unitarians to be theists in the social ethical tradition of Theodore Parker, whose writings had so strongly influenced Brahmos such as Keshub Chunder Sen and Protap Mazumdar, and Charles Dall's close friend Rakhal Das Haldar.[3] Sunderland had stood firm on the Western Conference charter words "Kingdom of God," whereas William Channing Gannett and others were moving away from theism and Christianity toward the wording, "Freedom, Fellowship and Character."[4]

What disturbed Sunderland about this controversy was that those who wished to exclude theistic and Christian wording from the statement of purpose claimed that they were theists who did not wish to impose the wording on anyone else. It was not a conservative-radical issue, Sunderland asserted, since he described himself as "a radical of the Theodore Parker and Emerson type." For him, it was a battle "distinctly between radical broad, progressive, ethical theism — theism in its most advanced and undogmatic form — and non-theism."[5] While Sunderland's position lost in the Western Conference, it won the day at the national conference held in 1894 at Saratoga,

New York, where Unitarians publically accepted "the religion of Jesus" and that "practical religion is summed up in Love to God and Love to Man."[6]

Sunderland's theological position, so clearly articulated before his departure for India, demonstrates how far mainstream Unitarianism had moved from the Channing-Ware-Dewey orientation Dall had brought to India with him in 1855. During the early years of his ministry Dall never explicitly discussed Emerson very much outside the pale of conservative Unitarianism. Although he had certainly never written Boston asking for Parker's works during Parker's lifetime, Dall quietly allowed the transcendentalist's works to slip into Calcutta libraries.

The Year in India

During the summer of 1895 Jabez Sunderland and his wife, Eliza, prepared to take a year's leave after seventeen years of service in Ann Arbor. They expected to spend the summer in Oxford, some of the year in Europe, and one winter month in Egypt. During their summer in England, however, leaders of the British and Foreign Unitarian Association, aware of Sunderland's leadership abilities, his correspondence with the Khasi Hills Unitarian Hajjom Kissor Singh, and concerned about the state of the fragmented Brahmo Samaj movement, asked Sunderland to consider spending a portion of the year in India. He wrote in his diary of an offer made on September 11, 1895, "to investigate the religious situation there, especially as to openings for Unitarianism, and as to the present condition of the Brahmo Samaj, they to pay my expenses in full on the other side of Egypt."[7]

September and October, 1895, were then devoted to reading, extensive correspondence, and broad publicity throughout the English Unitarian community. Sunderland's reading included such materials as Mary Carpenter's *Last Days in England of Rammohun Roy*, Mary Collet's *Brahmo Yearbooks*, and Mazumdar's *Faith and Progress of the Brahmo Samaj.*[8] By mid-November, Sunderland was on board ship for Bombay. Entries in his diary indicate how sensitive he already was to the situation of low-caste Hindu sailors who he witnessed eating rice and curry out of a common bowl, "sleeping wherever they can," and wondering how much pay each received.[9]

Sunderland's first two weeks in India were spent in a whirlwind of appointments and speeches in Bombay. Met at his ship by Brahmo B. B. Nagarkar, Sunderland attended a Brahmo Samaj service at his host's home his very first night in India. The reaction he has left in his diary was not entirely positive:

> The singing and chanting was according to Hindu music and not European and was very weird . . . it seemed to me all in a minor key, half a wail. The service was very devout.[10]

As the service was entirely in Marathi, it is no wonder Sunderland had difficulties in relating to it as worship.

His experience in meeting Justice Mahadev Govind Ranade[11] the following morning was a far more positive one. "He puts on no style and is very approachable," Sunderland noted in his diary, reporting on their conversation and Ranade's questions about English and American Unitarianism. Ranade informed Sunderland of the coming meetings of the Indian National Congress and National Social Conference of which he was General Secretary.[12] It was here Sunderland would receive his initiation into Indian political and social concerns, a dimension of Indian life which would involve him deeply for the remainder of his career. One week after his arrival, Sunderland addressed the Bani Israel Society, talking on Reform Judaism in America and leaving the works of Channing, Parker, and other Unitarians for their library. The following evening a crowd of 1,000 persons heard Sunderland speak on Unitarianism. The size of the crowd caused him some anxiety. He wrote in his diary,

> India is a land of orators and they speak without manuscripts or notes which I have not been accustomed to. I saw that I must *speak* here not read, and dreaded it. But I shall not dread it so much now.[13]

Toward the end of November, Sunderland spent a week in Madras. At the Elphinstone Hotel he was moved by the plight of the servants. He wrote that while each of the other guests called his servant, "boy," he did the same but was ashamed to do so. "I want to call him Mr."[14] Sunderland had not yet fully learned the harsh realities of caste and status in India. As Charles Brooks[15] and Charles Dall had done before him, Jabez Sunderland sought and finally found the second William Roberts, now seventy-five years old, still minister to the little Unitarian Church described by Sunderland as being "in pretty forlorn condition."[16] William, Jr., he reported, had been "faithful and devoted." When younger, Sunderland judged, he must have been fairly efficient but "at present his work has been pretty crippled from want of funds." He was depressed by the feeling that Madrasi Unitarianism had not changed much in one hundred years, that it was still small and weak. Sunderland preached to a congregation of eighty on December 1, however, describing his listeners as a "motley, curious throng, men, women and children, sitting some on chairs, some on benches and some on the floor, with bare feet, many of the men also with bare legs."[17] Roberts read the service in Tamil, and Sunderland preached and baptized Robert's one-year-old child and lead a discussion on the future of the school and the church. Sunderland found the church still to be divided, the schism going back to the issues of 1861 when Charles Dall had attempted mediation of charges by Abdul Masih,[18] that William Roberts had had an affair with Masih's wife. Madrasi Unitarians still believed that their only hope for progress and status would be the presence of a European missionary. This request dated back to the original letters of William Roberts, Senior to Thomas Belsham in 1818 yet it had never been fulfilled.[19]

While at Madras, Sunderland also addressed the Brahmo Samaj. Both in Madras and in the Khasi Hills, Unitarians existed along side Brahmos in the indigenous populations, but in both cases Unitarians were represented among the low-caste and tribal peoples while Brahmos were almost entirely reform-oriented Hindus of largely Brahmin background. Returning to Bombay, his headquarters for the trip, Sunderland next headed northeast for Ahmedabad, Jaipur, and Delhi. In Ahmedabad, he met with and addressed the Brahmos, visited a school founded by English Unitarian Mary Carpenter, and had his first encounter with two members of the Arya Samaj.[20] In Delhi, Sunderland resided with a British civil servant whose justification of British rule in India Sunderland found much with which to disagree. The first few weeks in India, even as the representative of the British and Foreign Unitarian Association, had already helped to solidify his feelings that British rule in India was not all that Charles Dall, for example, had believed it to be.

Going on to Agra, Sunderland lectured at Victoria College and met with Professor Dhur, leader of the small Brahmo chapter at Agra. At Lucknow, Sunderland delivered two lectures on Sunday, December 15. Meeting with Brahmo leaders, he noted in his diary, "It was the voice of nearly all that India is ripe for Unitarian thought and ideals. They believed that a Unitarian mission here would strengthen the Brahmo Samaj movement without compromising it."[21] These Brahmos expressed for the first time, out of the earlier Calcutta and Dall context, the feeling that Unitarianism and Brahmoism were, in fact, compatible and not necessarily competing for the same congregations. Sunderland's impression of the Brahmo missionary for the Lucknow area was likewise most positive. Of Lakshmana Prasad he wrote, "he seems like an earnest, intelligent and very devoted man. He gets no salary but lives upon what people choose to give him. I am quite impressed with his self-forgetting devotion."[22]

At Allahabad, Sunderland saw another side of pro-Unitarian enthusiasm in the person of the peripatetic Abdul Masih. Masih had first met Charles Dall in Calcutta in 1860, after which he had travelled to England where he received educational support from English Unitarians. In 1861, Masih returned to work with the Madras Unitarians. His brief ministry in Madras had proved far more disruptive than helpful, however. Since 1861, Masih had worked in various towns in the Northwest, translating Unitarian tracts into Urdu and corresponding regularly with Brooke Hereford, the English Unitarian minister who was now serving at Arlington Street in Boston. Sunderland discerned rightly that Masih was not an organizer but rather given to theological argumentation. He had spent his Unitarian years writing and publishing texts, aiming his polemics toward Muslims and "native Christians" whom he believed to be the best subjects for conversion.

Sunderland spent the last week of 1895 at Poona attending meetings of the Indian National Congress and National Social Conference. His first stop in Poona, however, was at the school of Pundita Ramabai, one of the first great women reformers of India whose career Sunderland had and would continue to follow closely.[23] What impressed Sunderland most about the meetings of both associations, in addition to the 6,000 persons in attendance, was that the leaders of both the Congress and the Conference were the same Brahmos he had been meeting on his lecture tours throughout India. Sunderland had not realized that the leaders of progressive religious movements were also involved in what were then the most progressive political and social movements. Sunderland was delighted with this discovery.

After sitting on the platform for the opening session of the Indian National Congress, he moved down among the Lucknow delegates wearing one of their badges. The third day of the Congress, Sunderland spoke on the need for more government support of education in India,[24] thus following in the tradition of William Adam and Charles Dall, both of whom had been staunch advocates of improved educational programs.

At the home of the noted scholar Professor R. G. Bhandarkar, Sunderland conversed again with Justice Ranade on the plight of Negroes in America, a subject of much embarrassment to Sunderland. On the train from Bombay to Calcutta following the conferences, Sunderland spoke frequently with Surrendra Nath Banerji, a Brahmo and noted Bengali leader of the Congress movement.[25]

Sunderland Among the Khasi Hills Unitarians

The Khasi Hills Unitarian movement was the legacy of Charles Dall. His schools had only continued for a few years after his death when his widow, Caroline Dall, decided to close the mission. Mrs. Dall felt, in her declining years and in her sorrow, that somehow no other missionary could fill the role her husband had served in for more than thirty years. The real Unitarian legacy which Charles Dall left was not in Calcutta, however; it was to the northwest in the Khasi and Jaintia Hills in the person of a Khasi tribesman named Hajjom Kissor Singh. In 1887, Singh, aged twenty-two, had courageously written to Jabez Sunderland, then editor of *The Unitarian*, of his encounter with Unitarianism via the works of Channing. Singh was a Khasi, a tribe which had been almost entirely converted to Christianity by Welsh Calvinists. The Khasis were not Hindus,[26] but rather had an indigenous tribal religion based on shamanistic practices. The tribe had emmigrated from Cambodia via Burma and had settled in the Khasi and Jaintia Hills near the borders of eastern Bengal. Before the missionary encounter, the Khasi language had not been written; hence, when the Welsh began to translate the Bible into Khasi, they rendered the language in Roman script. While Singh believed himself to be a good Christian, he had found himself questioning many doctrines, as had several of Charles Dall's earlier disciples. In 1887, the Brahmo Samaj had an active missionary in the Khasi Hills area. It was he who had already referred Singh to Dall and Dall's associate, Helen Tompkins, following Dall's death in 1886. Singh's request for Unitarian tracts and materials, published by Sunderland in March 1888, was the start of a forty-eight-year relationship between the Ann Arbor minister and the Khasi Unitarian movement.

In another letter published by Sunderland in December 1888, Singh reported that he had made one convert, Thom Singh. The two were holding prayer meetings every Sunday and though they had not been completely rejected by their orthodox friends, the latter would never attend Unitarian prayers. Calling on the American Unitarian Association to send some money so that he could publish Unitarian tracts in Khasi, Singh concluded his first letter by reporting that the Brahmos at Shillong, largest city in the Hills, had asked him to cooperate with them.[27] A letter published in the same issue and written in September 1888 reported that Singh had formed a "Unitarian Union" of five male Unitarians and had adopted a statement of beliefs:

> We believe (1) in the unity of God; (2) in the Fatherhood and motherhood of God; (3) in the Brotherhood of Man; (4) in Love, Union, Worship, and Faith; and (5) in Immortality.[28]

This statement, though essentially in the spirit of James Freeman Clarke's statement first published in 1886 and still repeated in many American Unitarian churches, showed some noticeable cultural differences. First was the statement including the "Motherhood of God" very much from Hinduism but also from the Khasi culture which had matrilineal descent as a family focus. "Unity" and "Union" also appeared as terms designed to make clear the Unitarian split with Trinitarian Christianity. Sunderland, in commenting that he was forwarding material from Singh to the Foreign Missions Committee of the American Unitarian Association, followed up the letters and his comments with an informational article on the Khasis reprinted from the *Calcutta Journal*.[29]

By the end of October 1890, Hajjom Singh proudly reported fifteen Khasi Unitarians scattered throughout several villages. In April 1891, Sunderland published excerpts from one of Singh's sermons, particularly significant for its attack on Khasi indigenous religion. He commented with the point that only humans, among all creatures, can distinguish good from evil, and only humans have the power to cultivate understanding thus making it possible for individuals to be at differing levels of understanding. "Man was not created by demons," he continued, attacking a cardinal belief of Khasi faith,

> nor by men, nor self-made, and he did not come out from stones, but was created by God, so that our father and mother are like *ayah* (nurse) and *behrah* (guardian). So we are sons of God and are ordered to obey his will, now in Khasi religion at present there are thousands of demons and many rites and customs. I believe our forefathers had few demons; and I have heard from old people that *at first* our forefathers worshipped and offered sacrifices to God and not to demons.[30]

Singh explained that the corruption of Khasi faith had occurred because there was no written record. Hence, each succeeding generation had brought errors to the faith. He now declared Khasi religion was untrustworthy and the time had now come when God's pure, simple religion was to be practiced. Attempting to convince his audience that love of God, the soul, and love of humankind were the essence of religious faith, he likened sacrificing to demons as an endless bribe,

> "If you give them nothing, you will be free. Now tell me, I offer no sacrifices to demons, and do not bow to them but only to God; and I am just as you are... Now accept the religion of God and you will be happy."[31]

Explaining to Sunderland that this was the manner in which he had to preach to villagers, Singh reported how he and his co-workers impressed villagers, giving them information about the nearest "church" and urging them to consider what he had told them. What is particularly significant about the Khasi Unitarian movement at its inception was that it developed in an indigenous style undominated by any American or British Unitarian mission presence. While the movement was eventually served and assisted by both American and British clergy, its teachings and point of view developed in response to what was already present both in the folk religious tradition and the Trinitarian Christianity imposed upon it. The movement grew spontaneously in mountain villages so that by the end of 1894, Singh could report to Sunderland that two new branches had been founded at Martiang and Raliang, the former with six and the latter with five members; that the congregation at Jowai,

Singh's home village, had twenty-one members, while that at Nongtalang had twenty-nine, both of these villages also having Khasi Unitarian schools. Jowai also had a post office mission from which English tracts were sent throughout the subcontinent. Singh believed the role of the Unitarian schools crucial "for enlightening the ignorant demon-worshippers and bringing them under the influence of 'the religion of God'."[32] Thus in the period shortly before Jabez Sunderland's visit to the Khasis, Singh was able to write with confidence in his cause but uncertainty for the future:

> The field is very large and the cause is becoming more widely known, but we cannot break fresh ground and establish new preaching stations, because there is no regular and competent superintendent of the Mission, and none of our day workers are as yet fit to be entrusted with the job of a missionary superintendent.[33]

Of all the visits Sunderland made in India, he was best prepared for his visit with the Khasi Hills Unitarians after a decade of correspondence with Hajjom Kissor Singh. The rugged nature of the Michigander's actual trip through the hills was something Sunderland could not have anticipated, however. En route from Bombay he passed through Calcutta for only a day or two and pressed on to Assam for a three-week journey among the Khasi Hills Unitarians. Travelling by boat up the Brahmaputra for three days and two nights, he finally reached Gauhati and continued up the mountain road by horse-drawn carriage. He was warmly received by Robin Day and a number of the Khasi Unitarians in Shillong on his first day there, both with Brahmo leaders and members of the Unitarian community.[34]

Sunderland was at once impressed by the Khasis. Visiting the Unitarian School, later named in his honor as the first "European" to visit the Unitarian community, he learned of their strong desire for an American or British missionary. Because of the sudden death of H. K. Singh's mother, the leader and founder of the Unitarian movement did not meet Sunderland until the latter went to Jowai, Singh's home village. On January 10, Sunderland, although suffering serious back pains, began an arduous journey through the mountains to visit Unitarians in four or five Khasi Hills communities. Riding the thirty-three miles to Jowai on horseback, he was deeply moved by the beautiful mountain scenery sharply in contrast with the flat dryness he had seen through North India. Two days later, at

Jowai, Sunderland met with Singh and the Reverend David Edwards, a Khasi convert from Methodism and the only seminary-educated Unitarian among the Khasis. Edwards served the small congregation at Mowkaiwow where Sunderland would visit on the trip out to Raliang. These three, with other Unitarian followers, worshipped together daily while discussing the needs of the Khasi mission programs.[35]

The two-day journey from Jowai to Nongtalong was undoubtedly the highlight of Sunderland's visit among the Khasis. H. K. Singh, David Edwards, and three others, in addition to nine accompanying servants, made up the party covering the difficult terrain. Sunderland commented pointedly that it took three or four servants in India to do the work that one would in America. Over the roughest cliffs, Sunderland rode in a *thappa*, that is, he was carried in a special basket on the back of one of the servants. This he at times found so frightening that he preferred to take the risks of climbing over the rocky cliff terrain himself. On this leg of the trip, Singh traced for Sunderland, as he had in earlier correspondence, his conversion from Methodism, the impact of William Ellery Channing's "Unitarian Christianity Most Favorable to Piety" upon his thought, and the helpfulness of Charles Dall in providing more Unitarian materials.

Nongtalong, the destination of the treacherous two-day climb, was the first village where Khasi Unitarians had gathered in worship some ten years earlier. There the Polang family had kept the community together despite harrassment by followers of Khasi traditional religion and some zealous Methodists. On Saturday, January 18, 1896, in the tiny church at Nongtalong, Singh and Sunderland led a council to ordain David Edwards formally into the Unitarian ministry.[36]

The impact of Jabez Sunderland upon the simple Khasi Unitarian community has continued to the present day. The school at Kench's Trace, Shillong, has been named after him and although he has been all but forgotten by the American Unitarianism that he served most of his life, he is remembered today as a patron saint, 10,000 miles from his home by a generation of people who never met him.

Sunderland wrote in his diary that he too had learned much from the Khasis:

> I find in these simple, earnest, warmhearted, hardworking, in their way intelligent and manly people much that attracts me. Their warmth of feeling towards me was very touching. They clung to me

> and could hardly let me go. And I confess it was with much feeling I parted with them. . . I have had so much to do from the first with starting the Unitarian movement among them that they seem to me almost like my children.[37]

Supporting the Khasis' desire to have a foreign missionary in their midst, Sunderland strongly believed that in order to gain the respect of the Government and to compete with Catholics and Methodists, a missionary should be sent. Thus, where the Madras community never succeeded in obtaining a full-time foreign worker, Khasi Unitarians have had a nearly continuous record of British Unitarian assistants including the late Margaret Barr who spent thirty-four years among the Khasis.

Negotiations With The Brahmos

The last weeks of Sunderland's Indian visit were spent in Calcutta essentially to study conditions in the Brahmo Samaj in order to discern what future the organization might have. After settling in at the India Club, Sunderland first attended a service of the Sadharan Brahmo Samaj, the mainstream faction which had broken with Keshub Sen after the Kuch Behar marriage in 1879.[38] Later the same day, Sunderland was guest at the home of a son of Debendranath Tagore, in a gathering of representatives of all three branches of the Samaj for a purely social event with music and readings from Rabindaranath Tagore's early poetry. This same day, Sunderland went home with Protap C. Mazumdar for tea, and together they went to visit Keshub's home and tomb.[39]

At the New Dispensation (Navavidhan) service Sunday evening, Sunderland was aware of the sharply differing Vaisnava influences at work in contrast to the Sadharan chapters that he had previously visited. "Just an hour given," he wrote in his diary, "to wild singing, chanting, beating a kind of drum, clanging cymbals, blowing conch shells, swaying body, hands and dancing." On January 27, a service with participants from all three Samajes was held at the home of Debendranath Tagore and seemed to indicate that Sunderland's presence as the first Unitarian clergyman in Calcutta since Charles Dall's death a decade earlier was a symbol of unity. Though Sunderland continued to attend *sankirtan* at the New Dispensation, and to have dinner with A. M. Bose, President of the Sadharan Samaj, he also continued his presence at joint receptions and ceremonies.

The time for discussions about unity in the Brahmo Samaj was ripe. Professor P. K. Roy proposed that regular services be conducted in English with a Unitarian missionary who could help strengthen the Samajes from an organizational and business standpoint. He also suggested that Brahmos might attend Oxford or Meadville seminaries to prepare for leadership, a program that would slowly develop during the next decades.[40]

On February 2, Sunderland noted in his diary that:

> Many here feel that the Brahmo Samaj is passing through a crisis. (1) Its old leaders are passing away; (2) The Samaj is divided; (3) There is no leader as there used to be under Rammohun Roy and Keshub Chunder Sen; (4) There is a great revival of Hinduism; (5) Theosophy which is hostile to the Samaj is flourishing here under Mrs. Besant (now here) and others.

This latter point was of greatest concern to Sunderland. He commented that Annie Besant was that very week in Calcutta lecturing on theosophy but also advocating caste and Hinduism "in its nearly or quite full form." This, he said, would do much harm, turn people back "to their old superstitions," and stop the reform movement. "Vivekananda," Sunderland declared, "is doing the same."[41]

Sunderland's assertions about Brahmo divisions and the leadership situation was largely unfamiliar to American Unitarians of his day. Except for P. C. Mazumdar's visit to America in 1893, a visit largely taken up by his activities at the Parliament of Religion and with the Lowell Lectures, the American Unitarian Association had had little contact with the Brahmos since the deaths of Dall and Keshub in the mid-1880s. Hence the British Unitarians had sent Sunderland specifically with the charge of investigating the Brahmo situation.

What is especially interesting about Sunderland's comments on Theosophy and Vivekananda is that he had encountered both Vivekananda and Mazumdar at Chicago in 1893. Vivekananda had received far more publicity, though Mazumdar had been appointed to the Program Committee through Unitarian efforts. His 1893 visit and his subsequent support had come from Unitarians as well. Sunderland's support of the Brahmos over against these two other surging religious forces was almost sectarian in its determination; however, it was also based firmly in Sunderland's social-ethical-theistic orientation which he had so clearly articulated in his reflective statement about "The

Issue in the West." Although Vivekananda's movement had a social service emphasis to it, and the British Annie Besant's "Hindu" ideas were certainly "theistic," both contained elements of mysticism and asceticism not in keeping with Sunderland's feelings about the nature of religious experience. The New Dispensation Brahmo Samaj also had its emphasis in Vaisnava devotional mysticism (bhakti), but it had had its roots in the rational reform movement of Rammohun Roy and its development in the progressive social reform of Keshub Sen before the latter had turned to asceticly-oriented devotionalism. The later phase of Keshub's career and the attitudes expressed in it Sunderland clearly disliked. Writing in his diary while reading the English works of Keshub, he wrote,

> There was a quality of real genius in him. But he was ambitious, égotistical and unbalanced! So it seems to me. If he had only been humble, unselfish, as sane and wise as he was brilliant, what a work he might have done! To what a height he might have lifted the Brahmo Samaj movement, instead of leaving it divided, distracted, almost ruined by his insane follies.[42]

Sunderland's bias and the limits of his understanding are clarified by these remarks. Though he sincerely wished to work out a settlement among the three samajes, his personal bias favored the Sadharan, or Progressive Samaj, the branch which stood in the middle between Tagore's Adi Samaj and Keshub's Navavidhan. Yet Sunderland's relations with Protap Mazumdar were cordial and understanding. This points up the differences between Keshub and his cousin Protap, but also it points up how Protap was capable of planting his feet in two directions: the bhakti asceticism of Keshub (though he was clearly neither a supporter nor instigator of it) and the more rational social-ethical orientation of English and American Unitarianism.

Protap, for example, even as a "left-wing" representative of the New Dispensation, was appointed Secretary of the Brahmo Samaj Committee formed at Sunderland's request. The basic object of the newly-founded committee was to overcome the petty rivalries in the Samaj and urge cooperation at levels of mutual interest. Furthermore, the committee would seek "to establish practical methods of cooperation . . . (with) the British and Foreign Unitarian Association."[43]

In letters between Sunderland and Protap written after Sunderland's return to England, the purpose and desire of cordial relations between Brahmos and Unitarians was fortified. How different this spirit was from that expressed twenty-five years earlier at the time Charles Dall declared himself a "Christian Brahmo" and the editor of *The Indian Mirror* did what he could to read Dall out of the movement! Writing that every day he had spent in Calcutta, even in India, had reassured him of the common cause Brahmos and Unitarians had, Sunderland asserted,

> Our faith is the same, our ideals are the same, our spirit is the same. Our names differ. But in what we are endeavouring to be and do we are one. Even in the matter of the spiritual leadership of Christ, I find, somewhat to my surprise, that there is practically no difference. While our Brahmo brethren hold, with us, that Christ was man, simply and only, I find that most of them hold as strongly as we do, that he is the greatest of the world's prophets and religious teachers . . . who has done more than any other to "show us the Father" and to win men to a holy life.[44]

At an organizational level, Sunderland made eight proposals, five of which were quickly pursued by the new joint Brahmo Samaj committee. These included urging British Unitarians to send a missionary who would work to promote Brahmoism and unity among Brahmos rather than re-establish a competing Unitarian movement; the creation of a joint Unitarian-Brahmo postal mission emanating from Calcutta; promoting and supervising the sale of Unitarian books in Calcutta; arranging to send young Brahmos to Manchester College, Oxford; and finally, direct financial aid from the British Unitarians to support their missionary and other educational and philanthropic work. The Brahmo Samaj Committee was composed officially of sixteen persons, six each from the Sadharan and Navavidhan and four from the Adi Samaj.[45]

Protap had written both the *Inquirer* and the *Christian Register* praising the work Sunderland had undertaken among the Brahmos. Reflecting in his letter to the *Inquirer* that Sunderland's visit had been anticipated by many who feared either that he was an evangelical missionary or that he was a secular universalist, Protap stressed how

> by his genial sympathies, broad culture, and genuine religiousness, he has proved that an enlightened Christian and an enlightened Hindu are very like and very close to one another, though certainly not the same. . . His whole testimony has been accepted by the whole Brahmo Samaj without a dissentiate voice so far.[46]

A committee such as Sunderland's presence had stimulated would have had no chance of success before he had come. He would make the ideal missionary but, failing the possibility of his return to India, Protap asked the British Unitarians to find a man of equal stature. Calling also for support in theological education and a post office mission, he concluded his letter by emphasizing that such an arrangement between the Unitarians and the Brahmos would not compromise either or identify one with the other totally.

Unable immediately to find a minister who would go to India for three years, the British Unitarians agreed to send the Reverend James Harwood on a lecturing tour. His visit included Calcutta and the Khasi Hills. While his stay in India was only for four months, it reconfirmed Sunderland's commitment to the Brahmos made the previous year. British Unitarians knew of the interest in their work simply from letters received. In 1896 alone they shipped 685 books and 12,429 tracts directly to persons in India requesting material.[47]

The first recipient of the hundred-pound British Unitarian annual scholarship to Manchester College went to Promotho Lall Sen, nephew of Keshub. Subsequent recipients were such notable Brahmo figures of the twentieth century as Bipin Chunder Pal, Hem Chunder Sarkar, and V. R. Shinde of Poona. When the British and Foreign Unitarian Association voted in its annual meeting of May, 1896, to support the Sunderland-Mazumdar requests, they could not know the significance of their action for a temporary renewal of the Brahmo Samaj and for the specific contribution it would make to three major Indian leaders of the coming decades.

However, the impact of Jabez Sunderland's journey to India went far beyond a revitalization of the Brahmo Samaj and a scholarship program in England for Brahmos. The impact of openness and interchange, following two years after the more idealistic and grandiose World Parliament of Religions, meant that acculturation was truly possible. Not only were Brahmos more responsive to Western religious liberalism, but American and English Unitarians as a result of Mazumdar visits and the Sunderland lectures upon his return, were also far more sensitive and informed. The hostilities of Charles Dall's later years seemed to have passed.

Two years later Sunderland retired from Ann Arbor, served a brief, unsuccessful ministry in Oakland, California, and a year in London before accepting a call to the church in Toronto where, coincidentally, William Adam and Charles Dall had served before him. Throughout these years as well as during subsequent ministries in Hartford, Connecticut, and Ottawa, Ontario, Sunderland lectured regularly on Indian religions, on the Brahmo and Arya Samaj reform movements, and on Christian missions in general. While still in Ann Arbor, he published the tract, "Christian Missions in India,"[48] his first of many indictments of Western and Christian influences in the subcontinent. In 1903, he published in *Unity* "Missionary Work in the Unitarian Churches,"[49] calling for a missionary spirit beyond the usual sectarian spirit.

The highlight of Sunderland's continuing concern for India was an article which appeared in the *Atlantic Monthly* for October 1908, "The New Nationalist Movement in India."[50] This was a popularized version of a pamphlet published a few years earlier, "The Causes of Famine in India"[51] which had offered considerable detail and statistics on famines in India under British rule. The *Atlantic* article made Sunderland's sharp indictment of British rule in India accessible to a broad American intelligentsia for the first time. From 1901 to 1906 he had lived in Toronto, actively engaged as a minister in community and university affairs. His sensitivity to the situation in which Indians found themselves had been heightened by his travels through India, his activities with the Indian National Congress and the National Social Conference whose newspapers and publications he had continued to receive, his continuing correspondence with Indians, and his living in Canada.

The initial argument of Sunderland's article was to compare the status of Canada and Australia, virtually "republics," to India with "no self-government, no representation; ruled absolutely by Great Britain."[52] From the Magna Carta to the present status of Canada and Australia, he argued, Britain had followed a principle of freedom and self-rule, a lesson she bitterly learned during the American revolution. Why has Britain followed a different principle with her dependencies, he queried

> Is another and different principle to be adopted here? Are there peoples who it is just to rule without their consent? Is justice one thing in England and Canada and another in India?[53]

Sunderland could find no real justification for why England

was in India since, unlike America, India was not an empty land to be settled and developed, but a fully populated nation which had been served by highly organized governments and religious cultures long before England had developed beyond tribal stage. Lord Curzon himself, speaking at the Delhi Durbar in 1901 had said that "India has left a deeper mark upon history, the philosophy, and the religion of mankind, than any other terrestrial unit in the universe." In the same address, Lord Curzon had also said that Britain's principal strength in India was the "faithful attachment and service of the Indian people." "British statesmen never tire of boasting," Sunderland commented,

> of "our Indian Empire"; and of speaking of India as "the brightest jewel in the British crown." Do they reflect that it is virtually a slave empire of which they are so proud; and that this so-called brightest jewel reflects no light of political freedom?[54]

Offering then an interpretation of the causes of the incipient nationalist movement for the American public, Sunderland cited poverty, famine, taxation, government bureaucracy, and military expenditures as the principal causes for the degradations suffered by India and her people. The benefits of British rule Sunderland saw largely in the palatial buildings, the railway stations, and the new physical facilities in India, facilities serving mainly the British themselves.

Famines, particularly rampant in the last quarter of the nineteenth century, and the millions of deaths resulting from them, were caused by more long-term inflicted poverty than anything else. With ninety percent of the population agricultural ryots or peasants, surviving on meager earnings and taxed a third of their incomes to support a government which did not serve them, it was no wonder that millions would starve in a famine when they could not afford to feed themselves even in years of plenty. The true cause of famines was not lack of rain, therefore, but poverty. Britain was practicing outright robbery in India, Sunderland declared, a practice which the English had deplored among the Romans in Egypt and Gaul and among the Spanish in America and Holland.

Sunderland offered suggestions for alleviating poverty in India. Lighten taxation. Reduce "unnecessary and illegitimate military expenses." "Stop the drain of wealth to England." Recognizing that these suggestions would serve the Indian interest but that India was powerless to do anything to her situation, Sunderland struck out in his strongest indictment against the British, writing,

> It is hard to conceive of a government farther removed from the people in spirit or sympathy than is that of India. There has been a marked change for the worse in this respect within the past twenty-five years, since the vice-regal term of Lord Ripon. The whole spirit of the Government has become reactionary, increasingly so, reaching its culmination in the recent administration of Lord Curzon.[55]

Sunderland contended, in 1908, that talk of self-rule was considered treason. The governmental bureaucracy, efficient as it might be, did not meet the needs of the people. As to the argument given that Indians were incapable of ruling themselves, what an indictment this was against England, he asserted. How could 150 years of English rule make Indians less capable of ruling themselves than in the centuries before the English came? True, the English hegemony emerged during a vacuum of power, "But everything indicates that if India had not been interfered with by European powers, she would have," Sunderland concluded, "soon been under competent governments of her own."

In the matter of education there had been virtually no improvement. While under princely rule, the states of Madras and Baroda had been spending far more, with the latter offering compulsory education. In contrast, British India offered only poor quality education to one boy in ten and one girl in 144. It appears, though Sunderland did not mention it, that the situation had not changed much since William Adam's appraisal nearly seventy-five years earlier.

CHAPTER TWELVE

Politics and the Pulpit: Sunderland as a Social Crusader

Sunderland's political yet religiously and ethically motivated public indictment of British rule in India was a prelude to a second career. In 1908, the year of the *Atlantic* article, Sunderland was sixty-six years old. During the next two decades he became a leading American spokesman for the Indian nationalist movement, aiding nationalists in exile, publishing books banned in India, supporting the cause of freedom for India wherever and whenever he could. What began for him as a journey seeking out information on Unitarianism and the Brahmo Samaj as a delegate of the British Unitarians became a fervent political crusade. If Sunderland went to India in 1895 with a feeling of sympathy for her people, he returned with a deep involvement with her people and her leaders at several levels, righteously committed to publicizing the just rights of Indians to the American public.

On his return from India, Sunderland began regularly and extensively lecturing about what he had accomplished, about his contacts with the Brahmo and Arya Samaj movements, Indian religion, and political issues as well. Serving as minister of the Unitarian church in Toronto from 1901 to 1905, Sunderland was outspoken both in the press and in the pulpit in his opposition to British colonialism. As early as November 1904, he was quoted in the Toronto *Star* denouncing the "race prejudice, superficiality and arrogance" of imperialism in Asia.[1] A week later, the Toronto *World* reviewed Sunderland's *Causes of Famine* in which Sunderland's statement that "India is an orange England is sucking dry" was prominently featured.[2]

In 1905, Benoydranath Sen, the nephew of Keshub Chunder Sen, whom Sunderland had met in Calcutta in 1895, came to North America to deliver a lecture sponsored by the Philosophy Department of the University of Toronto. Benoydranath was described by Sunderland as one of the "Mazumdar" faction of the Brahmos but "more socially liberal." In his Toronto lecture, Benoydranath demonstrated the impact of acculturation on what could best be described as a fourth-generation Brahmo by discussing the "contest" between the Vedas and "Western Religions." Explaining that the West had brought freedom of inquiry and rationalism to India, he then enumerated the Indian responses in five categories: (1) traditionalists, (2) radical rationalists exemplified by "Young Bengal" who stood far apart from the masses of people, (3) a group between these two "who perpetuate what they believe to be good" and strive to rid India of evils, (4) the eclectics (not further defined), and (5) groups advocating harmony or "organic unity" such as the New Dispensation church, a group going beyond mere eclecticism.[3]

While this speech was not especially noteworthy in the overall annals of Brahmo-Unitarian relations, it did point up Benoydranath Sen's perception of religious developments in India and also served, as did his entire tour, to reinforce the work already undertaken by Sunderland during the past decade. By 1906, Sunderland's records show that the British and Foreign Unitarian Association was successfully carrying on a postal mission from Calcutta under the leadership of Brahmo Hem Chander Sarkar. During the last six months of 1905, the mission had received 175 requests from Brahmo chapters and public libraries for materials. At Allahabad, Ramanda Chatterjee, later a close friend of Sunderland's as editor of the renowned *Modern Review*, had processed more than one thousand requests for books and tracts supplied by the British Unitarians. Two new tracts were aimed at Muslims and translated into Urdu.[4] More than a thousand copies of these had been distributed among "educated and liberal minded Mohammadans" while the noted V. R. Shinde had also distributed 1,739 Brahmo and Unitarian books in the Bombay area. For the first time it appeared that Brahmos and Unitarians were cooperating to spread a message of mutual concern well beyond the traditional Calcutta area, without the competitiveness and acrimony experienced during Charles Dall's ministry.

But Sunderland had already begun to turn his attention to social and political matters. Clippings in his files tell of the harassment of Indian students in England in 1908 following the period of national agitation in India when the partition of Bengal had taken place. While serving as minister to a church in Hartford, Connecticut, Sunderland joined in the establishment of an India House in New York City to aid Indian students studying in America. He also related himself to the newly-established Society for the Advancement of India, as a Vice-President, while the well-known attorney Myron Phelps served as President with New York's Rabbi Stephen Wise on the

Advisory Council. A letter from Phelps to Sunderland written in July 1908, urged Sunderland to undertake fundraising to promote the publication of an *Indo-American Review.*[5]

Sunderland, despite his perceptive article in the *Atlantic Monthly*, still held certain paternalistic views about India and Indians. In his lecture, "Present Religious Conditions in India," delivered at the Four Corners Club in Hartford on January 15, 1907, he asserted that three influences had awakened India: (1) the impact of Western civilization, (2) "native reform movements among the Hindus, the most important of which is the Brahmo Samaj together with its child, the Arya Samaj," and (3) Christian missions. Sunderland's arguments on the first two areas were natural, logical, and not original. On the third point, he wrote,

> India needs Christianity. India's religions need Christianity; but they need her not as a foe to antagonize and destroy their good. They need her as a friend and helper; as a wiser and stronger sister, to take them by the hand and lead them onward and upward . . . to the realization that God has given prophetic souls in India.[6]

Expressing strong criticism of traditional Christian missionary practices, as he had earlier in his career, Sunderland suggested, "Let Christianity try the experience of going to India in the spirit of Jesus, not to destroy but to fulfill." Though critical of both the missionaries who had converted relatively few Hindus and Muslims, and also of the British whom he deemed responsible for liquor and opium, Sunderland's meaning was in no way clear. He pointed to a few missionaries who "preach less theology and more love," but he never explicitly stated what Christians might do to improve India. At this point, for example, Sunderland did not express the notion that Christian missionaries might assist Indians in gaining independence. The relationship of Christian clergymen in America to the campaign for independence would not emerge until the 1920s.

The Role and Involvement of Poet Rabindranath Tagore

It would be an error to suggest that the bulk of Sunderland's concern with India prior to World War One was political. During the period from 1905 to the time of his second trip to India late in 1912, he worked diligently to maintain his contacts with both the Brahmo Samaj and the Khasi Hills Unitarians. In 1912, he worked diligently to maintain his contacts with both the Brahmo Samaj and the Khasi Hills Unitarians. In 1912, the fifty-year-old Bengali poet, Rabindranath Tagore, youngest son of the Adi Brahmo Samaj leader Debendranath Tagore, made the first of five visits to the United States. At the time this most famous of the Tagores was born in 1861, the young Keshub Chunder Sen was working closely with his father in the Brahmo movement and living in the Tagore home.[7] While the magnetic impact of Keshub must have worked more fully on Tagore's older brothers, the similarity of such ideas as the significance of Asia's message for the West, very much a part of Tagore's lectures in England and America and of Keshub's later preaching, cannot be ignored. After the split between the older Tagore and the social reformer Keshub Sen in 1866 and even more after the second Brahmo split in 1879 following Keshub's declaration that he was "an inspired prophet," the interaction between the young poet and Sen undoubtedly diminished.

In 1906, Rabindranath's son, seeking to choose a university where he could study agriculture, decided to attend the University of Illinois. In 1912, when Rabindranath travelled to England in search of a cure for a severe case of hemmorrhoids, he continued his journey, attracted by the possibility of a homeopathic cure in America, and spent several months living in Urbana with his son.[8]

While en route to America, Rabindranath stopped in England where he was introduced to the Irish poet William Butler Yeats who on reading a translation of Tagore's *Gitanjali* arranged to have it published in England and America. The poetry book was such an instant success in both countries that Tagore, who later in 1913 would receive the Nobel Poetry Prize for the work, was already well-known when he arrived in the United States.

One scholar has suggested that the months Tagore spent in the Midwestern university town of Urbana may have provided the kind of positive experience the big Eastern cities did not, and indeed, may have stimulated his first thoughts of the university he was to establish in Bengal at Santiniketan in 1921. But more significant for his contact with the West was the germ of an idea — that Tagore might be one way through which the ideas of India could be introduced constructively to the West. Swami Vivekananda and Protap Mazumdar had already started such a project in 1893, but as the struggles of Jabez Sunderland had already made clear, the American public knew and appreciated very little of what India had to offer.[9]

Tagore's first significant contact with Unitarianism took place during his months in Urbana. Again the acculturation motif enters the picture for in Urbana Tagore was invited to lecture on Sunday evenings at the local Unitarian church where the Reverend Mr. Vail had a comparative religions study group. It was from these lectures on the Upanishads that Tagore wrote his early religious work, *Sadhana: The Realization of Life*, published in New York in 1913.[10] Tagore was much sought after during his stay in the United States. He refused most invitations to lecture including one sent to him by Sunderland inviting him to the American Unitarian Association's annual meeting. The poet was caught between a desire to communicate with the West and a desire not to be exploited by it.

Both ideologically and practically, Tagore's sentiments were with the international liberal religious cause. In 1915, he was listed as President of the International Congress of Liberal Religions to be held in Bombay, a movement with which Sunderland would be deeply involved during his 1913 visit to India but which would never come to pass due to the First World War. A letter dated June 12, 1913, from Tagore to American Unitarian Association secretary and internationalist Charles Wendte written in London indicated Tagore's intention to attend the 1913 Congress of Religious Liberals held in Paris that year.[11] Earlier he had addressed the National Conference of Religious Liberals in Rochester at Wendte's request on the subject of "Race Conflict."[12]

During Tagore's 1916 trip to America, Sunderland, then active in New York, established contact with the poet and published articles about him in both the *Christian Register* and *Universalist Leader.*[13] By this time, Tagore was addressing huge audiences in places such as Carnegie Hall in New York. But by the time he returned to America in the twenties, his politics were too far left and increasingly in sympathy with the Communist revolution to give him much of a hearing either among Unitarians or any other significant audience.

Tagore is probably best remembered by English Unitarians for his Hibbert Lectures, "The Religions of Man," delivered at Manchester College, Oxford, in 1930. These lectures, published six times, expressed with a clarity of vision Tagore's understanding of the creative spirit in human and divine, of the religious prophet, the artist, and the mystic. The substantive final chapter set forth Tagore's view of the traditional Hindu four states of life and summed up his universalism and idealism.

> For this fourfold way of life India attunes man to the grand harmony of the universal, leaving no room for untrained desires of a rampant individualism to pursue their destructive career unchecked, but leading them on to their ultimate modulation in the Supreme.[14]

Sunderland's International Concerns

A growing interest in missionary outreach and inter-religious dialogue had been developing in the American Unitarian Association since the Parliament of Religions in 1893. Protap Mazumdar had returned to Boston in 1900 for the seventy-fifth anniversary of the American Unitarian Association held in conjunction with the newly-formed International Congress of Liberal Religion. This organization held some six meetings in Europe and America between 1900 and 1913. At the same time, the American Unitarian Association had established new contacts in Japan and the Philippines. After Sunderland's first trip both British and American Unitarian interest in India and the Far East was high. Professor Francis Greenwood Peabody of Harvard Divinity School reported on his journey as Billings Lecturer to Japan to a meeting of the "First Unitarian Missionary Conference" held November 11 and 12, 1913. Sunderland, as second Billings Lecturer, himself en route to India via Japan and China, was not, however, present.

Sunderland's message to the conference had already been published by the American Unitarian Association in the form of a pamphlet, "The World Mission of the Unitarian Faith." Here Sunderland articulated more clearly than he had previously his understanding of Unitarian outreach. "I believe that the liberal faith by its very nature is calculated for humanity as a whole," he wrote, "that its principles are world principles, that its gospel is a world gospel, that its ideals are ideals for all men."[15] Refuting those Unitarians who would insist that Unitarians had no duty to carry the message of modern Christianity "to other lands," Sunderland went into considerable detail on the expenditures of other denominations for foreign missions.

> All the history of the world shows that no religious body can live shut up within itself. 'To give is to live, to deny is to die.'[16]

Citing the positive effect missionary outreach had had on orthodox Protestantism, Sunderland suggested that Unitarians had suffered a great loss because they had not undertaken a dynamic missionary program. Quoting American Unitarian Association internationalists Reverend Charles Wendte and Samuel Crothers, Sunderland made plain his paternalism yet openness to expand liberalism among men of other faiths. "It is the service we can render to the peoples of the world who need us. We are not our own. We belong to God and our Brother."[17]

> Our aims are not aggression but fraternity. . . Our wish is to carry to non-Christian peoples a form of Christianity which is world-wide in its sympathies. . . We go not to destroy such venerable historical religions as Buddhism, Hinduism, Confuscianism or even Mohammedism, but to assist such of their followers to improve them, to purify them, to reform them, to let shine upon them the light of modern knowledge, and thus purge away their superstitions and their lower elements, and lift them up to the level of their own best teachings.[18]

The conclusion of Sunderland's views was to justify fully Charles Dall's earlier mission in India. Asserting that American Unitarians had never fully appreciated what Dall had done to spread Unitarian educational principles and literature without establishing churches, as such, Sunderland pointed to the fact that Dall's portrait hung in the Calcutta Town Hall "and was pointed to as that of one of the best friends that India ever had."[19] In addition, Sunderland cited the remarkable development of Unitarianism among the Khasis and the strong impression he had that Unitarians would be welcome throughout the Muslim world as further evidence for developing a major Unitarian mission movement in Asia.[20]

The Billings Lectures: Return to India

It was thus that Sunderland departed from Ottawa during the summer of 1913, appointed as American Unitarian Association Billings Lecturer to Japan, China, the Philippines, Ceylon, and India. The series began in Japan in October 1913 and terminated in India in February 1914. Sunderland was also specifically asked to investigate the possibilities of a Congress of World Faiths to be held in India in connection with an "around the world pilgrimage" sponsored by the American Unitarian Association for 1915. Printed publicity accompanying Sunderland described three series of lectures he was to offer: (1) "Religion in the Light of Modern Knowledge" including one lecture on "Liberal Religion as a World Movement." (2) Religion and Evolution, including one lecture entitled, "The Bible, Jesus and Christianity in the Light of Evolution." (3) "Great Writers of England and America," including lectures on Americans; Emerson, Longfellow, and Abraham Lincoln.[21]

Sunderland's second stay in India was considerably shorter than his first: it followed on an organizationally successful trip to Japan and China. Arriving in Calcutta on December 4, 1913, direct from Hong Kong, Sunderland was met by Brahmos M. G. Maitra, Principal of the Brahmo College, Shivanath Sastri, leader of Sadharan Brahmo Samaj, and Ramananda Chatterjee. Chatterjee had corresponded with Sunderland as early as 1907 from his former home in Allahabad, informing the American of his new role as editor of the *Modern Review* and soliciting articles from Sunderland. In 1909, Chatterjee had moved the journal to Calcutta where it would play an increasingly important role in the national movement. Sunderland would continue to publish articles in it, some appearing until late in 1936.

On this second journey, Sunderland seems to have packed in more meetings with high-level nationalist figures than during his first journey; his dinner with Gokhale at P. K. Roy's is a good case in point. The national movement had progressed considerably since 1896; Sunderland's known sympathies for it certainly facilitated his meetings with the major figures. There was no time for a visit to the Khasis this time, however, for Sunderland wanted to reach Karachi by December 21 for the start of the all-India Theistic Conference where he would have to make his essential contacts for the coming World Congress.[22]

The train trip from Calcutta to Lahore took one week. En route Sunderland stopped two days at Aligarh in the western United Provinces. There he visited with Principal Ahmad of the Anglo-Oriental Muslim College, founded a generation earlier by the noted Sir Sayyid Ahmad Khan, the liberal Muslim reformer of the late nineteenth century. Charles Dall, in correspondence with the American Unitarian Association as early as 1866, had taken note of Ahmad Khan's potential as an ally for Unitarianism.[23] Had Dall not been so much at odds with

English Unitarianism after his 1861 visit there, a far better relationship might have developed during Sayyid Ahmad Khan's year in England, 1869-70. While English Unitarians pursued Keshub Chunder Sen with great vigor, they seem to have been totally oblivious to Ahmad Khan's presence.[24] Sunderland's visit does not appear to have led to any new rapproachment between the college at Aligarh and either English or American Unitarianism, but the visit gave evidence of Sunderland's increasing concern for and interest in Islam and Muslim problems.

Although Sunderland's primary concern was to see the establishment of an international religious congress grow out of the Karachi meeting, he was also concerned about broadening cooperation beyond obvious Brahmo support. He appears to have at least received a commitment from the Arya Samaj he described as "a progressive and growing theistic body in the Northwest." In making this laudatory statement, Sunderland was obviously referring to the political and social teaching of the anti-caste, anti-British Samaj and not to its fundamentalist religious teachings. It was among the anti-British Samaj that Sunderland made his initial personal contact with Arya leader Lajpat Rai, with whom he was soon to work closely in New York. Similarly, he made contacts with Sikhs, Parsees, Theosophists, and other liberal Hindus and Muslims as well as a good number of Orientalist scholars. Among these were Professor Bhandarkar of Poona, whom Sunderland had met in 1895; Dr. J. C. Bose, the eminent Indian scientist who had twice lectured in America; the Principals of leading Brahmo, Arya, and Muslim colleges; the Muslim Justice Imam of the Calcutta High Court; and the poet Rabindranath Tagore. Furthermore, Sunderland obtained a commitment of funds from the Maharajahs of Kuch Behar, Pithipuram, and Baroda, who were all known to be sympathetic with progressive religious movements.[25]

Sunderland had made it clear to the Indians whose commitments he received that the goals of the Congresses were to be these:

> One was the promotion of better acquaintance between the various religions of the world. . . The different religions hold themselves aloof from one another far too much. . . Better acquaintance would do much to remove these jealousies and antagonisms, and to create a feeling of friendship and brotherhood.
> Second, the Congresses were designed to stand for the universal elements in all the religions. . . This would help the different reli-

gions to see how much they have in common.
Third, and most important of all, the Congresses would endeavor to create in all the religions a conviction that they have a great work to do together for the moral uplift of the World. Religion ought to be the world's greatest power for the moral regeneration of men and society.[26]

It is clear from Sunderland's statements of purpose that he had become more of a universalist than ever. The implicit Christian paternalism underlying the tract of 1913 on "The World Mission of Unitarianism" had been transcended in Sunderland's zeal to see these Congresses as a real stepping-stone to world peace and a reduction of social evils. At best, however, his idealism could only appeal to the handful of intellectuals and religious liberals, the kind of people capable of transcending their parochial religious identities. But, the Congresses, interrupted by the war, never were held. Although many American liberals believed with Woodrow Wilson that this was "the war to end all wars," a strong nationalist spirit was abroad in Europe and Asia. Sunderland's activities in New York with Lajpat Rai and other militant nationalists had, in fact, added to the spirit of nationalism opposing his earlier universalist idealism. The new desire for nationalism in India which Sunderland supported could never lead to a lasting peace until political and social issues were resolved.

Sunderland and Indian Nationalism

Jabez Sunderland's growing concern for the internal nationalist developments going on in India greatly increased after his return to America in 1914. That same year Sunderland received an honorary doctorate from Tufts College in Medford, Massachusetts, and moved to an apartment in New York City. He also became minister, at the age of seventy-two, to a small church in Poughkeepsie, New York, to which he commuted by train a few days a week. He remained minister in Poughkeepsie until his eighty-sixth year, retiring to Ann Arbor in 1928.

Although Sunderland's primary connections with India prior to his second trip had been with Brahmos, it was through his connection with the Arya Samaji, Lala Lajpat Rai, and with early anti-imperialist groups in America, that Sunderland first became militantly anti-British and a pro-Indian nationalist. Prior to the publication of his 1908 article in the *Atlantic*

Monthly, Sunderland had been motivated to reply at length to a letter praising British rule in India which had appeared in the Boston *Evening Transcript* in April 1906.[27]

In 1907, Sunderland had aided the founding of a Society for the Advancement of India based in New York and presided over by liberal New York attorney Myron Phelps, who had been active in the earlier anti-Imperialist League movement. While this society only existed for three years, it gained notoriety for an open letter signed by twenty-one members in response to a pro-British-imperialism speech by President Theodore Roosevelt in January 1909. Additionally, Sunderland wrote a twenty-nine-page response to the President's speech. The society's position was far from popular as was made clear from pressures brought to bear against a New York law firm in whose offices the society had held its meetings.[28]

Lala Lajpat Rai, leading spokesman for the Arya Samaj movement and a strong advocate of self-rule for India under British dominion, had visited America in 1905, coming into contact with the Anti-Imperialist League leadership. His extensive writings, critical of the British, in such periodicals as the Lahore *Tribune*, the *Modern Review*, and the *Dayanand Anglo-Vedic College Magazine*, had led to his deportment from India in 1907 along with Ajit Singh, another militant critic. Arrested and deported without trial on the basis of a law promulgated almost a century earlier under the East India Company, the action against Lajpat by the Government of India was a foreboding of the extremely tense situation to come to India following the War. Although Lajpat Rai returned to India for a short period at the time that Sunderland first met him at the Karachi Congress in December 1913, he soon departed for Japan and finally decided to return to the United States via the Pacific in December 1915.[29]

In California, Lajpat Rai wisely kept his distance from the Indian immigrants, mostly Sikh, belonging to the radical Ghadr organization. The Ghadrs, while attempting to foment revolution in India against the British, had expressed strongly pro-German sympathies throughout the war. After almost six months on the West Coast, Lajpat Rai arrived in New York on May 20. His presence was quickly made public by his letter of May 31 to the *New York Times*, in which he compared the Indian situation to the situation in Ireland which was already receiving widespread support in America. A later response by the *Times*, however, indicated that, though the paper had published his letter, it was not in agreement with Rai's position.[30]

Only one of many persons of Indian origin placed under surveillance during the war, as the result of an agreement between the British and American governments, Lajpat Rai worked actively nonetheless in the cause of Indian self-rule, garnering support of the liberal-left journals such as the *New Republic*, *The Nation*, and later *Unity* as well. Particularly helpful to Lajpat Rai was Professor Edwin Seligman of Columbia University who served as President of the New York Ethical Society from 1908 to 1921. Through Seligman, the Arya leader was able to arrange numerous lecture engagements and thereby to meet with Indian students and immigrants throughout the country.[31]

Sunderland had already made public his support of Lajpat Rai through an article on the Arya Samaj published in the *Universalist Leader* during September 1915. Writing in moderate tones, Sunderland pointed out that loyalty of Indians to India was not to be taken as disloyalty to the British. Crediting the Arya Samaj and its leaders with educating their younger generation and fostering in it a spirit of independence, Sunderland suggested that the British would have to learn that Indians only wanted the kind of status for themselves that Australians and Canadians now enjoyed.[32]

Sunderland's role in this pre-Gandhian stage of the Indian self-government movement took its most important turn in the founding of the Home Rule League of America on October 22, 1917. Based in a Broadway office building with Lajpat Rai as President and prominent Indians Narayan Subrao Hardiker and Keshava Deva Shastri as joint secretaries, a first election held by the membership in January, 1918 made Sunderland Vice-President and a member of the board of seven councillors. The organization's chief aim was to promote the cause of self-rule for India. For this purpose, the first issue of the journal, *Young India*, was distributed in January 1918. The publication survived for three years, with Sunderland as its editor during the last year. Throughout the three years, however, Sunderland contributed fifteen articles to the journal and came to symbolize the "American" half of the phrase "Indo-American" in the organization's by-laws.[33]

From the first issue, Lajpat Rai emphasized that neither he nor the Home Rule League had pro-German sympathies.

Despite his disclaimer and his care in associations, he reported in his "Farewell Address" published in the December, 1919, issue of *Young India* that he had constantly been harassed by the Department of Justice, had been followed by detectives, and had had his telephone tapped. There appears to be ample evidence from Department of Justice records that Rai was not exaggerating the situation.[34]

Young India was in financial difficulties from its inception. While Rai and Sunderland could depend for support on such liberals and socialists as Scott Nearing, Norman Thomas, Oswald Garrison Villard of the *Nation*, and publisher Ben Huebsch, there were never enough subscribers. To support the effort one Indian student contributed $175 of his summer earnings while an Indian dinner held at the Civic Club netted another $300 in mid-October 1918. In addition, radical Indian nationalist B. G. Tilak sent $5,000 via a Theosophist returning to America from India.

The first anniversary dinner of the Home Rule League, held November 20, 1918, at the Grand Hotel, was attended by more than 300 persons with speeches by not only Lajpat Rai and Villard but also Sunderland and the Reverend John Haynes Holmes, minister of the Community Church of New York. This appears to have been Holmes's earliest public support of the cause of Indian nationalism, preceding by more than two years his famous sermon on Gandhi. Admitting that he knew little about India apart from what he knew of the Brahmo Samaj movement, Holmes called on the audience not to lament the past but to look to the future "and testify to our firm belief that the people of India are destined to win, as all true people of the world."[35] Holmes placed great confidence in the liberal British mind and in the growing Labour party as a moderate way to approach the self-rule problem. The events of 1919 in India alone would prove him far too idealistic and, like Sunderland, a strong believer that, with the end of the war,

> was coming a new construction of the human race, a recrudescence of the democratic spirit of mankind, as embodied in inter-nationalism in self-dependence of the nations. It is in this world of tomorrow that India will surely come to its inheritance.[36]

Sunderland's speech that evening was far more perceptive and to the point. Noting the appalling ignorance of Americans about India, he credited this ignorance as much to prejudice as to the distance between the two countries. Citing the books of Lajpat Rai, Ramsey MacDonald, and H. W. Nevinson as accurate sources on India and chiding many works written by missionaries which "take a pleasure in upholding British rule in India in its harsh aspects," Sunderland emphasized how "such books give as little truth about the condition of the Indians as any book supposed to deal with the problems and conditions of the slave that was written by a slaveholder."[37] In a subtle reference to Holmes's confidence in British liberals, Sunderland reminded the audience how ineffective "highminded" and courageous Englishmen like Morley had been when faced with the internal civil service bureaucracy which ruled in India. There are two Englands as there are two Americas, Sunderland stressed.

> Today there is an America which is sympathetic with everything that strikes the liberal chord whose heart is in the work for right and justice, and wants to see all peoples including the peoples of India given a chance. This is the America we are of and in which we believe. On the other hand, there is an America that is reactionary, that is in favor of privilege, monopoly, autocracy, and imperialism with all it implies.[38]

Sunderland knew well what lay in store for the League of Nations through American isolationism. He was keenly aware of the growing post-war conservatism dominating American politics and of a similar kind of division in British politics.

Though *Young India* and dinners such as the one at which Holmes and Sunderland spoke only reached those already committed in some measure to the cause, the League's more effective work was in lobbying Congress and through the Indian Information Bureau and Library created in conjunction with the organization itself. While dinners served some propagandistic purposes when covered by the press, it was the effective work of Senators Frank Norris, Joseph France, and A. J. Gronna as well as Congressman William Mason of Illinois which brought the India issue to momentary public attention.[39]

Sunderland and his colleagues, horrified by General Dyer's massacre of some five hundred persons at Amritsar in April 1919, reported on the negative reaction of the American press to the Hunter Commission "whitewash" of the affair. The Indian Information Bureau, with perhaps the most direct pipeline to the Indian viewpoint on what was happening in the Punjab, served to disseminate information on the continuing troubles with the British. Meanwhile, Sunderland and Holmes collaborated on a strong article in *Young India*, "Repression — Road to Revolution," in which they pointed to historic examples of the futility of the kind of repression that the British were now practicing throughout India.[40]

Lajpat Rai's departure from America early in 1920 was a setback to the Home Rule League. Sunderland, who had collaborated with Rai on two books written during Rai's stay,[41] took over both the presidency of the League and the editorial work of *Young India.* At seventy-six, Sunderland was highly esteemed by the league membership but not nearly as knowledgeable as he should have been to carry on the work effectively. The church at Poughkeepsie took time. The truly pressing issue in America for Indians was the continuing harassment and discrimination against them. A new organization, "Friends of Freedom for India," began to take precedence as a defense organization for Indians threatened with deportation or delayed for citizenship clearance.[42] While neither Sunderland nor Holmes was involved in founding the new organization, its concerns became theirs. Taraknath Das, an Indian graduate and Fellow of the University of Washington who had been imprisoned at Leavenworth "for complicity in the California Conspiracy to violate neutrality laws in 1915" before America entered the war, later became a leading member of Holmes's church in New York. In April 1923, *Unity*, now edited by Holmes, published a major article by Iowa State professor Sudhindra Bose, "Indian Barred from American Citizenship," which took strong exception with American discriminatory immigration practices.[43]

India in Bondage

Besides Mohandas Kamcharand Gandhi, whose unusual personality and tactics had the major impact in leading India to independence in 1947, there were many other Indians and non-Indians who preceded Gandhi and also many contemporaries who played a great though far less publicized role in the freedom movement. Lala Lajpat Rai, for example, introduced Gandhi to America through the pages of *Young India* as early as July, 1918.[44] Gandhi became virtually the only figure in the Indian nationalist movement known to most Americans during the twenties and thirties. His role should not be minimized but

Lala Lajpat Rai, in conjunction with Jabez Sunderland, actually did more to build a base of support for the Indian cause in the United States.

During the 1920s Sunderland continued his work for the cause of Indian nationalism and Indian nationals in America through extensive writing and publishing, largely in the American Unitarian publication, *Unity*, and the Indian journal, *Modern Review*, edited since 1907 by Brahmo Ramananda Chatterjee. In 1924, Sunderland's increasingly nationalistic and anti-British bias appeared in his "Open Letter to Mahatma Gandhi and the Indian Congress leaders" on the subject of the forthcoming League of Nations Opium Conference. Crediting the United States with having attempted earlier to place severe limits on production of opium, Sunderland assailed the British, who opposed the limits, for claiming that limits would be "contrary to the desire of the Indian people." Sunderland called on the Indian Congress to send its own representatives to the meeting recognizing that the Indians who had been appointed representatives were as "camouflage" and a "deception" on the part of the British.[45]

The various articles and essays on India Sunderland had been writing during these years resulted in the publication of a 572-page book, *India in Bondage*, published in New York and Calcutta in 1929. When the Indian edition was promptly suppressed by the Government of India. Sunderland received considerable notoriety, including an article in *Time* Magazine.[46] *Time's* sensationalist approach to the issues raised in an equally sensational way by Sunderland's hard-hitting and highly opinionated text pointed up the "ridiculous" extremes to which British policy had gone to India in 1929. How incredible that Ramananda Chatterjee and his printer should be fined 1,000 rupees and sentenced to three months jail on sedition charges for publishing the book of a "snowy-haired upstanding Poughkeepsie clergyman."

> The sedition is supposed to lurk between the pages of the book, *India in Bondage — Her Right to Freedom.* Last week when Poughkeepsie reporters sought out the author, Dr. Jabez Thomas Sunderland, he was ready for them, ready to wield a potent verbal cudgel in defense of the two Indians who sat in a stinking Bengali jail.
>
> Suppressed last week, why was not the book suppressed sooner? It has sold in the thousands for a twelvemonth. A second Calcutta edition appeared last spring.[47]

Sunderland insisted to the press that if Chatterjee was guilty of sedition then so was the whole newly-elected British Labour government and Prime Minister Ramsey MacDonald, whose criticisms of British rule in India under the Conservatives he had quoted extensively in the book. Motivation for suppression, it was thought, might indeed have been these words spoken by MacDonald two years before becoming Prime Minister:

> The moral justification that has always been made for the existence of our empire amongst subject peoples has been that we are training them for self-government. The most typical of that is our Indian empire. A thousand and one reasons are given for a little more tutelage. . . Now plain practical common sense should come to our rescue. *Nobody can imagine that any harm will come from independence. Let independence be granted.*[48]

In effect, *Time* continued, if MacDonald said this two years ago, why cannot India receive her independence now? Describing Sunderland's work as "vital, comprehensive and militantly fair" the article played up Sunderland's sharp criticism of the Rudyard Kipling stereotype of the Indian as "new caught sullen peoples half devil and half child."[49]

Although one might be tempted to say that Sunderland's coverage by *Time* was surely his finest public hour, the culmination in publicity of thirty-five years of concern, a *New York Times* book reviewer was less kind and far more critical of Sunderland's sensationalist approach to India's problems. As he had been completing *India in Bondage*, Katherine Mayo's *Mother India*, a book very much in the Kipling imperialist tradition, had been widely disseminated. Several sharp responses to Mayo had already been written including Lajpat Rai's last major work, *Unhappy India.* While agreeing with the criticisms Sunderland raised in his book about Mayo's work, the *New York Times* said of him,

> In the main that criticism is entirely just. But what our author does not see is that every word applies equally to his own book. After reading it, one who knows the British in India at first hand is inclined to put it aside because the portrait is unrecognizable; just as one is inclined to discount the book he so severely criticizes for exactly the same reason. Mr. Sunderland is hardly conscious of the degree to which his prejudices color his facts.[50]

There can be little doubt that this reviewer could offer a perspective far more objective than the eighty-six-year-old

Poughkeepsie clergyman. Yet Sunderland's work had not gone unnoticed among major Indian figures. Letters of gratitude had come from Gandhi, Ramananda Chatterjee, and the poet Rabindranath Tagore, very much in the Indian tradition of praise. Tagore did not pretend to suggest that Sunderland had been objective when he wrote,

> Such a knight-errant on behalf of those who have been rendered defenseless, makes the name of the West still respected in India in spite of that domination from the West, which has robbed her of freedom and left behind a rankling sense of injustice. The facts, which the Reverend Dr. Sunderland has set down in his book, are impressive. They corroborate the great saying of Abraham Lincoln which he quotes on the title page, — "No nation is good enough to rule over another nation."[51]

Lala Lajpat Rai's sudden death, following a beating that he received under riot conditions in Lahore, deeply saddened Sunderland. His address in honor of Rai, presented before the Civic Club of New York on November 30, 1928, was later published both by the *Modern Review* and by *Unity*. Sunderland's personal attachment to Rai led him to conclude, perhaps rightly, that up to 1928 the Arya Samaj reformer was truly India's national leader, although certainly John Haynes Holmes and others would not have agreed with him.

In his last years, Sunderland was much honored by those who supported his political position on India. In April 1926, the editorial staffs of *The Nation*, *The New Orient* magazine of New York, and *Unity* gave a public reception and banquet in Sunderland's honor at the Aldine Club in New York. In May 1928, the India Society of America did likewise, presenting letters from Gandhi, Tagore, and Rai. In October and November 1928, he served as President of the India Conference of America held for some two weeks in New York. Most significant perhaps was the reception held at Vassar College at the time of Sunderland's ninetieth birthday in 1932. The speaker of the evening was Valabhbhai Patel, a noted figure from the nationalist movement who, while travelling in America, took time to join a final living tribute to Sunderland.

More moving than any of these, however, must have been the Memorial meeting sponsored by the Hindustani Community of New York and held at Holmes's Community Church on August 25, 1936. Participating with songs and prayers from their own traditions were Hindus, Muslims, Sikhs, Christians, Parsees, and Jews. Sunderland was declared by Haridas Mazumdar, who presided over the service, to be a "Maharishi," a great sage, one to whom all Indians whether in America or at home, could look with pride and awe.[52]

The full impact of Jabez Sunderland's career must yet be calculated by a complete biographical study. For the work of Unitarians in India, he marked a sharp turning point between the religious-missionary thrust of nineteenth-century Unitarianism and the socio-political approach of much twentieth-century Unitarianism. It would now remain for John Haynes Holmes to carry this political thrust much further in his relationship with the support of Mohandas Gandhi.

CHAPTER THIRTEEN

John Haynes Holmes and Gandhi: A New Kind of Mission

When John Haynes Holmes, minister of the Community Church of New York, met Mohandas Gandhi in London in 1931, he had already been espousing the cause of *satyagraha* or truth-force for a decade. Holmes's "discovery" of Gandhi had come while reading a journal article about Gandhi's South Africa experiences in the New York Public Library in 1918. He had already become familiar with the activities of Indian nationalists and their sympathizers in New York through Jabez Sunderland. Holmes's career was to be different than Sunderland's, however, and his interest in India was to focus primarily on the figure of Gandhi.

What were the forces leading John Haynes Holmes to Gandhi? Holmes was born in Philadelphia in 1879 but raised in Boston, graduated from Harvard College and the Harvard Divinity School as a Unitarian in 1904. That same year he was ordained to the ministry of the Third Church in Dorchester, Massachusetts, and also was married to Madeleine Hosmer Baker, a member of the Unitarian Church of the Saviour in Brooklyn, New York. In 1907 at the age of twenty-six, Holmes began what was to be a ministry of forty-two years to the congregation of the Church of the Messiah, later recognized as the Community Church of New York.[1]

No one was more keenly aware than Holmes especially when he arrived in New York, of the Edwardian-Theodore Roosevelt "fool's paradise" in which most Americans and Europeans of his time were living. He has described the beginning of his ministry as a time of "sweetness and light" when "nobody wanted to precipitate a quarrel."[2] But Holmes was moving increasingly in the direction of socialism "as the ordered solution of the confusions and injustices of our time."[3] In the midst of his early association with campaigns for legal and social justice, Holmes became an avid reader of current pacifist writers, the most significant of whom was the French Nobel Prize winner, Romain Rolland. Rolland, leader of the peace movement in Europe during World War One and exiled in Switzerland, was to become a major influence and correspondent of Holmes. Unfortunately Holmes twice missed the opportunity to meet with Rolland, who was later a great European supporter of Gandhi. The novelist was early aware of Holmes's outspoken pacifism, for Rolland wrote, in an essay "Free Voices from America," published in August 1917,

> Most notable (among the anti-war ministers of religion) is the pastor of the Church of the Messiah in New York, John Haynes Holmes by name, from whom I had the honor of receiving a magnificent letter in February, 1917, just before the United States entered the war. . . (Mr. Holmes) refuses to exclude any nation from the human community. The Church of the Messiah . . . will not respond to any militaristic appeal. His conscience constrains him to refuse conscription. He will obey his conscience at any cost. 'God helping me, I can no otherwise.'[4]

Holmes had spoken out against the war in Europe as early as 1915 not only negatively but offering a four-point positive program under which he, as a pacifist, would operate. Describing his as a ministry of reconciliation, he vowed to serve his country "in wartime by serving the dream of international brotherhood."[5] Although his freedom of the pulpit was sustained by a vote of the trustees, many objected strongly to Holmes's position and several members resigned from the church. Throughout the war, Holmes was to find relatively little support in New York for his position. It is little wonder then, that when he first discovered Mohandas Gandhi in 1918, Holmes was deeply moved by the Indian's experiences in South Africa.

Reflecting on his discovery of Gandhi through the pages of an article in the British Unitarian *Hibbert Journal* during 1918, Holmes, in fact, made a similar judgment about himself. The article in question had been written by Gilbert Murray and was a study of conscientious objection in wartime as dramatized in the case of Stephen Hobhouse, an English Quaker, who, like Holmes, had remained a staunch pacifist throughout the war. Murray used Gandhi as a point of comparison. He only knew that Gandhi had returned to India from South Africa in 1914 and "that his influence in India (was) now enormous, almost equal to that of his friend, the late Mr. Gokhale."[6]

Murray was both exaggerating and misstating the case. During his first three years back in India, Gandhi had become active in moderate Congress politics and certainly had mourned the early death of moderate leader Gokhale. His primary concerns, however, had been to get an *ashram*, or religious community, organized near Ahmedabad in his native area of Gujerat. Relatively little could be known about Gandhi at this time not only because of his decision to confine much of his work to the area of India where he could speak in the vernacular, but also because, at best, his work seeking out grievances among the peasants of Champaran in a remote area of Bihar in Eastern India (in 1917) was the first major civil disobedience project Gandhi had led.

Erik H. Erikson's major study of Gandhi in relation to the Ahmedabad textile strike of 1918 has pointed out that Gandhi received virtually no coverage in the English language press either in India or in England.[7] As a result, Murray and Holmes could not have known that in April 1915, Gandhi had defended the British war effort at a public dinner in Madras, talking of "the British ideal of liberty." In 1918, he defended the war effort again, saying that Indians should fight so as to win greater respect from the British.[8]

It was Murray's two-page description of Gandhi's non-violent campaign in South Africa over the twenty-year period from 1893 to 1914 "against the white man's government and on behalf of his downtrodden fellow countrymen, dark-skinned coolies" that had singularly impressed Holmes. Jolted out of his pre-war idealism and deeply and morally perplexed by the war situation, Holmes had studied the teachings of Jesus and Christianity on non-violence. He had examined the pacifist sects growing out of the leftwing of the Reformation, notably the Quakers. He had encountered Romain Rolland and through him Tolstoi "who appealed to religion, as Romain Rolland to culture, to make an end to war as foe to every higher interest and nobler ideal of man's life."[9] It was Tolstoi who, with Thoreau and the Jesus of the Gospels, had helped to direct Gandhi to his *satyagraha*, his truth-force for nonviolence in South Africa almost twenty-five years earlier.

John Haynes Holmes's discovery of Mohandas Gandhi and his immediate sense of excitement and commitment to the emerging Indian leader came from his feeling of moral and religious kinship with Gandhi, not out of an immediate understanding or identification with religious, national, or ideological problems of India. With little factual evidence and deep frustration that no one could tell him much about Gandhi, Holmes, less than three years later, preached his famous sermon at the Church of the Messiah, "Who is the Greatest Man in the World?"

The answer, to the amazement of all who heard, was Gandhi!

No one can read *My Gandhi*, written when Holmes was seventy-four years old, without feeling that he deeply needed saints and heroes with whom to identify. It is otherwise difficult to understand why Holmes, possibly with assistance from a younger Gandhi scholar, might not have traced his personal encounter with Gandhi much more in terms of his growing concern for and knowledge about the political situation in India. For example, neither in *My Gandhi* nor in *I Speak for Myself* is there any reference to Jabez Sunderland, Lajpat Rai, Indian nationalist activities in America, or the consistent role which *Unity*, the journal Holmes edited, played as an outlet for information on India not available in most American media. Holmes's collected papers indicate that throughout his entire ministry his interest in India's affairs went far beyond that which he has reported in his autobiography or *My Gandhi*.

In 1919, he published, jointly with Jabez Sunderland, a brief article, "Repression — Road to Revolution," in *Young India*. Developing recent statements of President Woodrow Wilson, Holmes and Sunderland cited the examples of George III and the American revolution down to the current uprisings in Russia in calling for England to cease her suppression of India in the wake of the massacre at Amritsar in April 1919. Arguing that repression only makes public the case against the repressor, and that "men act not so much when their minds are convinced as when their emotions are stirred," the authors went on to state that the unfair repression of one individual leads to feelings of indignation in the dozens of friends and relatives of that person. Equally disasterous, they claimed, was the love for the enemies of a repressive government engendered in the hearts of the repressed. Most serious of all they contended, was that repression "sets the pace for the use of violence."

> When a government refuses to listen to the people, declines to give accused men fair trials, declares that the remedy for political and industrial discontent is the policeman's club or the machine gun, asserts that the place for an agitator or a reformer is in a prison cell — it is simply appealing from reason and justice to force and violence. How can it wonder if its own methods of violence and force are answered by violence?[10]

In this 1919 article, Holmes showed himself willing to stand with the kind of commitment to freedom and justice in the

Indian context in which Sunderland himself had already engaged since his return from India in 1914. Holmes's interest in India also began to show up in the pages of *Unity* as soon as he became editor, following the death of Jenkin Lloyd Jones in September 1918. During the summer of 1918, Sunderland had published two articles in *Unity* directly related to Indian political questions, "Political Conditions in India" and "Is Rabindranath Tagore pro-German?"[11] Throughout 1919, Sunderland published seven "controversial" articles on India in *Unity* attacking the status of untouchables, supression of freedom of the press in India, and "Britain's Carpetbag Government.[12] In 1920, Sunderland published seven more articles about India in *Unity* as well as other articles on women's suffrage, morality, and religion, and a three-part series on William Ellery Channing.

The Gandhi Sermon

In 1921 Holmes and *Unity* publicly presented Gandhi. The week of Holmes's famous Gandhi sermon, Sunderland published the essay "India's Attempted Revolution Without Bloodshed" in *Unity*. As president of the New India Information Center on Broadway, Sunderland had continuing access to possibly the only vernacular and English language nationalist publications coming to the United States from India. Stressing how India had always been a peace-loving nation that "abhors bloodshed," Sunderland wrote, possibly for the first time in an American publication designed for an American audience, of Gandhi's program of "non-cooperation" and "suffering." Sunderland quoted Gandhi at length, about whom he and Holmes could now correctly state, "he" has enormous influence. His word everywhere is:

> We must have no bloodshed. We have a right to our liberty; it is dearer to us than life; we will obtain it or die. But we will do no wrong; we will not kill; we will not hurt our oppressors; we will not even hate them; but we will not cooperate with them in any way, in their work of tyranny and wrong, in their work of carrying on an unjust government in this country which does not belong to them; and thus we will compel them to give us our rights and our freedom.[13]

Here was the statement of Gandhian idealism on which Holmes and Sunderland based their sympathies and feeling for the Indian revolution. Regrettably, the revolution was not to proceed without bloodshed or communalism between Muslims and Hindus. From the start, both men seem to have been largely blind to the political side of Gandhi and to the difficulties he had in keeping easily inflammable urban communities from violence. Gandhian idealism was fine in its own right; but by 1922, violence rather than nonviolence had taken such a toll in India that Gandhi would be forced to call off his national campaign.

Holmes's sermon of April 10, originally published as part of a Community Church sermon series, received only brief reference in *My Gandhi* and in *I Speak for Myself.* Its publication in late April 1921 in two installments in *Unity* has preserved the text of a sermon which Holmes later looked upon as an act of incredible audacity.[14] Opening with an allusion to the Versailles Peace Conference two years earlier, Holmes stated that it was surely there that one would have looked for the "greatest man" in the world in 1919. However, of all those at the peace conference failure, Holmes could cite only General Smuts of South Africa as a man "who saw mankind and not himself in the glass."[15]

Turning away from Versailles to the post-war world, Holmes described three other men whom he believed might well qualify for the position. The first of these was Romain Rolland, the French novelist to whom Holmes already admitted owing much of his ideology. Rolland, Holmes asserted, more than any other man, was responsible for "any civilization . . . any light shining through the gross darkness of the present chaos" in Europe. In sharp contrast to Rolland the idealist, Holmes next cited Lenin the realist, whom he described as the man with the most personal power in the world. Urging his hearers to overcome their prejudices toward Soviet Communism, Holmes cited the *New York Times* as an example of a source which "an unguarded moment . . . referred to him as 'the most remarkable personality that the World War brought into prominence.' " His materialistic successes in Russia impressed Holmes greatly, but his tyrannical methods and lack of "ethical or spiritual principle" would limit Holmes's ability to designate Lenin as the greatest man of that day.[16]

Holmes then turned to his third possibility and his final choice — Mohandas Karamchand Gandhi, a man of whom he had first heard only four years earlier and whose writings he had not directly encountered until shortly before the sermon. Holmes divided Gandhi's career into its South African part up to 1913 and its much shorter Indian period of only eight years. Describing the situation of "color prejudice" practiced in South Africa against the 150,000, mostly indentured laborers in Natal, Holmes then mistakenly stated that Gandhi had been called to South Africa as a lawyer in 1893 to help Indians in the fight for their civil rights. Actually, Gandhi was asked to represent an Indian Muslim merchant in a civil suit. The connection had been made in Gandhi's home city of Porbandar where his older brother served as attorney for the Indian office of the company concerned.

Gandhi had begun his South Africa experience in Durban, not in Johannesburg. He had also realized quickly that all Indians in South Africa were not coolie laborers, nor were they any more united than in India; they spoke different languages and represented not only the Hindus and Muslim populations but also there were Parsees and Christians. Gandhi's commitment to working against color prejudice had come during an incident in which he was violently removed from a first-class train compartment. Holmes quite correctly went on to describe how Gandhi organized the Indian community of Durban into strikes and nonviolent resistance.

Of Gandhi's young independence movement in India, Holmes reported the Mahatma's refusal to move against the British during the war and of British "opression . . . visited upon the Indians" since the war, a tyranny which had led Gandhi into the new noncooperation revolution. About this revolution, Holmes suggested that

> What we have here — under Gandhi's leadership, is a revolution — but a revolution different from any other of which history has knowledge. It is characterized by four distinctive features.[17]

Holmes's first point about the revolution was its intention to free India from alien rule and injustice. Second, Holmes stressed Gandhi's lack of hatred for the British in spite of his unwavering opposition to them. Closely allied to this was the Gandhian policy of *ahimsa* or nonviolence. Going beyond nonviolence, however, Holmes suggested that Gandhi's positive policy of noncooperation practiced on a massive scale among peasants and professionals alike "would little by little bring paralysis to the government as the hemlock brought inch by inch the chill of death to the limbs of Socrates." Finally, Holmes's fourth point in explaining Gandhi perhaps told as much about Holmes's understanding as it did about Gandhi:

> Gandhi seeks the moral and spiritual regeneration of India on the lines of Indian thought, Indian custom and Indian idealism. This means the exclusion, so far as possible of the influence of the west, with its industrial slavery, its materialism, its money worship and its wars. The first step in his endeavor, is to wipe out the barriers which divide the Indians from one another, and make them one great united brotherhood. Thus he seeks the obliteration of caste distinction and religious differences; Mohammedan must live peaceably with Hindu, and Hindu with Mohammedan. Then must come a leadership of mankind with peace and amity. "I believe absolutely," says Gandhi, "that India has a mission for the world." His idealism therefore transcends the boundaries of race and country, and seeks to make itself one with the highest hopes of humanity. "My religion," he cries, "has no geographical limits. If I have a living faith in it, it will transcend my love for India herself."[18]

That Holmes could not yet understand the full context or political manner of Gandhi's program was quite clear from these remarks. He drew from Gandhi, in 1921, the reform, the universalism, and the sense of brotherhood, the pacifism, the conservative rejection of technology, the attempt to bring Hindus and Muslims together. This spoke to the idealism and the realism in Holmes's religious and socio-ethical philosophy. Where one might compare Rolland to Tolstoi or Lenin to Napoleon, Holmes in 1921 was prepared to compare Gandhi to Christ.

Whether fully accurate or not, Holmes's sermon was important somewhat in the way Channing's "Baltimore Sermon" preached 102 years earlier was important for making public the Unitarian cause in America. Holmes's sermon gained wide publicity and it was received with much acclaim in India. One result was that before long Holmes would strike up a correspondence with Gandhi, leading eventually to their two meetings in 1931 and 1947. In America, however, Holmes's sermon was significant because it called public attention to Gandhi, who like Channing before him or Martin Luther King, Jr., after him would become a highly controversial, and at first, little understood figure. If Holmes's pacifism during the war had not stood him in good stead in his church, among the general public, or even among Unitarians, his words of praise for a man who opposed British presence in India and did so by breaking the law, by organizing strikes, and by behaving in unexpected ways, did little more to endear him.

The leading Unitarian internationalist, the Reverend Charles W. Wendte, was by contrast an early public critic of Gandhi's "simple" approaches in an age of complex industrialism. In an essay published in *Unity* during the summer of 1922, "Gandhi and Modern India," Wendte reported on a highly publicized letter which Gandhi had written from prison in Ahmedabad. Wendte believed that the letter clearly revealed that Gandhi's definition of *swadeshi* was "a rejection of modern culture and civilization, and a return to the ancient ideas and institutions of India."[25] Wendte quoted Gandhi's statement of aims and beliefs, denouncing them as "reactionary utterances." Reflecting both progressivist and paternalistic views typical of much religious liberalism of the day, Wendte expressed his natural distaste for Gandhi's approaches:

> They seriously call in question the sanity of his judgements and his fitness to be a leader of his people in their attempts to secure freedom and self-government. There never was a time when the well-informed mind of civilized man was less inclined to a worship of the unintelligent and slavish past, when past sanctions, beliefs, customs and institutions received less reverence or affection, or were so readily surrended for present effectiveness and the ideals and hopes of the future.[19]

Citing positive examples of development in China and Japan, Wendte feared the worst for India were she to "shut out the light of modern intercourse, knowledge, science . . . and to become a nation of peasants only . . . to fall at last a victim to her own oppressors." Wendte believed that India had the right to freedom and independence, but he insisted on the liberal model of Ireland, Australia, or Canada. What he did not seem to perceive was the radical cultural difference between India and the other countries, a difference which Gandhi was the first to exploit to its fullest. Where most early moderate nationalists in India were English-educated and appreciative of the English contribution, appealing to middle-class sentiment of the Brahmo Samaj variety, Gandhi, perhaps preceded in some small measure by Tilak, was the first man to mobilize entire peasant communities in the cause of *swaraj* and *swadeshi*.

It is certainly a tribute to Holmes, that although clearly in the Unitarian minority in seeing the significance of Gandhi, he would allow the pages of *Unity* to be used as a forum as much against Gandhi as for him. One month later a rejoinder to Wendte was published in *Unity*, written not by Holmes but by Alice Stone Blackwell. Pointing out how Wendte had been misled by anti-Gandhi propaganda, she cited the example of George Washington, who may have held many erroneous beliefs in his own time but whose charismatic qualities and leadership abilities made him overwhelmingly appropriate to be the leader of the American revolution. "We venerate him in spite of his intellectual errors," she commented. What was important about both Gandhi and Jesus, she continued, was their doctrine of non-resistance, with which Gandhi "had quickened the spiritual life of millions in a way unequalled by any man of modern times."[20] Pointing to the shortcomings of Western industrial civilization which she felt Gandhi rightly criticized, Blackwell also stressed Gandhi's social reform campaigns against caste, child marriages, and "ill-usage of widows" emphatically denying Wendte's assertion that Gandhi was slavishly immitating the past. She was quick to admit that Gandhi had made mistakes, but she also wanted to make it clear that Gandhi's ideals, if carried out internationally, could have the greatest possible positive significance. Alice Stone Blackwell was an international idealist of the Holmes variety in contrast to Wendte, an internationalist who wanted to impose the best of Western civilization upon the world. Neither type really understood Gandhi or the context out of which he was working, but the idealists whose personal religious attitude was naturally sympathetic to Thoreau, Ruskin, and Tolstoi could not help but also deeply support Gandhi.

Sunderland's Death: 1936

During the eighteenth year that John Haynes Holmes served as editor of *Unity*, the ninety-four-year-old Jabez Thomas Sunderland died. The issue of Monday, September 21, 1936, was dedicated almost entirely to the memory of Sunderland, reporting the Memorial Meeting that had been held at Community Church, reprinting two Sunderland articles, both universalist in their emphasis, and opening with a eulogy editorial by Holmes himself.[21] Tracing Sunderland's contribution to both Indian nationalism and Unitarianism in America, Holmes concluded his essay with a personal tribute:

> It was my privilege to know Dr. Sunderland for more than twenty-five years. I wish to place on record that he helped me on many occasions, as he did other Indians like the late Lala Lajpat Rai and any who sought his cooperation. The example of Dr. Sunderland's life has given me courage in hours of depression to carry on the struggle. His life will always serve as a source of inspiration to me. He was undoubtedly one of the noblest Americans I have come to know; and he served the cause of India better than many Indian patriots. Indians all over the world and especially Indian patriots pay homage to Dr. Sunderland's memory.[22]

Holmes made clear his debt to Sunderland in this memorial issue of *Unity*: yet, it is strange that nowhere else in Holmes's published writings about India or freedom or in his extant letters is there much to demonstrate that Holmes was ever deeply connected with Sunderland, especially in those years from 1914-1928 when Sunderland was in the New York area. Apart from his presence at the first anniversary dinner of the Home Rule League at which he admitted how little he then knew of India, Holmes's name does not appear in connection with the Home Rule League or its 1921 successor The Indian Information Bureau.

Meeting Gandhi

Although John Haynes Holmes did not meet Gandhi personally until 1931, he kept as closely informed about him as possible. A 1923 letter from Jane Addams to Holmes written from the Cecil Hotel in Delhi, spoke of Addams's frustration at being unable to see Gandhi even though she had visited the Sabramati Ashram in Gandhi's absence and was singularly impressed by the leadership that he was offering.[23] A letter from Holmes to Romain Rolland in 1924, following the publication of Rolland's book on Gandhi in *Century Magazine*, mentioned that after several years of press obscurity, Gandhi had suddenly become quite prominent and was the subject of one American book as well. The regular importing of *Young India* by radical publisher Ben Huebsch was another important factor helping to build Gandhi's image.[24]

Looking back on his "discovery" of Gandhi, Holmes expressed the excitement of those days in the early twenties in the closing paragraph of the first chapter of *My Gandhi* in this way:

> All this (Gandhi as saint, seer, and statesman) I felt when I first found Gandhi. All this I confirmed as passed the years which bound him close and ever closer to my heart. The drama of this experience of discovery was terrific. Here was our world rent to ruin by mad resort to force and violence. Out of this vast convulsion there emerged this single man who put all his trust in truth and love. While the world gave itself over to self-destruction, Gandhi found the way of life and triumphantly walked therein. History has known nothing like it since Christ and Caesar.[25]

Perhaps the greatest problem in analyzing Holmes's deferential attitude toward Gandhi is the lack of material which might trace Holmes's relationship to Gandhi. *My Gandhi* was published in 1953, thirty-two years after Holmes preached his first Gandhi sermon. It is difficult to know on what, if on more than his memory, Holmes based the chapter describing his first meeting with Gandhi in 1931. This took place in London by arrangement through the Reverend Charles Freer Andrews, an Anglican minister and most probably Gandhi's closest European supporter outside the ashram community itself.

Gandhi had come to London to attend the much-heralded Round Table Conference on Indian affairs. While touring in Switzerland during the summer of 1931 Holmes read in the newspapers that Gandhi would attend the conference. Holmes, therefore, readjusted his schedule and headed for London in order to be there when Gandhi would arrive. Gandhi was accompanied by his closest followers: his son Devadas, the Englishwoman disciple Mirabehn (Madelaine Slade), his secretary Mahadev Desai, an early biographer who died before independence was achieved, another secretary, and Gandhi's greatest biographer, Pyarelal Nayyar, as well as the noted Indian poet and orator, Mme. Sarojini Naidu. These Holmes described with an aura of expectancy as "my friends — but friends I had never seen!"[26]

Holmes seems genuinely to have been caught between two extremes of emotion — that of the young boy aggressively moving heaven and earth for a moment of meeting his hero figure and that which "was appalled at the spectacle of my own audacity in seeking intrusion upon so important, even historic, an occasion."[27] Led on to Folkestone by Reginald Reynolds, a Quaker supporter who had met Gandhi during an earlier stay in India, Holmes backed away from his Yankee reluctance and was welcomed at the door to Gandhi's cabin. Holmes's first impressions stayed close to him for a lifetime for he was often asked what they had been. First, Holmes was amused to see that Gandhi in real life looked so much the way he did in cartoons and photographs. Second, Holmes found that despite his small and awkward appearance, Gandhi was a man of "infinite charm and grace."

One must honestly say that this visit from Holmes was far less important in Gandhi's context than William Adam had been for Rammohun Roy or Charles Dall for Keshub Sen. His influence extended only in two minor directions. First, he interposed himself in such a way as to prevent a meeting sought by Mayor Jimmy Walker of New York with Gandhi. Holmes had long been a foe of the corruption rampant in the Walker administration. He was sickened by the thought that Walker, then in London, should use Gandhi for publicity purposes. Holmes was certainly also aware how badly the Western press distorted Gandhi and his cause. The second issue in which Holmes engaged was that of dissuading Gandhi from visiting America. Holmes felt strongly that too much disrespect would be shown the Mahatma and, further, the proper preparations for such a trip had not been made. Though he spoke for himself in insisting that Gandhi not come, Holmes states that on his return, this opinion was corroborated by several leaders of the Indian community in New York with whom he spoke.

Holmes's anecdotes about Gandhi presented in true religious sincerity are probably the most moving and significant aspects of his book. Although nothing Holmes says of Gandhi is said in a scholarly or critical way, his comments demonstrate the view of the serious devotee as opposed to a view from the liberal religious tradition. He reported the story of Gandhi's Muslim Pathan disciple, Badshah Khan, in which the Pathan said that he could never easily question Gandhi's decisions because Gandhi always referred his problems to God and listened to God's command. In this light Badshah Khan saw Gandhi as much more a Muslim than a Hindu. "It is in this sense," Holmes wrote,

> that Gandhi must be understood primarily and fundamentally as a religious being. Almost alone among the great statesmen of history, he spoke and acted from spiritual motives and to spiritual ends. Outwardly one saw only a man rigorously faithful to ideals, but inwardly there was the spectacle of a man seeking to find and to surrender to the mystic promptings of the spirit.[28]

Holmes's second encounter with Gandhi more than seventeen years later was far more significant than his first. That Holmes and Gandhi had corresponded frequently over the intervening years and that Holmes's support from America was greatly appreciated was clear from the Mahatma's response to Holmes's letter requesting an interview. Gandhi replied,

> You have given me not only exciting but welcome news. The news appears almost too good to be true, and I am not going to believe it in its entirety unless you are physically in India.[29]

The trip to India was to be a lecture tour under the sponsorship of the Wattenmull foundation. Sailing for India on September 18, with a week's stop in London and another in Bombay, Holmes finally arrived in Delhi, with his son, Professor Roger Holmes of Mount Holyoke College, on October 12, 1947. Delhi was under martial law in the aftermath of communal rioting which in turn had resulted from the partition of the country and the creation of Pakistan. Within a few days Holmes was to discover that his lecture in Agra was cancelled because trains could not get through unmolested.

Holmes took no notes during or after the interview with Gandhi. Except for the whitening of his hair, Gandhi appeared virtually the same to Holmes as when they had met sixteen years earlier. The memory of the first encounter was fresh in Holmes's mind:

> I could feel that it was only the day before that I had been with him at Kingsley Hall, and that all the years between had been rolled back and were now as though they had never been. Here was a man who had mastered the regimen of life — had broken the barriers of the flesh, and had entered already into the pure realm of the spirit.[30]

Holmes asked whether he might be able to travel about India with the Mahatma during his three months' lecturing tour there. But Gandhi felt his place for the present was in Delhi where vast numbers of refugees, Muslims fleeing to Pakistan and Hindus arriving homeless from Pakistan, were gathered waiting for resettlement. Many were dying of starvation. Lack of adequate facilities led to frequent outbreaks of violence. Holmes now understood why Gandhi had long opposed partition of India. He urged Gandhi to do what he could to see that both Hindu and Muslim refugees received available food equally. Gandhi published Holmes's plea in his newspaper, *Harijan.*[30]

Holmes had been home barely a month when word of Gandhi's assassination came at the end of January 1948. The news came as so great a shock to Holmes that he wept uncontrollably for some time. As if he needed to justify the outburst of feeling natural to someone devoting his life to the cause of humanity and society, Holmes in his later writings documents similar experiences in the lives of Jane Addams and Eleanor Roosevelt.[31]

In *My Gandhi*, Holmes asserts that Gandhi was at his greatest in the last period of his life, when the strains of partition and the riotous disruptions which followed it required Gandhi, then past seventy-five years old, to be ready for any contingency at any time. Just prior to leaving India, Holmes wrote Gandhi what turned out to be the American Unitarian's last letter to the Mahatma. Holmes has excerpted a portion:

> Of course you have been saddened, well nigh overborne, by the tragedies of recent months, but you must never feel this involves any breakdown of your lifework. Human nature cannot bear too much — it cracks under too great a strain, and the strain in this case was as terrific as it was sudden. But your teaching remained as true and your leadership as sound as ever. Single-handed you saved the situation and brought victory out of what seemed for the moment to be defeat. I count these last months to be the crown and climax of your unparalleled career. You were never so great as in these last dark hours.[32]

The seeming exaggeration of Holmes's praise could certainly be justified. Gandhi did much to bring India its independence and much to alleviate the communal tensions during partition. Without Nehru and many others, however, others who stressed different kinds of values and development for India, the independence movement could not have succeeded. Gandhi, no doubt, remained true to the principle of *ahimsa* or nonviolence all his life, but many critics believe that Gandhi's policies led others to violence. Gandhi himself had real doubts despite what Holmes wrote to him. A letter from Gandhi in response to Holmes, but not included in Holmes's book, reveals something of Holmes's failure to understand Gandhi in his own context:

> I wonder if the claim (Holmes's praise) can be proved. That much more than Dr. Holmes observed can be proved of Ahimsa, I have not the slightest doubt. My difficulty is fundamental. Have I attained the requisite qualifications for exhibiting the virtues of Ahimsa, however imperfectly, I see every reason for the utmost caution in advancing claims that cannot be proven beyond a doubt.[33]

John Haynes Holmes certainly realized that *My Gandhi* met with far more criticism in the press than praise. In Unitarian circles, generally uninformed about Gandhi beyond what Holmes had taught them, the story in all its emotional fervor meant much. More sophisticated reviewers saw its limitations. George Catlin, writing in the *Middle East Journal* suggested that while any book which served to publicize Gandhi and his message was to be welcomed, it was essential that the West get the right perspective on Gandhi. Catlin felt that Holmes had "unduly simplified Gandhi's 'Experiments with Truth' to the point of removing their quality."[34]

A Gandhi symposium held in Hawaii in 1969 on the centenary of the Mahatma's birth similarly explored the "meanings" of Gandhi in a contextual and sophisticated way. The editor in fact pointed to Holmes, Albert Schweitzer, "and other Gandhi partisans" for avoiding careful analysis of the issues which could shed true understanding on Gandhi's life and career. Karl Potter's philosophical article exploring Gandhi's theory of nonviolence, for example, raises serious questions not with Gandhi's method, but with the whole concept of *ahimsa* taken out of its ancient Indian frame of reference.[35]

Although Gandhi's life and work were a pivotal emotional symbol for John Haynes Holmes throughout his career and Holmes was certainly the first person responsible for fully publicizing Gandhi in America through the publication of the *Autobiography* serialized in *Unity*, neither the religious or political problems of India were the primary focus of his ministry. Where William Adam, Charles Dall, and Jabez Sunderland devoted the crucial years of their lives to working with and among Indians, Holmes's relationship was maintained through correspondence and publicity work. After Gandhi's death, Holmes continued correspondence with Gandhi's sons, as well as with Nehru and Pyarelal, Gandhi's principal biographer. In 1950, he edited and assisted in the publication of the letters between Gandhi and his English disciple, Mirabehn. Throughout his ministry, Holmes worked tangentially with groups attempting to support the freedom movement in India as well as with groups seeking to promote international understanding. This dimension of his work marked the new kind of mission twentieth-century Unitarians would undertake.

Notes for Chapter One

1. David Kopf, *British Orientalism and the Bengal Renaissance* (Berkeley and Los Angeles: University of California Press: 1969) p. 4-5.
2. Samuel Johnson, *Oriental Religions* (2 vols.) (London: Truebner and Co., 1879).
3. James Freeman Clarke, *Ten Great Religions: An Essay in Comparative Theology* (Boston and New York: Houghton Mifflin Co., 1871).
4. David Kopf's study of the Brahmo Samaj, though cited here, is a work-in-progress, without a specific date of publication as this work is published.
5. For details on Margaret Barr's work among the Khasis, see Margaret Barr, *A Dream Come True: The Story of Kharang* (London: The Lindsay Press, 1974) and the more recent booklet by Y. S. Paul, *Margaret Barr: A Universal Soul* (Udaipur, India: 1975).

Notes for Chapter Two

1. For a good survey history of India since 1400 A.D., see Percival Spear, *A History of India*, Volume 2 (Baltimore: Penguin Books, 1956).
2. For a full discussion of this period as it relates to government and educational developments in Bengal, see David Kopf, *British Orientalism, op. cit.*
3. Kopf, p. 47.
4. Kopf, pp. 75-76.
5. Material for this section is taken from Earl Morse Wilbur, *A History of Unitarianism in Transylvania, England and America* (Cambridge, Mass.: Harvard University Press, 1952).
6. Joseph Priestley, *A Comparison of the Institutions of Moses with Those of the Hindoos and Other Ancient Nations* (Northumberland, Pa.: published privately, 1799).
7. Priestley, p. 7.
8. For a full discussion of these issues in their context, see especially C. Conrad Wright, *The Beginnings of Unitarianism in America* (Boston: Beacon Press, 1955), and more recently, Jack Mendelsohn, *Channing: The Reluctant Radical* (Boston: Little Brown Co., 1971).
9. The court case contesting which of two groups would retain the building and property of the First Church and Parish in Dedham, 1818, was the most notable example of this struggle between Congregational Calvinists and Unitarians.
10. Kopf, *op. cit.*, p. 71ff.
11. For a detailed study of Charles Grant and his role in supporting evangelical Christianity in India, see Ainslee Embree, *Charles Grant and British Rule in India* (New York: Columbia University Press, 1962).
12. Kopf, *op. cit.*, p. 156.
13. Kopf, *op. cit.*, p. 196.

Notes for Chapter Three

1. The Roberts story is drawn from material found in the *Christian Reformer*, Vol. VI, No. LXXVII, London, 1818.

2. *Ibid.*, p. 6.
3. Priestley's work is discussed in Chapter 2, above.
4. *Christian Reformer, op. cit.*, p. 8.
5. *Ibid.*, p. 9.
6. *Ibid.*, p. 1.
7. *Christian Reformer*, Vol. VI, No. XLIX, p. 4, 1819.
8. *Ibid.*, p. 3.
9. *Ibid.*, p. 251.
10. *Christian Reformer*, Vol. VII, No. LXXXIV, pp. 398–399, 1821.
11. "Letters from William Roberts . . . to Dr. Thomas Rees and the Reverend Thomas Belsham," London, 1820, pp. 6–12.
12. Extracted from a letter published in the *Monthly Repository*, 1824 dated October 3, 1823.
13. *Monthly Repository*, "Unitarian Fund Register," VII, report of May 25, 1825, pp. 57-59.

Notes for Chapter Four

1. The most complete biography of Rammohun Roy is that of Sophie Dobson Collet as edited in 1962 by Biswas and Ganguli of Calcutta. Originally published in England in 1900 posthumously, the 1962 Calcutta edition corrects and reinterprets the original text at many crucial points.
2. David Kopf, *op. cit.*, pp. 196-197.
3. Thomas Rees (editor), quoted from the Preface of his American edition of Rammohun Roy's *The Precepts of Jesus* (New York, 1825), p. VI.
4. *Ibid.*, pp. 8 and 11.
5. The most recent edition of Rammohun Roy, *The Precepts of Jesus* with the *Appeals* is found in *The English Works of Raja Rammohun Roy* ed. by Nag and Burman (Calcutta: Sadharan Brahmo Samaj, 1948) Pts. V–VI.
6. M. M. Thomas, *The Acknowledged Christ of the Indian Renaissance* (London: S.C.M. Press, 1969), p. 2.
7. Thomas, quoted from p. 4.
8. *Ibid.*, p. 10.
9. *Ibid.*, p. 12.
10. "Letter to the Unitarian Society of London," *Christian Reformer*, Vol. IV, No. LXXVII, January 1818, p. 1-2.
11. *Ibid.*, p. 3.
12. *Ibid.*
13. "Review," *Monthly Repository*, Vol. XIV, p. 561, identified in Collet as a letter from Rammohun to John Digby, pp. 71 and 109.
14. "Review," *ibid.*, pp. 565-566.
15. *Monthly Repository*, Vol. XV, No. CLXIX, January 1820, p. 2.
16. *Ibid.*, p. 3.
17. Cf. Collet, p. 109, on this point with the view of William Adam as reported by the Reverend Charles Dall in his notes of an interview he had with Adam while in London, 1861. See below, Chapter 5, for further details of the interview.

18. Nag and D. Burman, *The English Works of Rammohun Roy*, Part V (Calcutta, 1948), p. 4 of the "Introduction" to *The Precepts of Jesus.*
19. M. M. Thomas, *The Acknowledged Christ, op. cit.*, quoted from p. 9.
20. *Ibid.*, quoted p. 12, from Parekh.
21. *Ibid.*, p. 13.

Notes for Chapter Five

1. Sophie Dobson Collet, *Life . . . of Rammohun Roy, op. cit.*, p. 122.
2. *Missionary Register*, XVII, 1822, pp. 682-690; and XVIII, 1823, pp. 164–170 as published at the end of bound annuals of the *Monthly Repository.*
3. *Ibid.*
4. *Ibid.*, p. 166.
5. S. C. Sanial, "The Rev. William Adam," *Bengal Past and Present*, Vol. VIII, (January-June, 1914), pp. 251-252. Sanial's description of Adam's family relations seems odd and cannot be corroborated elsewhere. That Yates was his brother-in-law and that the family played no role in their disagreement over the New Testament translation with Rammohun also seems strange.
6. *Ibid.*, p. 252.
7. *Ibid.*
8. Charles H. A. Dall, Minutes of a conversation with the Reverend William Adam, London, 1861, from the unpublished diary notes in the Dall papers, pp. 2-3.
9. William Adam, "The Claims of Jesus" (Calcutta, 1821), p. 23.
10. "The Rev. William Adam's Letter to the Rev. William Yates, one of the Calcutta Baptist Missionaries on the Original Grounds of the Missionary Controversy with Rammohun Roy (May 1824)" in *Rammohun Roy and Progressive Movements in India* (Majumdar and Datta, editors), *op. cit.*, pp. 59-61.
11. *Ibid.*, pp. 61-67.
12. *Ibid.*, p. 70.
13. *Ibid.*, p. 73.
14. Sanial, p. 260.
15. *Ibid.*, p. 261.
16. Dall on Adam, p. 10 of manuscript.
17. Sanial, p. 262.
18. *Ibid.*, p. 264.
19. W. Adam, *Report on the State of Education in Bengal* (Calcutta, 1838), p. 132.
20. *Ibid.*, p. 135.
21. *Ibid.*, p. 178.
22. *Ibid.*, p. 239.
23. Charles Dall, note on Adam, pp. 11–12.
24. William Adam, "The life and labours of Rammohun Roy" (ed. Rakhal Das Haldar), (Calcutta, 1879).
25. Minutes of the Society for the Propogation of the Gospel in India. See note 16, Chapter 6, below.
26. William Adam, "Malcom's *Travels*," *Christian Examiner*, Third Series, Vol. VIII, 1893, p. 387.

27. *Ibid.*, p. 391.
28. *Ibid.*, p. 392.
29. *Ibid.*, p. 399, a reference to the Christian missionary accompanying Malcom.
30. William Adam, *The Law and Custom of Slavery in British India* (Cambridge, Mass., 1840), p. 6.
31. *Ibid.*, p. 9.
32. *Ibid.*, pp. 235-237.
33. *Ibid.*, pp. 239-240.

Notes for Chapter Six

1. William Adam, *A Lecture on the Life and Labours of Rajah Rammohun Roy* (1838), Calcutta edition by R. D. Haldar, 1879, reprinted by P. K. Sen in *Biography of a New Faith*, Vol. 1, (Calcutta: 1951), p. 411.
2. Collet, *op. cit.*, p. 125.
3. Collet, p. 132.
4. *Unitarian Miscellany and Christian Monitor*, Vol. 2, No. 14, February 1822, pp. 205-213; *ibid.*, Vol. 3, No. 17, June 1823, p. 80.
5. *The Christian Disciple*, Boston, N.S., Vol. V., No. 28, July and August 1823, pp. 295-313; No. 30, November-December 1823, pp. 363-392.
6. *Ibid.*, pp. 380-381.
7. *Ibid.*, p. 392.
8. *Christian Register*, Vol. 3, 39, May 7, 1824, p. 154.
9. The two letters to Sparks dated October 27, 1822, and December 9, 1822, have been published in Collet as being addressed to "A Gentleman in Baltimore"; see p. 133. The originals were located by this author in the Sparks papers at Harvard University's Houghton Library. For details of this discovery see "Rammohun Roy and the Rev. Jared Sparks" by this author in *Bengal: Past and Present*, Autumn 1975.
10. *Christian Register*, *ibid.*, p. 154.
11. *Ibid.*
12. *Correspondence Relative to the Prospects of Christianity in India* (Henry Ware, Senior, editor), Cambridge, Mass., 1824, p. 135.
13. *Ibid.*, p. 137.
14. *Monthly Repository*, "Unitarian Fund Register," 1823, p. 2.
15. *Ibid.*, p. 20.
16. Notes taken from an unpublished book of Minutes located in the Unitarian historical archives at Harvard Divinity School, Andover-Harvard Library. I am indebted to Professor C. Conrad Wright for calling my attention to this and to the Reverend Alan Seaburg, archivist, for his assistance throughout this study.
17. "Report of the Committee of the Unitarian Fund," May 25, 1825, published in *The Christian Reformer*, Vol. XI, No. CXXXVII, pp. 182-187.
18. Joseph Tuckerman, "On the Causes by which Unitarians have been withheld for Exertions in the Cause of Foreign Missions" (Weekly Lecture of May, 24) *Christian Examiner and Theological Review*, Vol. 1:3, May and June 1824, pp. 182-196.

19. William Ellery Channing, "Remarks on Associations" in *Channing's Works*, Vol. 1, Boston, 1849, pp. 281-332 and "The Universal Father," in *The Works of William Ellery Channing: The Perfect Life*, Boston, 1892.
20. Joseph Tuckerman, "Letter on the Principles of the Missionary Enterprize," American Unitarian Association tracts, (1), pp. 175-193, Chelsea, June 8, 1826.
21. Joseph Tuckerman, "Is Rammohun Roy a Christian?", *The Christian Examiner*, Vol. 3:5, September-October, 1826, pp. 361-369.
22. *Ibid.*, p. 363.
23. *Ibid.*, p. 369.
24. "Intellegence," *The Christian Examiner*, Vol. 3, No. 2, March-April 1826, p. 169.
25. William Adam to E. S. Gannett, August 3, 1826, unpublished letter in the American Unitarian Association letterbook collection, Andover-Harvard Library, Unitarian archives.
26. Collet, p. 211. The editors of Miss Collet's biography have commented on this passage as an "example of the narrowness... of Mr. Adam..."
27. "Answer of a Hindoo to the Question, Why do you Frequent a Unitarian Place instead of the Numerously attended established Churches," reprinted in The English Works of Rammohun Roy, Part II (Calcutta: 1946), pp. 193-194.
28. Collet, pp. 217-218.
29. Letter to Joseph Tuckerman, September 1, 1828, quoted in Collet, p. 211.
30. Collet, p. 226.
31. Collet, p. 227.
32. See Mary Carpenter, *The Last Days in England of Rammohun Roy* (London and Calcutta: 1866).
33. For this letter from Joseph Tuckerman to William Ellery Channing, I am grateful to Mr. Bayard Tuckerman of Westport, Mass. It has not previously been published.
34. See Anna Letitia LeBreton (editor), *Correspondence of William Ellery Channing, D.D., and Lucy Aiken from 1826 to 1842* (Boston: Roberts Brothers, 1874), p. 191.

Notes for Chapter Seven

1. M. M. Ali, *The Bengali Reaction to Christian Missionary Activities* (1833-1857), (Chittagong, 1965), pp. 6-9.
2. Shoshee Chunder Dutt gives a contemporary view of the "Young Bengal" movement in his essay of that title; see his *Essays*, (Calcutta, n.d. [1852?]) and discussion below.
3. M. M. Ali, *ibid.*, 12.
4. *Ibid.*, pp. 16-20; see also and cf. Sivanath Sastri, *History of the Brahmo Samaj*, Vol. 1, (Calcutta, 1911), pp. 86-88.
5. M. M. Ali, *op. cit.*, p. 21. The statement appeared in Debendranath's *Autobiography* and was republished in the article by J. N. Farquhar in the *Encyclopaedia of Religion and Ethics*, (Edinburgh: T. & T. Clark, 1909), p. 815.

6. *Ibid.*
7. Ali, pp. 33-34.
8. Ali, p. 34. See also Rakhal Das Haldar, *The English Diary of an Indian Student* (1861-1862), (Dacca, 1903) and Sukumar Haldar, *A Mid-Victorian Hindu*, (Ranchi, 1921).
9. Charles W. Wendte, "A Memoir," in Charles Brooks, *Poems, Originals and Translated*, (Boston: Roberts Brothers, 1885), p. 3-34.
10. Wendte, p. 49.
11. *Ibid.*, p. 51.
12. "Extracts from Letters," *American Unitarian Association Journal*, Brooks to American Unitarian Association, Vol. No. 2, pp. 62-64.
13. *Ibid.*
14. *Ibid.*, p. 64.
15. Brooks to American Unitarian Association, *op. cit.*, p. 66.
16. Brooks, Diary for April 30, 1854. I am indebted to Mrs. Mary Harding of Jamestown, Rhode Island, a descendent of Reverend Brooks, for providing me with the original diary manuscript.
17. Brooks, Diary for May 13, 1854.
18. *Ibid.*
19. Shoshee Chunder Dutt, "Young Bengal," *op. cit.*
20. Brooks, *Diary*, May 11, 1854.
21. S. C. Dutt, p. 34.
22. *American Unitarian Association Journal, op. cit.*, Vol. I, No. 2, pp. 69-73.

Notes for Chapter Eight

1. John H. Heywood, *Our Indian Mission and Our First Missionary* (Boston: George Ellis, Co., 1887), pp. 5-8.
2. Charles H. A. Dall, "Lecture on the Poor," describes in graphic detail the conditions in which Dall found the poor in England during a visit in 1842. The handwritten manuscript has been transcribed by this author from papers in the Dall collection at Harvard.
3. Heywood, *op. cit.*, p. 12.
4. *American Unitarian Association Quarterly Journal*, Vol. II, No. 3, p. 325, from a letter dated February 12, 1855.
5. *Ibid.*, p. 343.
6. Heywood, p. 33.
7. *American Unitarian Association Quarterly Journal*, Vol. III, No. 2, p. 272.
8. *Ibid.*, p. 266-269.
9. *Ibid.*, p. 275.
10. *Ibid.*
11. See Nirmal Sinha, *Freedom Movement in Bengal: Who's Who* (Calcutta 1968), pp. 124-125.
12. *Ibid.*, pp. 181-187.
13. *Ibid.*, pp. 100-104.
14. *Ibid.*, pp. 143-149.
15. *Ibid.*, pp. 149-152.
16. Dall to American Unitarian Association in *Quarterly Journal*, Vol. III, No. 2 & 3, pp. 276, 278, 425.

17. Charles H. A. Dall, *Some Gospel Principles* (Calcutta, 1856).
18. C. H. A. Dall, *A Discourse Occasioned by the Death of Abbot Lawrence* (Calcutta, 1855), p. 10.
19. C. H. A. Dall, "Unitarianism and its Progression in America" in *ibid.*
20. C.H.A.Dall, "Christian Liberty: Assent and Dissent" in *Gospel Principles.*
21. Dall, "A Unitarian View of Christ," p. 13.
22. Dall, "Human Brotherhood: The True Church of Jesus," p. 4.
23. *American Unitarian Association Quarterly Journal,* Vol. III, No. 4, pp. 601-602.
24. *Ibid.*, p. 602; see also "Hindu Metropolitan College," in *Bengal Harkaru Press,* January 8, 1856.
25. *Ibid.*, pp. 616-624.
26. Dall to American Unitarian Association, September 13, 1856, in unpublished American Unitarian Association letterbook collection.
27. C. H. A. Dall, "Lecture on True Patriotism in Bengal" (Calcutta: J. F. Bellamy, Englishman Press, 1958).
28. *American Unitarian Association Quarterly Journal,* Vol. IV, "Extracts from Letters," p. 377, November 25, 1856.
29. *Ibid.*, p. 383, December 8, 1856.
30. *Ibid.*, p. 517, January 8, 1857.
31. Sinha, *op. cit.*, pp. 15-20.
32. *American Unitarian Association Quarterly Journal,* Vol. V, pp. 125-126.
33. *Ibid.*, p. 118.
34. *Ibid.*, p. 128.
35. *American Unitarian Association Quarterly Journal,* Vol. V, pp. 81-82.
36. Vol. V, *op. cit.*, pp. 374-375.
37. Vol. VI, *op. cit.*, pp. 288-289.
38. "Intellegence: Reverend J. C. Gangooly and Missions in India," *Christian Reformer,* London, Vol. XBI, N. S. No. CLXXXVIII, August 1960, pp. 516-517. See also Gangooly's unpublished letter to Dall confessing his adultery and also a facsimile of his baptismal certificate signed by Dall in the Dall papers.
39. "Intellegence," *op. cit.*, p. 519.
40. *American Unitarian Association Monthly Journal,* Vol. I, 1861, pp. 340-342, 381.
41. *Ibid.*, p. 382. For details of Abduh Masih's departure from India see *Unitarian Herald,* London, for July 13, 1861, pp. 125-126.
42. Full details of this intrigue may be found in the Dall papers.
43. "Intellegence," *Christian Reformer,* Vol. XVII, p. 188 (March 1861).
44. See Rakhal Das Haldar, *English Diary, op. cit.* For details of the Haldar-Dall controversy see the *Unitarian Herald,* August 3, 1861, p. 147.
45. See Haldar, *op. cit.*, pp. 37-38; see also report in *Unitarian Herald,* August 3, 1861.
46. *Unitarian Herald, op. cit.*, pp. 157-158.
47. "Rakhal Das Haldar's Religious Position," C. H. A. Dall, *ibid.*, p. 158.
48. "The Reverend C. H. A. Dall and Rakhal Das Haldar," August 10, 1861, p. 172.

49. "Indian Mission," *American Unitarian Association Monthly Journal,* VI, 1861, p. 382.
50. Dall to American Unitarian Association; see letterbooks, August 26, 1863.

Notes for Chapter Nine

1. For details, see Chapter 8 above for Dall's early contacts.
2. Protap Chunder Mozoomdar, *The Life and Teachings of Keshub Chunder Sen* (Calcutta: Navavidhan Publications, 1931 (edition)), p. 65.
3. Dall, from notebook "Combined Powers," unpublished.
4. Keshub Chunder Sen, *First Report of the Colatula Evening School* (1855-1857) (Calcutta: P. G. Roy, 1857), p. 3.
5. Mozoomdar, *Sen, op. cit.,* p. 65. Dall always addressed his Unitarian colleagues as "Brother. . ."
6. C. H. A. Dall, "The Brahmo Samaj of India led by Baboo Keshub Chunder Sen With Facts Historical and Personal," in C. G. Banerjee, *Brahmananda Keshub Chunder Sen,* Vol. II, pp. 374-375, 1874 (? Date of original publication). See also Dall's "Lecture on Rajah Rammohun Roy" (Calcutta: 1871), pp. 4-5.
7. *Ibid.*
8. Dall, unpublished notes on Keshub Chunder Sen, 1884.
9. Miscellaneous Notes, 1857-1859.
10. Dall, "The Brahmo Samaj of India. . ." *op. cit.,* p. 362.
11. Dall to American Unitarian Association, letterbook, April 18, 1884.
12. Mozoomdar, *op. cit.,* p. 67.
13. Dall to American Unitarian Association, September 8, 1863.
14. *Unitarian Herald,* London, February 10, 1866.
15. *The Inquirer,* London, February 5, 1870.
16. C. N. Banerji, "The Rise and Progress of the Brahmo Samaj," *Indian Evangelical Review,* III, 1877, p. 87.
17. Dwijadas Dutta, *Behold the Man: Or Keshub and the Sadharan Brahmo Samaj* (Calcutta: 1930), p. 57.
18. Mozoomdar, *op. cit.,* p. 332.
19. *Ibid.,* p. 68.
20. *Ibid.,* p. 69.
21. Mozoomdar, *op. cit.* (1938 ed.), p. 270.
22. Quoted in Prem Chunder Basu (ed.), *Life and Works of Brahmananada Keshev* (Calcutta: Navavidhan Publishing Committee, 1940), p. 64.
23. P. K. Sen, *Biography of a New Faith, op. cit.,* Vol. I, p. 275.
24. Keshub Chunder Sen, "Jesus Christ: Europe and Asia," in *Lectures,* p. 21.
25. *Ibid.,* pp. 35-36.
26. Keshub Chunder Sen, "The Religion of Love," in *Essays: Theological and Ethical,* fifth edition, Calcutta, 1916, p. 26.
27. P. C. Basu, *op. cit.,* p. 75.
28. "Education in Bengal," *Calcutta Review,* XL, 1864, p. 153, quoting the *Report of Public Instruction,* 1862-1863, Appendix A, p. 14.
29. Keshub Chunder Sen, "Young Bengal: This is For You," in *Essays, op. cit.,* p. 6.

30. Keshub Chunder Sen, "Jesus Christ: Europe and Asia," in *Lectures in India* (Calcutta, 1954), p. 20.
31. Sastri, *op. cit.*, Vol. I, pp. 163ff.
32. Sen, "Great Men," in *Lectures in India, op. cit.*
33. Keshub Chunder Sen, *Essays: Theological and Ethical*, "The Spirit of Christ," pp. 178-181.
34. *Ibid.*, p. 178.
35. *Ibid.*, p. 179.
36. All these lectures are included in the volume, *Lectures in India, op. cit.*
37. "The Kingdom of Heaven," in *Lectures*, p. 192.
38. Dall to American Unitarian Association in letterbooks, May 21, 1866.
39. Dall to American Unitarian Association in letterbooks, June 22, 1866.
40. Mary Carpenter, *Six Months in India* (London: Longman Green and Co., 1868), pp. 167-168.
41. *Ibid.*, p. 177.
42. *Ibid.*, p. 185.
43. *Ibid.*, p. 189.
44. "Miss Carpenter at Howrah," clipping in the Dall papers.
45. Dall to American Unitarian Association, December 14, 1869.
46. Text found in J. E. Carpenter, *Life and Work of Mary Carpenter* (London: Macmillan & Co., 1879), pp. 259-260. Letter dated June 12, 1859.
47. For a detailed discussion of these points, see Krishna Lahiri, "Mary Carpenter and the Early Crises in Teacher Training for Women in Calcutta," unpublished paper (University of Pennsylvania, 1976).
48. Keshub Chunder Sen, *Diary in England*, in *Keshub Chunder Sen in England*, 3rd edition revised and enlarged (Calcutta: 1938), p. 26.
49. Frances Power Cobbe, "The Brahmo Samaj," in *Hours of Work and Play* (London: 1867), pp. 59-83, originally published in *Fraser's Magazine*, August 1866.
50. *Ibid.*, p. 63.
51. G. S. Leonard's *History* was published in 1879.
52. Keshub Chunder Sen, *Diary*, *op. cit.*, p. 37; see sermon text, pp. 61-70.
53. "Welcome Soiree" in *Keshub Chunder Sen in England, op. cit.*, p. 72.
54. *Ibid.*, pp. 89-90.
55. *Ibid.*, pp. 100-101.
56. See addresses in *Keshub . . . in England*, "England's Duties Towards India," pp. 300-307; "Indian Reforms," pp. 307-315; and "The Duties of Christian Missionaries in India," pp. 315-329.
57. "Christ and Christianity," p. 229.
58. *Ibid.*, p. 234.
59. Dall in published but untitled letter in Dall papers, May 19, 1870.
60. Dall to American Unitarian Association, September 4, 1871.
61. Dall to American Unitarian Association, December 28, 1869.
62. Dall to *Indian Mirror*, published November 7, 1871, Calcutta.
63. *Ibid.*
64. *Indian Mirror*, November 30, 1871.
65. Dall to *Indian Mirror*, April 7, 1872. See *IM*, April 3, 1872, for an article on the disbelief of Liberal Christians and Charles Dall's Unitarianism.

66. For details, see S. D. Collet, editor, *Brahmo Yearbook*, 1879, pp. 43-52.
67. Keshub Chunder Sen, "Am I an Inspired Prophet?" quoted from *ibid.*, p. 70.
68. Dall to *Brahmo Public Opinion*, n. d. offprint.
69. Dall to *Brahmo Public Opinion*, another offprint.
70. "The Reverend Mr. Dall's Schools," *Englishman*, Calcutta, February 26, 1877. Mary Chamberlain died in 1879. A major biographical obituary appeared in the London *Inquirer*, April 11, 1879.
71. Caroline Healey Dall, *The Life of Anandibai Joshee*, Boston, Roberts Brothers, 1888.
72. "The Latest Mystic," *The Inquirer*, June 21, 1879.
73. See the article, "From Theism to Superstition," *The Inquirer*, July 29, 1882, with its review of Collet's 1881 *Brahmo Yearbook.*
74. "Thoughts on Unitarianism," from the *Indian Mirror* as republished in *The Inquirer*, April 17, 1875, p. 254.
75. *Ibid.*
76. Keshub Chunder Sen, "The Disease and the Remedy," in *Lectures in India*, pp. 271-292, *op. cit.*
77. "On the Reverend C. H. A. Dall," *Indian Mirror*, April 18, 1877.
78. "Keshub Chunder Sen on Unitarianism," *The Inquirer*, May 12, 1883.
79. *Ibid.*
80. *Ibid.*
81. "The New Dispensation in India," *The Inquirer*, August 11, 1883, pp. 501-502.
82. *Ibid.*, p. 502.
83. Untitled article from *The Inquirer*, June 2, 1883, p. 345.
84. "The Funeral of Keshub Chunder Sen," quoted from *The Inquirer*, January 12, 1884, p. 17.

Notes for Chapter Ten

1. See Keshub Chunder Sen, "Diary in Madras," for details of Protap's journeys.
2. See articles in *The Inquirer* for the period, and also relevant sections in Bose, *Life of Protap Chunder Mozoomdar*, Nababhidan Trust, Calcutta, 1927, 2 vols.
3. Protap C. Mozoomdar, *The Faith and Progress of the Brahmo Samaj* (Calcutta: 1882).
4. Friedrich Max Mueller, *Biographical Essays*, "The Letters of Protap Chunder Mozoomdar to Max Mueller," August 20, 1881 (Charles Scribner and Sons: New York, 1884)., p. 146.
5. M. M. Thomas, *The Acknowledged Christ . . . op. cit.*, p. 89, quoted from Mozoomdar's *The Spirit of God*, pp. 239ff. See also his *The Oriental Christ* (Boston: 1883).
6. *The Oriental Christ*, pp. 10-11.
7. *The Spirit of God*, pp. 39, 41, 50-51.
8. *Ibid.*
9. *Ibid.*, p. 239.

10. Protap C., *Mozoomdar, Tour 'Round the World*, 2nd edition, Calcutta, 1940.
11. *Ibid.*, p. 6.
12. "Editor's Notebook," *Unitarian Review*, Boston, February 1884, p. 165.
13. *Ibid.*, p. 168.
14. See editorial sections of the *Unitarian Review* for October 1883, and April 1884.
15. The definitive biography of Conway is that of Mary Elizabeth Burtis, *Moncure Conway: 1832-1907.*
16. Moncure D. Conway, *My Pilgrimage to the Wise Men of the East* (Houghton, Mifflin and Co., Boston and New York, 1906), p. 221.
17. *Ibid.*, p. 223.
18. Ameer Ali, *Life and Teachings of Mohammed* (London: Williams and Norgate, 1873).
19. John Henry Barrows (ed.) *The World's Parliament of Religions,* (Chicago: 1893), (2 vols.).
20. Jabez T. Sunderland, "The World's Parliament of Religions," *The Unitarian.* October 1893, pp. 441-442.
21. *Ibid.*, p. 448.
22. Protap Chunder Mozoomdar, "The Brahmo Samaj" and "The World's Religious Debt to Asia," in *Lectures in America and Other Papers* (Calcutta: 1955), pp. 4-29.
23. P. C. Mozoomdar, "Letters to the Brahmo Public," in *Lectures in America, op. cit.*, pp. 43-44.
24. *Ibid.*, p. 50.
25. John Henry Barrows to Protap Mozoomdar as published in *Lectures*, p. 244.
26. *Ibid.*, pp. 147-148.
27. *Ibid.*, p. 150.

Notes for Chapter Eleven

1. Sunderland did not even rate a reference in Earl Morse Wilbur's major work on Unitarianism nor in Stow Person's *Free Religion.* Moreover, Sunderland is the subject of considerable negative discussion in Charles Lyttle's volume *Freedom Moves West.* He discusses Sunderland's role in the *Controversy in the West* (Beacon Press, 1952); see especially pp. 161-164 and 176-191.
2. For Sunderland's biography, see *Who Was Who.* It was first included in the current edition for 1929.
3. Keshub Chunder Sen had been introduced by Dall to the works of Channing and Parker as early as 1857. They had remained close associates until Keshub's death in 1884 at which time Dall was the only Christian participant in Keshub's funeral. Rakhal Das Haldar was a Brahmo, a close associate of Dall's, who alienated Dall because of his refusal to finally convert to Unitarian Christianity. Haldar accompanied Dall on a trip to England in 1861. See Chapter eight for details.
4. From an undated manuscript in the Sunderland papers entitled "The Historic Issue in the West," p. 3.
5. *Ibid.*, p. 4.

6. *Ibid.*, p. 6.
7. Sunderland's unpublished "Diary in India," 1895, entry for Wednesday, September 11.
8. Mary Carpenter's *The Last Days in England of Rammohun Roy* was published in London in 1866; Sophie Collet's Brahmo Yearbooks appeared annually from 1876 to 1882; P. C. Mozoomdar's *Faith and Progress of the Brahmo Samaj* was published in Calcutta in 1884.
9. Diary, November 13.
10. Diary, November 17.
11. Mahadev Govind Ranade was a leading moderate of the Indian National Congress movement. A recent definitive biography has been offered by Richard P. Tucker, *Ranade and the Roots of Indian Nationalism*, University of Chicago Press (microfiche edition), 1973.
12. Diary, November 18.
13. Diary, November 25.
14. Diary, November 29.
15. The Reverend Charles T. Brooks served his entire career as minister in Newport, Rhode Island. The details of his life and travels in India appear in Chapter seven, *supra.*
16. The origins of the Madras Unitarian movement may be traced to correspondence between William Roberts, Sr., who had been influenced by the works of Priestley and Lindsay during travels to India as a servant, and the Reverend Thomas Belsham, leader of the English Unitarian movement in its early days c. 1820. For details of this relationship and development, see Chapter three, *supra.*
17. Diary, December 1.
18. For details on Akbar Masih see p. 7ff. on Sunderland's meeting with him at Allahabad a few weeks later.
19. The letters from William Roberts, Sr., to Thomas Belsham were published in issues of the *Monthly Reporter* from time to time during 1818 and 1819.
20. Mary Carpenter, daughter of the Unitarian minister Lant Carpenter, had been deeply influenced by her father's descriptions of Rammohun Roy's visit to and subsequent death in England (1830-33). In 1866 she made the first of several journeys to India to establish a number of schools for women and to aid in the reform of other institutions. For details of these trips and her controversy with Charles Dall, see Chapter eight, *supra.* Sunderland appears to be the only American religious liberal ever to have responded favorably to the socially radical but theologically fundamentalist Arya Samaj. Notes from his lectures located at Meadville Theological School indicate his strong interest in this group as well as in the Brahmos.
21. Diary, December 16, 1895.
22. *Ibid.* Sunderland may not have realized that in the thirty-five years in which Brahmo missionaries had operated, they were never paid a salary and had to depend on the charity of their members for support. This was certainly in keeping with the Indian monastic and temple traditions.
23. Sunderland's obituary of Pundita Rambai appeared in the *Christian Register* (c. 1922).

24. Diary, December 23-30, 1895.
25. Diary, January 1, 1896.
26. For background on the history and culture of the Khasis see Hamlet Barch, *The History and Culture of the Khasi People* (Calcutta: 1967).
27. Hajjom Kissor Singh to Jabez T. Sunderland, in *The Unitarian*, December 1888, pp. 526-527.
28. *Ibid.*, p. 527.
29. *Ibid.*, p. 528.
30. *Ibid.*, April 1891, p. 172.
31. *Ibid.*, pp. 172-173.
32. *Ibid.*, May 1895, p. 210.
33. *Ibid.*
34. Sunderland's Diary, January 7.
35. Diary, January 9-13.
36. Diary, January 15-19.
37. Diary, January 20.
38. When Sunderland arrived in Calcutta, the Brahmo Samaj had existed in three ideologically separate groups since 1879. The Brahmos he had met around India had primarily associated themselves with the mainstream Brahmo Samaj of India (Sadharan Brahmo Samaj) which had broken with the conservative Adi Samaj of Tagore in 1866. The split with Keshub in 1879 leading to the creation of the third New Dispensation Brahmo Samaj (Navavidhan) had been specifically precipitated by Keshub's agreeing to the marriage of his minor daughter to the Maharajah of Kuch Behar despite Keshub's earlier work to outlaw child marriage.
39. Diary, January 24-27, 1896.
40. Diary, January 28-30.
41. Diary, February 2.
42. Diary, February 6.
43. Suresh Chunder Bose, *The Life of Protap Chunder Mozoomdar*, Vol. 2, Calcutta, 1929, p. 238.
44. *Ibid.*
45. The details of the new organization are described in Surendra Nath Dutt, *The Life of Benoydranath Sen*, Calcutta, 1928, pp. 154-161.
46. Bose, *op. cit.*, p. 241.
47. *Seventy-Second Annual Report of the British and Foreign Unitarian Association*, 1897, pp. 16-17.
48. "Christian Missions in India," 21 pgs. n. d. (1896, or 97?).
49. "Missionary Work in the Unitarian Churches," *Unity*, Chicago, 1903, 27 pp.
50. "The New Nationalism in India," *Atlantic Monthly*, October, 1908, Boston.
51. "The Causes of Famine in India," no publisher, n. d. (1905-1907?).
52. "The New Nationalism. . ." *op. cit.* (pages from reprint), p. 4.
53. *Ibid.*
54. *Ibid.*, p. 5.
55. *Ibid.*, p. 11.

Notes for Chapter Twelve

1. *Toronto Star*, clipping located in scrapbook within the historical collection of the First Unitarian Church, Toronto, dated November 28, 1904.
2. *Toronto World*, December 4, 1904, scrapbook, *op. cit.*
3. Notes and clippings about the lecture by Benoydranath Sen in the Toronto scrapbook.
4. "A Message to Musselmen" by James Harwood and "Materialism and Atheism Refuted" by James Freeman Clarke.
5. This journal was never published as far as this writer's research can determine.
6. Unpublished lecture from notes in the Sunderland papers at Meadville/Lombard Theological School, Chicago, Illinois.
7. Stephen N. Hay, *Asian Ideas of East and West: Tagore and His Critics in Japan China and India*, Harvard University Press, Cambridge, Mass., 1970, p. 23.
8. Stephen N. Hay, "Rabindranath Tagore in America" *American Quarterly* 14:3, Fall, 1962, p. 440.
9. *Ibid.*, p. 441.
10. Rabindranath Tagore, Sadhana: *The Realisation of Life*, The Macmillan Company, New York, 1913.
11. Letter from Tagore to Charles W. Wendte from S. Kensington, England dated June 12, 1913, in Unitarian archives at Andover-Harvard Library, Cambridge, Mass.
12. For coverage of the Rochester Congress and Tagore's role in it see the *Christian Register*, Vol. 92, issues 3, 5, 7, 8. A report by Wendte in the February 20 issue states: "Mr. Tagore held up to the meeting the high social ideals and reverence for the divine in the human which alone could permanently solve this question (of race conflict)."
13. "Rabindranath Tagore as an Educator," *Christian Register*, September 1, 1916, and *Universalist Leader*, August 19, 1916, p. 788. See also "A Distinguished Visitor from India," *Unity*, January 30, 1913, pp. 345-346.
14. Rabindranath Tagore, *The Religion of Man*, George Allen and Unwin, London, 1931.
15. J. T. Sunderland, "The Mission of the Unitarian Faith," American Unitarian Association pamphlet, Boston, 1913, p. 3.
16. *Ibid.*, p. 7.
17. *Ibid.*, p. 10.
18. *Ibid.*, p. 11.
19. *Ibid.*, p. 15.
20. *Ibid.*, pp. 15-18.
21. From printed publicity on the Billings Lecture Foundation, located in the Sunderland papers, Ann Arbor.
22. Data about Sunderland 1913-1914 journey is sparse in comparison to that in his 1895-96 diary.
23. See Chapter six, *supra*, for the earlier contacts of Charles Dall with Sayyid Ahmad Khan, founder of the college at Aligarh.
24. See Ahmad Khan's diary of his English journey, Mufasirun Lundun.

25. J. T. Sunderland, "Liberal Religion in the Orient": "Personal Experiences in Japan, China, Ceylon, and India," 1919, pp. 18-20.
26. *Ibid.*, pp. 20-21. Sunderland's conception of internationalism was developed further in his presidential address at Karachi. It was republished in *The Indian Messenger*, January 1, 1914 (Calcutta).
27. N. G. Rathore, *Indian Agitation in the U.S.: A Study of Lala Lajpat Rai and the Indian Home Rule League of America*, 1914-1920 (Columbia University, Ph.D. dissertation (unpublished), 1965, p. 15.
28. Rathore, pp. 16-24. As a result all twenty-one were placed on a list of undesirables maintained by the Government of India.
29. *Ibid.*, p. 66; see also Lajpat Rai's *Autobiography*, edited by V. C. Joshi; (New Delhi University publishers 1965) for his version of the experiences.
30. *Ibid.*, pp. 67-73. See Rai's letter to the *New York Times*, May 31, 1916.
31. *Ibid.*, p. 82ff.
32. J. T. Sunderland, "The Arya Samaj of India," in the *Universalist Leader* September 18, 1915.
33. Rathore, pp. 98ff. See also *Young India* as edited by Lajpat Rai.
34. Lala Lajpat Rai, "My Farewell," *Young India*, 2:12, December 1919, pp. 276-278.
35. *Young India*, 1:2, p. 24.
36. *Ibid.*
37. *Ibid.*, pp. 24-25.
38. *Ibid.*
39. Rathore, *op. cit.*, pp. 156ff.
40. "Repression — Road to Revolution," *Young India*, 3:7, July 1920.
41. Lala Lajpat Rai, *The Political Future of India* (New York: B. W. Huebsch, 1919) and *Young India* (New York: B. W. Huebsch, 1916).
42. See the tract, "Indian Freedom in the American Courts," published by "Friends of Freedom for India," April 1919.
43. Suhindra Bose, "Indians Barred from American Citizenship," *Unity*, April 19, 1923, pp. 123-125. See also unpublished lecture of Taraknath Das, "Some stateless persons in the U.S. of A." delivered before the American Society for International Law, April 24, 1925, Washington, D.C., The Hon. Charles Evans Hughes, presiding.
44. *Young India*, July 1918, p. 6.
45. J. T. Sunderland, "An Open Letter to Mahatma Gandhi. . ." unpublished according to the knowledge of this writer, pp. 1-2.
46. "India: Devil People?" *Time*, August 26, 1929, p. 30.
47. *Ibid.*, p. 31.
48. *Ibid.*
49. *Ibid.*
50. Charles Johnston, Review of "Five Books on India," *New York Times Book Review*, January 5, 1930.
51. Letter from Rabindranath Tagore, Columbo, Ceylon, June 4, 1928.
52. See *Unity*, September 21, 1936. for news article and memorial biography by John Haynes Holmes.

Notes for Chapter Thirteen

1. See J. H. Holmes, *I Speak for Myself*, pp. 1-108 for details of his early life. New York: (Harper and Row, 1959).
2. *Ibid.*, p. 110.
3. *Ibid.*, p. 112.
4. *Ibid.*, p. 166.
5. *Ibid.*, p. 179.
6. J. H. Holmes, *My Gandhi* (New York: Harper and Brothers, 1953), p. 1.
7. Erik H. Erikson, *Gandhi's Truth* (New York: W. W. Norton and Co., 1969).
8. Geoffrey Ashe, *Gandhi* (New York: Stein and Day, 1969), p. 147.
9. Holmes, *My Gandhi*, pp. 24-25.
10. John Haynes Holmes and Jabez T. Sunderland, "Repression — Road to Revolution," *Young India*, Vol. 2, pp. 159-162.
11. See J. T. Sunderland in *Unity*, Vol. LXXXI, June 13, 1918, pp. 247-248 and June 27, 1918, p. 280.
12. Volumes XXXIII and XXXIV.
13. Quoted in Sunderland's "India's Attempted Revolution Without Bloodshed," *Unity*, Vol. XXXVII, No. 9, p. 136.
14. *My Gandhi*, p. 29.
15. J. H. Holmes, "Who is the Greatest Man in the World Today?" *Unity*, LXXXVII, No. 10, p. 151.
16. *Ibid.*, p. 152.
17. *Ibid.*, p. 171, No. 11.
18. *Ibid.*, p. 172.
19. Charles W. Wendte, "Gandhi and Modern India," *Unity*, Vol. XXXIV, No. 21, p. 330, August 3, 1922.
20. Alice Stone Blackwell, "Gandhi and Modern Civilization," *Unity*, Vol. XXXV, No. 1, September 11, 1922.
21. See *Unity*, September 21, 1936, Vol. CXIII, No. 2. The Sunderland articles included were "A World Wide Brotherhood" and "A New and Better Bible."
22. John Haynes Holmes in *ibid.*, "Jabez T. Sunderland: 1842-1936," p. 28.
23. Letters from Jane Addams dated February 6, 1923, in Holmes papers, Library of Congress.
24. John Haynes Holmes to Romain Rolland, January 15, 1924.
25. Holmes, *My Gandhi*, p. 33.
26. *Ibid.*, p. 34.
27. *Ibid.*, p. 35.
28. *Ibid.*, pp. 58-59.
29. *Ibid.*, p. 111.
30. *Ibid.*, p. 115.
31. *Ibid.*, pp. 117-119.
32. *Ibid.*, pp. 135-137.
33. Gandhi in a letter from New Delhi, January 3, 1948, in Holmes papers.
34. George Catlin, "India," Book Review Section, *Middle East Journal*, Summer 1954, p. 347.

35. Paul Power (ed.), *The Meaning of Gandhi* (Honolulu: University of Hawaii Press, 1971; see especially Karl Potter, "Explorations in Gandhi's Theory of Non-Violence," pp. 91-119).

INDEX